The Aesthetic Economy of Fashion

Dress, Body, Culture

Series Editor: **Joanne B. Eicher**, *Regents' Professor, University of Minnesota*

Books in this provocative series seek to articulate the connections between culture and dress which is defined here in its broadest possible sense as any modification or supplement to the body. Interdisciplinary in approach, the series highlights the dialogue between identity and dress, cosmetics, coiffure and body alternations as manifested in practices as varied as plastic surgery, tattooing and ritual scarification. The series aims, in particular, to analyze the meaning of dress in relation to popular culture and gender issues and will include works grounded in anthropology, sociology, history, art history, literature and folklore.

ISSN: 1360–466X

Recently published titles in the series

The Aesthetic Economy of Fashion
Markets and Value in Clothing and Modelling

Joanne Entwistle

Oxford • New York

English edition
First published in 2009 by
Berg
Editorial offices:
First Floor, Angel Court, 81 St Clements Street, Oxford OX4 1AW, UK
175 Fifth Avenue, New York, NY 10010, USA

Berg is the imprint of Oxford International Publishers Ltd.

Library of Congress Cataloging-in-Publication Data

Entwistle, Joanne.
The aesthetic economy of fashion : markets and value in
clothing and modelling / Joanne Entwistle. — English ed.
p. cm. — (Dress, body, culture, ISSN 1360-466X)
Includes bibliographical references and index.
ISBN-13: 978-1-84520-473-0 (pbk.)
ISBN-10: 1-84520-473-5 (pbk.)
ISBN-13: 978-1-84520-472-3 (cloth)
ISBN-10: 1-84520-472-7 (cloth)
1. Clothing trade. 2. Fashion. I. Title.
HD9940.A2E58 2009
381'.4574692—dc22
2009020435

British Library Cataloguing-in-Publication Data

A catalogue record for this book is available from the British Library.

ISBN 978 1 84520 472 3 (Cloth)
ISBN 978 1 84520 473 0 (Paper)

Typeset by Apex CoVantage, LLC, Madison, WI, USA
Printed in Great Britain by the MPG Books Group, Bodmin and King's Lynn

www.bergpublishers.com

For my girls, Isabella and Rosa

Contents

Acknowledgements

This book has been a long time in the making. Not only did I conduct the fieldwork some time ago, the writing of it has taken far longer than I could ever have imagined, not least because I gave birth to two babies during that time and took extended maternity leave. The fieldwork at Selfridges could not have been undertaken without the generous support from an Economic and Social Research Council small grant (Award reference: R000223649). I am also indebted to the women's wear staff at Selfridges (all of them long gone) for their remarkable hospitality, honesty and friendliness. They are the ones that made this book happen by virtue of the amazing access they gave me over many months. I am also very grateful to the many model agencies, models and model bookers who kindly agreed to talk to me, in particular, Storm, Models One and Take 2, in London and Boss and Karins in New York.

Except for the time spent in the field, the business of writing this has been rather lonely at times. I am, however, grateful for the support of friends, family and colleagues who have helped in shaping it. During the early years, while at the University of Essex I was supported by my colleague Sean Nixon for conversations over coffee at the British Library. I am also grateful for the comments of anonymous reviewers of journal articles as well as those institutions, too numerous to name, who invited me to talk about my work over this time. My friends in New York, Elizabeth Wissinger and Sam Binkley, provided me with some very good opportunities to speak about my work in the early years and I am grateful for their company and intellectual friendship on my numerous trips Stateside. I am grateful to Patrik Aspers and Lise Skov for inviting me to the Copenhagen Business School in 2005 to present a paper at 'Encounters in the Fashion Industry' (now Chapter 8 in the book) and for their comments on what became a *Current Sociology* journal article. I owe a debt of gratitude also to Peter McNeil and Vicki Karaminas in the Faculty of Architecture and Design at the University of Technology in Sydney, Australia, for their kind hospitality while hosting me on a visit during Spring 2006 where I completed two chapters. But it is to my life partner Don Slater that I owe the biggest thanks for supporting me throughout the duration of this work and for many heated debates, quite literally, over boiling bowls of Vietnamese soup in Crouch End. The final book is my own work but it would have been a quite different book without all this input. I dedicate it to my two daughters who, while slowing down its progress, made the journey through it that bit more interesting and rewarding.

The author and publisher would like to thank the following for permission to use copyright material:

Sage Publications for paragraphs in Chapter 3 from 'The Aesthetic Economy: The Production of Value in the Field of Fashion Modelling' by Entwistle, J., *Journal of Consumer Culture*, 2 (3) pp. 317–340.

Sage Publications, Chapter 8, 'The Cultural Economy of Fashion Buying' by Entwistle, J., *Current Sociology*, 54 (5), pp. 704–724.

Introduction

Consider the following. A 'new' model is heralded as the 'next big thing' and is photographed on the cover of half a dozen major fashion magazines globally. The colour cobalt blue is decreed to be 'hot' this season and a 'sea' of garments in the hue hits every store. A 'new' designer is celebrated at London Fashion Week and the Collection hailed a 'success' that will 'put London back on the fashion map'. A range of denim from Los Angeles arrives in London to a fanfare of fashion press and, despite the cost—almost £200 for a pair of jeans—sells out within a week. There are waiting lists for the 'It' designer bag of the season and it is featured in the Most Wanted lists of every major UK fashion magazine. Bootleg jeans are officially declared 'dead' by a leading fashion magazine only to be championed the following month. Supermodel Kate Moss augments her already well-established position as an international style icon when she launches her latest Collection for London store Topshop to a frenzy of press and fans. Out on the streets, women queue to see inside her latest collection as they did weeks earlier for the opening of the latest 'fast-fashion' store on London's Oxford Street. 'Designer shoes are the next best thing to sex,' according to the latest survey on women's desire by a popular women's magazine.

These stories (some real, some fiction) depict the kind of ordinary fashion events which are written by journalists and consumed by readers of fashion magazines, women's magazines and newspapers. These styles, trends, garment ranges and stores will, in various ways and with differing degrees of success, find their way into the everyday consumption choices and practices of ordinary women—appropriated, translated, re-worked in the process. As Simmel (1971) argues, 'fashion' is expressive of the tension between individuality and group identity. Bearing this in mind, we might view these events as shaping the meanings and the styles defined as fashion, as well as framing the myriad choices consumers make as to the clothes, bags, shoes, and the like, they wish to buy. Understanding the interconnections between the collective and the individual bodies of consumers thus requires that we examine the many ways in which fashion is made up from the daily practices and activities of a great number of spatially dispersed actors circulating raw materials, trend ideas and stylized images in the pages of magazines and finished garments, and displayed in department stores and boutiques.

And yet, how much do we know about the inner workings of fashion and the actors who help to shape it? To start with, there are plenty of things we *do* know about fashion. We know a lot about the work of particular designers from careful historical and contemporary accounts of their work (Chalayan 2005); we can see examples of their work through thematic books, exploring aspects of fashion (Wilcox 2001; Koda and Bolton 2005), and exhibitions of design (Haywood 1998); we know much about the structure of UK fashion education and employment in fashion design (McRobbie 1998); we are aware of some aspects of fashion retail in the United Kingdom (Crewe, Gregson et al. 2003; Gregson and Crewe 2003); we can read salacious stories about the lives of models and sympathize (or not) with their struggles in the business (Bardot 2003; Gross 2004; France 2009); if we are engaged in a course on cultural studies or fashion at college or university we can find out how to 'read' fashion texts (Barthes 1985; Jobling 1999) or analyse the role and significance of fashion in historical and contemporary Western society (Evans 2003; Breward and Evans 2005) and the role of fashion in the construction of identities (Cole 2000; Woodward 2007). These studies have contributed much to our knowledge of fashion but, since fashion is so multi-dimensional, covering everything from art, design, business, manufacturing, technology and retail, there remain many areas that have not been examined and many aspects of fashion which are unexplained. A fuller account of fashion (as in fashionable clothing), as an economic and cultural practice, is required if we are to investigate the many dimensions of this industry in all its varied forms. Indeed, from high street to haute couture, fashion is not one thing or one industry, but is made up of related yet separate sectors or markets.

Despite this wealth of literature, there are still many things unexplained or little examined. We know little about the emergence of particular trends and styles *as* fashion: how does the latest 'hot look', be it that of a new fashion model, or a new style of dress, come to be defined and how do those in the system of fashion recognize the next big trend? How are such commodities selected and sold to consumers? What are the risks inherent in such fast-changing markets and how are they calculated and managed? We know little about the work of fashion journalists who translate the catwalk collections of designers into fashion 'stories', and next to nothing of the identities and work of fashion buyers whose choices directly shape our own by making particular styles available for purchase. We may have television programmes on fashion modelling, such as 'America's Next Top Model' and its various spin-offs, but still remain puzzled as to what it takes to become a fashion model or how model agencies select and promote models consumed by readers of fashion magazines.

These many aspects of fashion have been neglected, especially by sociologists and economists for whom it is, perhaps, too trivial to study, or maybe because so many of them pay so little attention to their own bodies and thus are oblivious to their dress: at the risk of offending some colleagues, sociologists are not noted for their fashion sense (see Crewe 2008 for a similar point relating to geographers). In other words, despite its global reach, economic significance, and obvious cultural appeal, fashion has been marginalized within mainstream sociology and economic sociology, and, thus, a sociologically informed account of fashion has only partially emerged. Related areas, like cultural studies and business, may study fashion, but the focus is on either the 'cultural' or the 'economic' aspects, respectively, without analysis of the obvious hybridity of fashion as business *and* culture. Some attempts have been made to capture these simultaneously, as in Fine and Leopold's (1993) analysis, but there still remain many unexamined aspects of fashion.

This book does not plug all the gaps in our knowledge of fashion but is concerned with some of the material practices that go to making up the phenomenon of fashion. In this Introduction I summarize the empirical and theoretical material I draw on in this book to flesh out our understanding of the particularities of fashion as an *aesthetic market*. On one level this book builds on my earlier work and attempts to map some of the practices constitutive of fashion, as in fashionable clothing (a precise definition is outlined below). As I have argued previously (Entwistle 2000a), dress is a 'situated practice', and that instead of grand theories about what motivates fashionable dress, we need to look at the multiple and overlapping practices that constitute fashion, from the many actors who make it—designers, photographers, models, fashion buyers, journalists and the like—to the many people who wear it. If possible, we should try to trace some of the connections between them all. Such an analysis is beyond the scope of any one book and certainly more than I can promise to deliver in this one. Instead, what I am suggesting is akin to a research agenda that would involve a number of linked projects to which this book would be just one contribution.

However, this book is not just about fashion; it is also a book about markets, in particular, aesthetic markets, which have often been neglected by sociologists and economists. These markets in cultural products warrant our attention, not just because they are economically and culturally important (Pratt 2004b), but because in examining them we extend our understanding of different market practices. Fashion markets are demonstrably concerned with the body and the orientations are specifically towards bodily aesthetics. The commodities themselves are obviously destined for bodily display and this fact has implications for how this market operates. Indeed, fashion throws into sharp relief the importance of bodily display and performance by actors inside the market, who must embody the very style or aesthetic they seek to commodify. That is to say, fashion markets are enacted through embodied style, with fashion knowledge performed on the bodies of those actors inside the market. However, while embodiment is important in aesthetic markets, it is evident that all markets are embodied—performed and enacted by embodied agents—yet this feature is little analyzed by economists, sociologists and business theorists. Aesthetic markets are, therefore, an interesting case study, raising new awareness and questions that draw attention to this and other hitherto neglected or repressed features of markets. This is not to say that aesthetic markets are the only ones concerned with bodies: medicine and health are similarly concerned (see for example Mol and Law 2004), but they are focused on the bio-medical workings of the body rather than with aesthetics. The qualities of aesthetic markets, and the ways in which these markets are embodied, have yet to be examined.

However, this book is not a comprehensive account of all aesthetic markets, or even all markets inside fashion, but focuses attention on insiders in two quarters of the fashion world: fashion modelling and fashion buying, although by accident rather than design, more attention is paid to the latter. The book is divided into two parts. In Part I, I spell out theoretical resources and ways of thinking about aesthetic markets. Here I draw specifically on my study of fashion modelling (developed further in Chapter 3) to indicate some of the ways in which fashion's aesthetic value is networked and collectively produced. This small scale study was the theoretical starting point of my work in this area and, though I did not know it at the time, formed the foundation for what was to become a more ambitious study of fashion buying at Selfridges, detailed in Part II. Thus, as I describe in the methodology section below, while the models project was critically and theoretically very important, it provided only a small amount of the data upon which I draw, compared to what I amassed during my six-month ethnography at Selfridges. However, together they support one another and enable me to make connections I would otherwise not have seen. Indeed, the similarities across these two markets were impossible to ignore, as I describe below, and led me to consider bringing them together in one book on aesthetic markets.

Let me begin by introducing the case studies and methodology in the first section of this chapter. I then move on, in the following section, to demonstrate the convergences between the two studies, both in terms of the empirical realities of the work they do in fashion, clothing and modelling markets, and in terms of the theoretical issues they both touch upon.

Case Studies and Methodology

The two case studies upon which this book is based—male fashion modelling and fashion buying—were conducted quite independently of one another and initially began from different research questions. The models project was my first foray into the world of high fashion. This study focused on male fashion modelling markets and was largely interview-based, supported by observations inside the model agencies I gained access to. Over the course of 18 months (between Spring 2000 and Summer 2001) I interviewed 24 male fashion models and six model agents or 'bookers' in three agencies in London—Storm, Models One, two of the larger agencies and Take 2, a 'boutique' agency—and two agencies in New York—Karins and Boss. In addition, I spent time observing models at castings in the agencies. I tried but failed to gain access to photo shoots but these are notoriously difficult to get inside, with stylists and photographers usually closing the set. I also collected large amounts of data on model agencies from the large industry-linked Web site based in New York, www.models.com, and mainstream publications. In addition, in the course of my second study of fashion buyers (February 2002 to October 2003) I observed models at fashion shows. Much of what I say in relation to male models is applicable to female models, although from the outset some notable differences should be referenced. Modelling is one of the few occupations where women earn significantly more than men (pornography is another obvious one). At every rung on the modelling ladder, female models are paid more than men, often considerably more for the same job. The extraordinary differences in salary between male and female models was brought home to me when I ran into an Australian model in the lobby of the Gerswin Hotel in New York, shortly after completing my fieldwork in 2001. He had recently been on an advertising campaign shoot with the Brazilian model Gisele Bundchen who was, at that time, the 'face of' Dolce and Gabbana and earning an estimated $3 million (US). Although only in the background of the photograph, he was paid a few hundred dollars for basically performing the same work. This may be partly explained in terms of the different political economies of male and female modelling. In female modelling, there are far more 'big' contracts, with cosmetic companies paying the highest (in the region of millions of dollars). Such contracts do not exist for men and the markets for men's fashion are neither as large nor as prominent as those for women's wear. However, the difference may also arise out of the closer association of women with the body and the higher cultural value placed on female 'beauty'. Indeed, as many feminists have pointed out (Coward 1984; Mulvey 1988; Bordo 1993; Haywood 1998), women's bodies remain more highly scrutinized and evaluated in terms of physical appearance. The high earnings are off-set by the generally shorter career of women in fashion modelling. The high premium on youth and beauty means that a female model's career can often be winding down just as a male model's is just taking off: while 25 is old for a female model, her male counterpart may be just starting to earn a decent income if he can transfer over to commercial work orientated to older men favouring older models. Despite these differences, many of the day-to-day calculations made by model bookers vis-à-vis models' careers are the same, regardless of gender. Further, male and female models move across the same network of value and prestige, with the major designers, photographers, stylists and magazines, responsible for promoting male and female models' careers, and thus they share the same concerns regarding the cultural value of particular forms of work.

My study of fashion buyers, conducted in 2002, was far more intensive. Unlike the models project which carried on over a long period of time during which I was lecturing, this project was fully funded by the Economic and Social Research Council (ESRC)[1] and was an in-depth ethnography, based on observations of the women's wear department at Selfridges between late March and late September 2002. In addition to observation, I conducted interviews with all the buyers and merchandisers in three areas of the women's wear department, as well as the then director of the store, the head of the women's Buying Office and the head of the Fashion Office responsible for such things as general trend direction and store promotion. Although the store does have a large concessions department, I was interested in what is known as 'own-bought' commodities—i.e. the commodities selected and purchased by buyers. Since the own-bought purchases were from high-end, designer labels, my analysis is, in some senses, specific to this sector of the fashion industry, and along with the models project, forms part of a picture of 'high fashion'.

My observations covered a whole range of activities buyers are involved in. I observed meetings at the store, followed buyers on their 'floor walks' around the shop floor, sat in on meetings with suppliers, and followed buyers on 'buys' in studios around London, New York, Milan and Paris. On buying trips I could talk to buyers informally about their work and pick up issues from my observations as they arose. Since so much of the fashion buying season is organized around 'fashion week', I also observed the Autumn/Winter collections at London Fashion Week (LFW) just prior to my fieldwork starting in February 2002 and followed the buyers around at the Spring/Summer 'collections' during September and October 2002 in London, Milan and Paris. Indeed, my ethnography took me on the journey around one season—from planning and buying stock to the arrival of the stock in the store months later.

Significantly, as noted above, these two projects were initially conceived and conducted as separate independent projects. In each case I began with different research questions. The first study started life as a continuation of earlier work on gender and sexuality at work (Entwistle 1997, 2000b). I came to study male fashion models because I was interested in how male models, working in a very non-traditional occupation, managed their (hetero)sexual identity in what is a feminized occupation where women are dominant and where models are sexualized workers often encountering gay men. I found male modelling to be a 'queer' occupation in that it confounded typical notions of heterosexual masculinity (Entwistle 2004).

However, in the course of the fieldwork, my observations led me to ask new research questions. Increasingly I found myself interested in the work of the 'bookers', who book the models for jobs and who select, promote and manage models' careers. I began to question the forms of knowledge and expertise they drew upon to select their chosen model bodies and their ways of calculating and managing the risks inherent in this market—those of how to calculate what 'look' to promote, and how to manage a fashion model's career so as to increase his value. Since this look did not often correspond to anything one would conventionally define as 'beauty' or 'good looks', I became interested in how the fashion model look is given value by bookers and others within the market. That is to say, the generation of value, for want of a better term, let's call it *aesthetic value* as it is concerned with a model's look, is inherently unstable and changing; it therefore has to be *stabilized* and *valorized* by actors within the market. I proposed the idea that this was a particular sort of market, an 'aesthetic economy', (Entwistle 2002) in that the main criterion of value—a key criterion within any market—was constituted out of a mix of seemingly nebulous 'cultural' concerns that determined the 'economic': who 'found' the model and how influential are they? what photographer, stylist or designer selected the model? which highly valued editorial spreads were they selected for? for which influential magazines or fashion campaigns? Thus, the success of any model and their *economic* value is, therefore, seamlessly woven into a web of *cultural* issues.

These concerns and questions inevitably spilled over into my second fieldwork project although, from the outset, I began with different questions. My initial interest was in fashion buyers as 'cultural intermediaries' between producers/suppliers and consumers. While this remained a concern, continuities and similarities I could not ignore began to emerge between this project and the models. Again, I found myself considering the particularities of fashionable dress as a market where the quality of the aesthetic was unstable and always shifting. And so the nature of *aesthetic value* in highly unstable markets became a critical concern with this project as well as the models. However, we are not talking about some Kantian pure aesthetic but something much more profane. Fashion value, as I argue, is defined through the collective activities and practice of actors inside the market. However, while I offer some theoretical resources that I consider to be very useful for understanding fashion markets and apply these to understanding two fashion markets, I do not claim to have a definitive theory of the aesthetic market or even a general theory of aesthetic marketplace of fashion. My analysis advances our knowledge about how aesthetic markets are put together but it is not and cannot be the definitive or final word on the matter.

Unlike classical economics, I approached this issue of value not as something 'the market', as some abstract mechanism, would determine. Instead, the issue of value seemed closer to more sociologically informed accounts of the markets and particularly led me to the work of Pierre Bourdieu (1984, 1993a, 2005) and Michel Callon (Callon 1998a, 1999; Callon, Meadel et al. 2005). Despite obvious theoretical and methodological differences between these two, I suggest, in Chapter 2, that there are many points of contact between them, not least their critique of classical economics and the way in which they see the market, or more specifically, *markets,* as practised social arrangements which knit together 'cultural' and 'economic' concerns. Throughout this book I draw on concepts derived and/or developed in the work of both theorists—concepts such as 'capital' and 'habitus' (Bourdieu 1984, 1993a,b) and 'qualification' and 'network' (Callon 1991, 1999; Callon, Meadel et al. 2005)—as I did not see any reason to choose between them when they were both so apt for unpacking the characteristics of the two related markets I observed.

Having spelled out the background to my two case studies, let me now say some more about the ways in which they are connected by examining four points of convergence between them.

Convergences

The World of High Fashion

Models, model bookers and fashion buyers share similar conditions of work and similar professional spaces of production, although with obvious differences in occupational settings and ethos. Thus, while the specific work of these agents differs, they occupy the same corner of the world—high-end or designer fashion—which means that their work overlaps at various times; at fashion shows, models parade on the catwalk beneath which buyers sit, and in design studios 'fit' models display the clothes that buyers may select. This simple fact has other implications. The world of fashion places an enormous weight and significance, not surprisingly, on the body and its presentation, a feature which will be discussed in more detail throughout this book. This world is predominantly white and relatively few black or ethnic workers are in evidence (most notably, in fashion modelling); it is also a world noted for its celebration of youth, 'beauty' and the 'thin' body. Models, bookers and buyers share these characteristics even while they might be from very different class backgrounds: indeed, class is not nearly as important in this industry as it might be in others. Thus, while they are situated at different points in the wider field of fashion, these different quarters of the fashion-making world look remarkably similar and examining the patterning of them together enables a fuller picture of the world of high fashion to emerge.

What do I mean by fashion? Fashion is a surprisingly vague term; at times a verb—*to fashion*—which can refer to almost anything, and at other times a short-hand for describing particularly modern dress. I would suggest, in line with others (Braudel 1981; Wilson 2003; Kawamura 2004), that fashion refers to a system of stylistic innovation, i.e. not to any specific product category (we can for example talk about fashion in architecture, design, even academic thought). The other way to put it is to say fashion is 'change for change's sake': it defines a constant movement for the sake of movement. Fashion has obsolescence built into it but not for reasons of necessity (not because things wear out or are replaced by better things) but simply because there is a *desire* (not of individuals but built within the system) for some movement or change. This characteristic of fashion (as a verb) can be found in a whole range of activities and cultural forms.

Fashion, especially fashionable clothing, is a particularly modern phenomenon, since the relentless movement of ideas, styles, and the apparent 'speed' at which they change are characteristic of modernity itself (Wilson 2003; Breward and Evans 2005). Precisely how modern is debatable. Many of the leading historians (Braudel 1981; Breward 1995) trace fashionable dress back as far as the fourteenth century, when styles of dress began to change more rapidly than before. However, at this time, fashionable clothing was confined to a very small minority, royalty and the aristocracy. The majority of people were not able to wear fashionable dress until much later, indeed, it is not until the twentieth century that something like a 'fashion system', i.e. regulated systems for the production of clothing (a 'mass' market) could be said to have emerged. However, fashionable clothing remained highly differentiated. Haute couture still produces very expensive unique clothing for a rich minority; prêt-a-porter still expensive but more accessible; and the high street reproduces this designer style for a fraction of the cost.

Fashionable clothing, then, involves two things: fashion refers to regular (i.e. biannual) stylistic innovation, and a production system that is geared to making and distributing these clothes. However, fashion is not just about changing clothes, it is also about changing *ideals* as to the design and look of clothes. In other words, fashion is about *aesthetics,* not simply new clothes, but clothes that are promoted and popularized as 'attractive', 'beautiful', 'stylish', or 'chic'. Hence, when we talk about fashionable dress we need to bear in mind not only the production of actual garments, but the production of aesthetic value around such garments. Clothes are selected for their ability to 'look good' within the terms of taste of the day.

One still useful way of thinking about fashion spaces and encounters is found in an early and rare sociological analysis of the fashion industry by Herbert Blumer (1969). In this article, Blumer outlines the institutional relations and processes of 'collective selection' that determine what constitutes 'fashion' in any one season. Rather than depicting fashion as a mysterious force which is the expression of some inner psychic force, as some explanations have tended to do, (Flügel 1930; Veblen 1953 [1899]), Blumer argues that fashion is socially produced by the institutional, social and cultural relations between a number of key players in the industry; principally between designers, fashion buyers and journalists. Thus, fashions come into being as the result of selective choices made by designers (who choose what garments to show in their collections) and by journalists and buyers (who select some items as the 'look' for a particular season). Designers are aware that their garments will be filtered through these cultural mediators, but can never predict what garments will be picked up. Blumer also notes that there is a remarkable similarity between these key players as to what elements they select and this he puts down to the fact that these cultural innovators and mediators are immersed in the same culture and seek out inspiration for new trends and tastes from the same sources. They are therefore well placed to pick up and translate what he calls 'incipient taste', the emerging aesthetic dispositions of the particular time. Although his analysis focused on the selection of fashionable clothing, his description of the networks of social relations which go to selecting particular key 'looks' each season can be utilized to describe how the look within fashion modelling comes into being through the interconnecting networks within the fashion system.

As with the 'collective selection' of fashionable clothing, there is a remarkable similarity in the model looks and fashion clothes chosen by key players inside the these two markets. Bookers and fashion buyers and other insiders move across the same networks and develop this same aesthetic sensibility and knowledge of what may or may not be 'in fashion' a few months ahead. Having said that, there are no guarantees of success. Bookers cannot always know what clients, photographers, magazine editors and designers want in terms of model looks, although they are better placed than you or I to make calculated guesses. The same is true for fashion buyers, who cannot predict with total certainly what their consumer/s want next season, but who are well placed inside the fashion network to understand and translate burgeoning trends. Much like the fashion designers who cannot predict in advance of their shows what items will be picked up by the fashion buyers and journalists and thus popularized, bookers and buyers cannot predict with absolute certainty what will make it precisely because they cannot know in advance what selections others—designers, photographers, customers—will make. However, their actions help to 'qualify' (Callon, Meadel et al. 2005) the goods, selecting, promoting and sending them on a journey towards other critical actors in the network. The process does not stop at any point in the network as looks selected feed-back and inform further choices. By describing the 'networks' and 'circuits of value' within two fashion markets, especially in Chapter 3, I hope to elaborate on Blumer's idea of 'collective selection'.

An Aesthetic Marketplace

As I have already suggested, fashion modelling and fashion clothing are examples of *aesthetic markets*. Although I offer a fuller definition and analysis in Chapter 3, I want to briefly define what I mean by this term. An aesthetic market is one in which an aesthetic quality—be it a look or style—is commodified, that is, defined and calculated within a market and sold for profit. Many products and services are styled and this is part of the product they sell. However, I am interested in markets where an aesthetic quality is the *core commodity*, rather than when the aesthetic is important in the process of selling something else. Take boutique hotels whose success may depend to a large extent on their aesthetic style. They may trade on their style, but are not solely in business to sell a look or style: they sell a service as well—hospitality, relaxation, maybe spa features as well. The aesthetic is important but not the only quality being traded in the marketplace. In fashion modelling and fashion clothing, the look or style takes primacy as the key quality transacted and, moreover, the aesthetic quality is in constant flux: fashion models and clothing come in and out of fashion with the seasons. In other words, in aesthetic markets, aesthetics are not something 'added on' as a decorative feature once a product has been defined; *they are the product/s* and, as such, are at the centre of the economic calculations of the practice. I am not so much interested in the content of the style itself—skinny or bootleg jeans, 'weird' or 'pretty' faces—since the content keeps changing. Instead,

I am interested in the *social* and *material* practices inside these markets. In other words, I am interested in how aesthetic values are generated *within economic action* by actors and increasingly essential to carrying out economic practices.

It is important to note here that I am not suggesting that these markets are radically different from other sorts of markets, or imply we have entered into some new 'epoch', that is some postmodern era of signs, signification and aesthetics, as arguments about the 'aestheticization of everyday life' suggest. Indeed, I would resist any attempt to suggest that we can dispense with older arguments based on political economy and reduce 'economy' to 'culture'. Instead, I concur with Jackson, Lowe et al. (2000: 1) who, drawing on the work of Latour, argue that 'the world is what might be called the "authentic hybrid" ... that is commercial cultures.' Aesthetic economies are examples of this 'authentic hybrid' and assert the necessity of understanding these markets as 'economic', and not merely 'cultural' or 'aesthetic'.

As recent literature on the 'cultural economy' (Ray and Sayer 1999a; Jackson, Lowe et al. 2000; Du Gay and Pryke 2002; Pratt 2004a) testifies, all markets are, to some extent, cultural, since all markets depend upon meanings and shared values as to what constitutes the 'market' and how to go about buying and selling within it. The 'economy' can never be extracted from cultural concerns, as some pure logic or 'law'. Indeed, as Gertler (2003: 88) puts it, 'culture and economy are two sides of the same coin. Seemingly natural structures such as markets are now understood to be deeply embedded.' It is for these reasons that my analysis draws heavily on economic sociology, particularly the work of Callon (1998c; see also Callon, Meadel et al. 2005) and Bourdieu (Bourdieu 1984; 1993a,b; 2005), to understand how 'cultural' and 'economic' categories are merged in the everyday calculations of actors inside the particular marketplaces of modelling and clothing. Thus, examining these aesthetic markets involves assembling a range of theoretical resources that enable one to consider the ways in which the aesthetic is calculable. It means examining the ways in which 'culture' and 'economy' are merged in market practices. These two terms have long histories within modern thought and developed independent intellectual trajectories, although more recent literature on the 'cultural economy' and within actor-network-theory has emerged to challenge this dualism. I discuss this literature in detail in Chapter 2 as it forms the context for my analysis of fashion.

To understand these markets, indeed *any* market, it is necessary to consider how value is arrived at; through what mechanisms and practices is a commodity's value secured? (Callon 1998a; Aspers 2001; MacKenzie 2004; Callon, Meadel et al. 2005). I am particularly concerned with *how the aesthetic quality acquires value within aesthetic markets.* Since we know that aesthetic value in a fashion market is a value attached to things that are constantly moving 'in' and 'out' of fashion, this question of value becomes a two-fold problem. Firstly, there is the problem of how those inside the market come *to know* what will be 'in' fashion, which is complicated by the temporal arrangements for fashion markets that require calculations to be made ahead of the season in which they will sell, adding a huge element of uncertainty to the calculations. Thus, secondly, the question becomes one of how this value—the quality of fashionability—can be *stabilized* long enough for fashionable commodities to be traded. In other words, fashionable commodity value is always diminishing but not because the product deteriorates in physical way (as food or flowers do), but because they will no longer be 'in fashion' once the season is over. However, temporality in fashion is a much more ambiguous thing; some things can hold their fashionable value longer than others, if trends stabilize over more than one season, as skinny jeans for example have managed to do for several seasons (at the time of writing); other things lose their value quicker than expected, as when trends for particular colours fail to sell in volume if 'for example' too many consumers find lime green unpalatable, or the weather proves to be too wet to sell linen trousers. However, the problem—for people such as fashion buyers—is that these factors may not necessarily be apparent until after they have made their orders and committed themselves to receiving the stock.

The flip side of this question concerning value is the issue of *calculation* which is at the heart of modernity, money and markets (Simmel 1990). That is to say, value—as something socially produced through market activity—directs attention to the ways in which this quality is rendered meaningful and its value determined through particular mechanisms. This can be translated into the question, *how is the aesthetic a category of economic calculation?* Aesthetic marketplace calculations have their own particularity or 'local rationality' (Abolafia 1998). Fashion modelling and fashion clothing exhibit the same features as other markets, such as the concern to push commodities and maximize profit, but this profit motive depends to a very great extent upon the incalculable value of nebulous, highly unstable qualities and categories of 'culture'—status and prestige, for example. They may appear more nebulous since at first glance they seem far more 'subjective' or 'immaterial' and thus far less 'stable'. The inherent properties of 'beauty', 'style' or 'design' (however defined) upon which the 'value' of aesthetic products seems to rest appear at first to be rather too ill-defined to be subject to 'rational' economic calculations. However, aesthetic values do not come out of nowhere; they certainly do not reside in the disembodied signs of contemporary capitalism, but are generated *internally* to the market itself, by the routine actions and practices of individuals and institutions. Hence, like Pratt (2004a) and others (Du Gay, Hall et al. 1997; Du Gay and Pryke 2002), I argue for a 'production of culture' approach to understanding work in such markets. In the world of modelling, the models' looks are constantly changing in response to the fluctuations of the fashion system and the differing needs of clients. In high fashion clothing, styles can vary dramatically from season to season, or develop organically from the previous season. These swings, seemingly without a central organizing principle, are, nonetheless, translated and managed by those inside the market in order to be meaningfully assembled into a market. The question, as I have already suggested, is how do those in the market calculate the product—a model's look, or designer clothing range? This leads automatically to a consideration of what forms of knowledge are required to understand and operate within a market.

Aesthetic Knowledge

To calculate inside a market, one must know something about it. This third point relates to the sorts of knowledge and the forms of 'capital' (Bourdieu, 1984) demanded in such markets. Knowledge is about *making sense*, but in aesthetic markets like fashion, sense-making engages non-cognitive abilities rather than cognitive and rational forms of economic knowledge familiar to economic sociologists and theorists of business. It is partly a *sensual* knowledge, formed through sensual encounters with the material objects themselves in marketplace experience, and it is *embodied* since this knowledge is performed on the body. Aesthetic knowledge is difficult to verbalize precisely because it is largely tacit in nature. Indeed, bookers and buyers struggle to describe it but often use very similar embodied metaphors to describe their knowledge, all stressing the importance of 'gut instinct' or having an 'eye'. It is summed up by Ingrid, of Clear Model agency, who, in an on-line interview with an industry site, explained how, after only nine months with the agency, she made Director of the Men's Board. Although, as she noted, 'I didn't want to be the Director of any board … I was like "I don't know if this is what I want to do and I don't know what I'm doing!" the owner of the agency insisted, suggesting, "you do know what you're doing honey. You have an *eye*. That's the first step." ' (www.models.com, emphasis added)

These embodied metaphors of the 'eye' and 'gut' are thus appropriate to describe knowledge in these markets, which is in some way *about* the body. They refer implicitly to the embodied *sense* and *sensibility* necessary in order to calculate and operate within an aesthetic market. This ability cannot be taught on a course, acquired through formal training or staff development; it is learned 'on the job'. That is, it can only be acquired *inside* the market and this is evident in the career paths of bookers and buyers. Most bookers start out as a 'tear-sheeters' (people in agencies who collect model images for inclusion in their books) and it is only once the necessary experience and cultural capital has been acquired that a tear-sheeter may be promoted to a booker or scout (someone who works for the agency, scouting out talent across the world). Other routes into model management come from previous experience in the fashion industry, as a stylist, or model, (the latter was the case for two of the bookers I interviewed). Buyers similarly acquire their knowledge through experience and would not be given a budget to manage until they had 'cut their teeth' in retailing. However, while traditionally buyers often started out on the shop-floor, today they are more likely to enter into graduate training programmes. Having said that, their knowledge is similarly built up through years of experience, first as assistant buyers and later as head buyers.

Knowledge is not just disembodied, dislocated information, but always embodied and situated, and for this reason, I am concerned with the spatiality of 'tacit aesthetic knowledge'. My argument, noted above, is that the first 'territory' of space and knowledge is the body itself, although this remains invisible in most accounts. We might pose the questions on a more mundane level. How do particular clothes end up in the shops? Why do model agencies form local markets in particular cities (and particular areas of the city) even while they feed globally distributed clients? These questions can be answered with reference to current research within economic geography and a burgeoning literature on retail geography that focus attention on the spatial dimensions of markets and commodities, attempting to define and characterize how such markets are spatially ordered in terms of 'commodity chains' (Jackson 1999, 2002) or 'systems of provision' (Fine and Leopold 1993) or 'commodity circuits'. I pick up these terms in Chapter 5 in order to understand the circulation of high fashion and the local and global dimensions of markets in fashion models and fashion clothing. The issues of the spatiality of knowledge in terms of embodied interactions and performances are further developed in Chapters 6 and 7. Here I examine some specific spatial encounters that contextualize fashionable commodities and focus on the geographically located and embodied processes and relationships.

Without pre-empting my discussion in these chapters, let me suggest how space is critical to the two markets I examine. Different spatial scales, from the very local to the global, explain something of the character and locatedness of these markets. It is not an accident that fashion model agencies are located in key cities like London or New York, with concentrations of agencies in particular parts of the city—SoHo in New York and the Kings Road, Covent Garden and latterly, Hoxton in London. This locality ensures that model agencies are neighbours to one another and located near to important clients in the city. So while models travel the world for work, it is also the case that model agencies in each city serve the needs of very particular local clients. Further, these spatial relations help to ensure the production and reproduction of particular aesthetics associated with these cities—the 'hunky', musculature look of the Los Angeles male model versus the 'skinny', 'odd'-looking London model—and these different aesthetics are precisely what enable these cities to locate themselves within the global fashion modelling market, establishing the identity of agencies and their unique 'selling point'. The local 'character' of the models is, therefore, a feature that is not only embedded within the local economy of fashion in the city, but has a global meaning and currency.

The same is true of the major department store observed. Selfridges occupies a prominent position on one of London's main shopping streets, Oxford Street. Its location is critical to its identity—it is the 'flagship' store in the United Kingdom—and this fact steers the store in the direction of particular products appropriate for this status. The location of the store alongside a number of competitors in the 'high fashion' market, such as Browns on South Moulton Street, is also critical. To maintain an identity alongside these, the store must sell products of similar status and caché although the product spread must not be identical if it is to maintain a unique identity. However, the store's competitors are also located abroad. Catering as it does for cosmopolitan customers, as well as local ones, the store locates itself in relation to competitors abroad as well—Barney's in New York, for example. Securing contracts with top-end designers depends upon maintaining a high status identity both within London and globally.

To understand these commodities and their circulation it is necessary to ask, who are the people responsible for making particular commodities available? That is, who aids their circulation and mediates between the producers of goods, on the one hand, and their target consumer/s on the other?

Models, Bookers and Buyers as Cultural Intermediaries

A fourth and final convergence focuses on the actors themselves who might be described as *cultural intermediaries* (Bourdieu 1984; see also Featherstone 1990) or 'taste-makers' within fashion, and also on their work of *mediation*. To take the first point, my study focuses on some of the influential fashion players responsible for helping to form and promote fashion aesthetics and taste inside these two markets. Much attention has been focused of late on the work of such cultural intermediaries, deriving from Bourdieu's (1993a, 1984) influential work on taste and fields of cultural production. These mediators, among them journalists (Bourdieu 1984), advertising agents (Du Gay and Nixon 2002; McFall 2002; Cronin 2004), men's magazine editors (Crewe 2003), music producers (Negus 1992, 1999) and fashion designers (Skov 2002) have been attributed an important role—some might argue, controversially, a more important role now than ever before—of bringing a range of cultural things to market: goods, images, tastes, aesthetics. In other words, they have been seen as influential mediators of culture, moving between the two realms of production and consumption and therefore responsible for framing or promoting culture in all its various guises within the capitalist marketplace. Most of us are, in some way and in differing degrees, touched by the work of these mediators through our encounters with images and products, so, while we never meet them directly in face-to-face interaction, we do encounter them indirectly, through the various cultural forms they work to produce.

However, this duality—production/consumption—is a false one, since neither production nor consumption are monolithic structures or discreet entities, but themselves complex processes that are critically interlinked. Part of the problem is that the literature within cultural studies and in the social sciences has tended to split off production from consumption. As Fine and Leopold argued in the 1990s, production is severed from consumption, the two seen as distinctly different realms rather than crucially intertwined. Studies of production may focus on production technologies, factory and sweatshop systems while studies of consumption focus on shopping habits and practices. However, we know little about the ways in which these two interact and the unsung multitude of people who exist in the many spaces 'between' who help to circulate and promote goods. In other words, the networks of distribution, dissemination and mediation are often neglected. Thus, Fine and Leopold's (1993) argument made in the early nineties is still largely relevant in the early part of the twenty-first century.

Bearing all this in mind, let me say a few more words about the three agents whose work I examined—buyers, models and model bookers—and why I see them as cultural intermediaries. I suggest that in different ways fashion buyers, models and model bookers are cultural intermediaries, each, in their own way, mediating between (for want of better terms) 'production' and 'consumption'. Although they sit at different interfaces between producers on the one hand and consumers on the other, models, bookers and buyers are in positions of influence within the fashion world and serve as connecting points between producers and consumers.

On face of it, fashion buyers are obvious and key mediators between production and consumption in the fashion industry: through their selections they mediate the products set out by designers, selecting them on behalf of their imagined or 'virtual' consumer (Carrier and Miller 1998). As Fine and Leopold (1993) argue, what they call distributors or 'middlemen' [*sic*] in the fashion industry—fashion buyers by another name—are crucial 'linch-pins', in the fashion system, bringing products to market that would otherwise languish in factory storerooms (or indeed, never get designed or manufactured at all). Their selections are, therefore, the critical yet invisible link between producers and consumers yet this tells us very little and begs further questions: how do they buy and how do they know what they know? Other questions concern who they encounter and what happens at these encounters, and thus how they select on behalf of their consumer/s. We might also ask, as I do in Chapter 8, what is it they actually mediate? This is an important question to ask if we are to understand their work of cultural mediation. I argue that buyers do not merely mediate garments, but also mediate trends, aesthetics, taste, 'style', i.e. they promote 'fashion' in its totality. In addition, numerous other things are mediated in the process—the identities of designers/producers/brands/their retail business, and, indeed, their own identity.

In what respect can models and bookers be said to be cultural mediators? As I argue, fashion is about more than simply clothes, promoting, in complex ways, the 'body beautiful'. The point is, of course, that clothes cannot be separated from the body beneath, but shape, drape, mould, expose, hide, define, emphasize or otherwise relate to the body and promote certain kinds of body in the process (Hollander 1993). These ideals are widely disseminated across a range of media and are themselves constantly changing and not always easily read as 'beautiful' by conventional standards. The work of modelling—performed by models themselves and bookers—is implicated in this dissemination of body aesthetics. Of course, models and model bookers perform different work and they have both been singled out of late for promoting unrealistic images of beauty, or for destructive versions of femininity. While not side-stepping this issue altogether, let me examine the ways in which models might be said to mediate body aesthetics.

Models have unwittingly become role models to many young women, as public debate surrounding Kate Moss demonstrates. Early in her career, Moss was single-handedly blamed for promoting anorexia and heroin abuse, and later, in September 2005, she was the centre of another scandal surrounding her alleged drug-taking. However, models do not single-handedly determine how they look or are perceived. To take the first point, at the beginning of her career, Moss was remarkably skinny and this was commented on in the press. However, she was not in sole charge of her image at this time. She needed to be selected by others—first by Sarah Doukas of the agency Storm and later by clients, such as photographer Corinne Day and Calvin Klein—for her look to be popularized.

Models are hired for their ability to sell us clothes, via the images they appear in. Models, particularly those who become household names as celebrities, are both *conscious* embodied mediators of style, fashioning themselves through various forms of 'aesthetic labour' (Entwistle and Wissinger 2006) to secure work in this competitive industry; they are also *unwitting complicit components* in networks of image production that mediate style, fashion and body aesthetics. Again Kate Moss is a particularly good example of the complexity of models' work. Moss mediates numerous things, not just the clothing she might wear in advertisements or editorials. She mediates the identities of brands she is the 'face of' (such as Burberry or Dior until September 2005). She is positioned in the field to act as a mediator for more general trends or fashion. Take 'grunge' which emerged in the early to mid 1990s, and styled frequently around Moss. She was a component in the dissemination of this style, along with the fashion designer Marc Jacobs and influential photographers, such as Corinne Day and Juergen Teller. However, she was not only the raw material upon which photographers and stylists worked, she also carried the style over beyond her model image. Indeed, her growing celebrity status has made her a *conscious* agent of style: she is photographed frequently by the paparazzi and her personal style is frequently singled out by fashion journalists as highly influential in promoting particular clothing and particular aesthetic styles and trends. Further evidence of her ability to mediate taste, fashion, and clothes comes from her current new role as consultant/designer at the UK retailer Topshop.

The point is that models are significant nodes in the dissemination of aesthetics; as component parts in the image machinery over which they do not have total control, and as conscious human agents who may style themselves effectively. In other words, the work of mediation is a complex one, not limited to conscious human agents. A photograph of a fashion model can disseminate ideas about fashion and style and the body through the complex ways in which it is put together and through the very media itself. This idea of *mediation* goes far beyond anything Bourdieu described with reference to cultural intermediaries. Indeed, his analysis did not focus on mediation as such, but the identities of the mediators themselves, a point McFall (2002) argues is too narrow. Thinking about mediation in this way, one can examine the influence of models far beyond their apparent role in selling goods. Models might be said to promote a host of things: aesthetic standards of dress, body and demeanour, a particular lifestyle, particular patterns of consumption (including the consumption of illicit drugs) that help to create and sustain a very particular urban scene and particular consumption habits focused around bars, restaurants, clubs, and so on (see Wissinger 2007b; Wissinger 2009).

In what ways might bookers be said to be cultural intermediaries? While far less visible agents of bodily aesthetics, they nonetheless exert some influence along the fashion network through their work of selecting and promoting fashion models to potential clients. In doing so, bookers help to shape the fashion model aesthetic, for men and women. While they may argue that their job is simply to pick up on trends and the needs of clients, in fact their work cannot be seen as simply a passive 'reflex' to demands of an abstract 'system', whether we call it the 'market' or not. Indeed, as I argue in Chapter 3, their work 'qualifies and requalifies' (Callon, Meadel et al. 2005) the model aesthetic; that is to say, they are instrumental in the circulation and validation of model looks precisely because they are well placed, in their work of promotion, to help generate value around any particular model looks.

That the look is a constantly qualified one is apparent when looking at the range of different models popularized at different times. The fashion model look today, found inside the pages of many niche fashion magazines, is often described as 'edgy' or 'quirky', while more conventional 'good looks' may be found in mainstream fashion editorial and commercial imagery. Bookers are hooked into a network of similar fashion workers—meeting and socializing with clients, designers, photographers—at industry events, parties, fashion shows and the like. From this location in the network they are best placed to pick up on 'incipient taste' (Blumer 1969) of clients and able to calculate which looks will sell to which clients. Their work of promotion involves a number of techniques, from 'talking up' the 'new faces' they sign to the agency, so as to help them secure their first vital meetings or 'go sees', to keeping more established models in work by calculating on how to adapt or change their image to stay 'fresh' on the market. These points I take up in more detail in Chapter 3.

In sum, all three workers contribute in some way to the configuration of high fashion tastes—in bodies and clothes. Although the precise content of the fashion aesthetic constantly changes, the *process of valorization* within each of these markets is remarkably similar. Buyers, models and model bookers contribute to the production and circulation of fashion by promoting some styles and not others, and by communicating this aesthetic sense, or taste, to consuming audiences.

Conclusion

This book addresses a gap in our understanding of fashion by asking questions of the *processes,* and *people,* in this instance, the buyers, models, model agents (but the list could and should be longer, including journalists, photographers and stylists), who configure the high fashion world. At a more general level, as I have indicated above, the book attends to the ways in which such markets are put together and to critical questions of value in markets as they pertain to aesthetic commodities. How is value generated around effervescent commodities; that is to commodities whose content is constantly in flux? To answer these questions, I am interested in the processes, knowledge and calculations that are required on the part of these influential insiders to identify, select, promote and thereby lend value or prestige to these commodities. As I go on to argue in Chapter 2, the 'cultural' and 'economic' aspects of these markets are inevitably intertwined in particular ways.

Part I
Understanding Aesthetic Markets

2

An Aesthetic Marketplace: Assembling 'Economy' and 'Culture'

Characteristics of Aesthetic Markets

What are the characteristics of aesthetic markets? Specifically, how are the aesthetic qualities of commodities rendered; that is to say, why are some things selected, promoted, distributed and sold as 'beautiful', 'stylish' or simply 'fashion' or 'on trend'? As noted Chapter 1, these questions are ones which focus attention on the sorts of processes, knowledge and calculations of actors in particular marketplaces in order to make sense of particular goods and bring them to market. These questions, the central ones of this book, are where I begin this chapter. However, before we can go any further, it is necessary to define and delineate the terms of this analysis. What do we mean by a market or marketplace and, more particularly, what kind of market is an aesthetic market? Essentially, these questions concern how something 'economic' (a business geared to profit) can be constructed out of otherwise non-economic, i.e. 'cultural', qualities (style, aesthetics, value, etc). Therefore, a good place to start is to examine how these two—'economy' and 'culture'—have been constructed as opposites, how they are often analytically separated, and how we might reconstitute their relation to understand markets for aesthetic commodities.

As many have claimed (Ray and Sayer 1999b; Du Gay and Pryke 2002; McFall 2004), culture and economy are two of the most complex and problematic terms in social and human sciences. They are often treated as analytically separate and distinct realms of life, as stable and coherent entities with their own internal logic when, in practice, the delineation between culture and economy is very difficult to sustain because 'culture and economy are ... provisional and historically contingent' and 'constituent dimensions of material practice, not discrete spheres.' (McFall 2004: 62). Nonetheless, the distinction is an important one in intellectual history and one that we must acknowledge before unpacking the constituent ways in which they inform the material practices within aesthetic markets.

Economy

Classical economics and more recent neo-liberal incarnations are peculiarly 'modern' ways of thinking about social life that 'arose in response to the complex transformations that produced the conditions of modernity' (Slater and Tonkiss 2001: 6). Instead of seeing the things of social life in their totality, modern economics is dominated by something called the 'market' which is an abstract system for the provisioning of daily life, with its own 'laws' that ensure it operates effectively. Thus, the market in modern European thought is 'a conceptual, strategic, abstract space of calculation and commercial opportunity' (Slater and Tonkiss 2001: 14). The idealized, abstract market beloved of economists separates out economic activity from the rest of social life as a special sphere of activity. Thus, it is evident that the market implies a number of things. Callon (1998b: 3) approvingly cites Guesnerie: 'a market is a co-ordination device in which a) agents pursue their own interests and to this end perform economic calculations which can be seen as an operation to optimization and/or maximization; b) the agents generally have divergent interests, which lead them to engage in c) transactions which resolve the conflict by defining price.'

There is, at the heart of this conception, the idea of 'the economy' as an impersonal realm of activity where action is rational, instrumental or goal-orientated. This view of the 'economy' emerged out of a separate sphere of analysis, namely, 'economics', and is at its most extreme in branches of liberal and neo-liberal thought. Thus, as Bourdieu (2005: 1) argues, 'The science called "economics" is based on an initial act of abstraction that consists in disassociating a particular category of practices, or particular dimension of all practice, from the social order in which all human practice is immersed.' The 'market' becomes a separate and idealized realm organized by 'laws' of supply and demand and price regulation, and divorced from ordinary experience. There is, therefore, a distinction to be drawn between the 'market' and actual 'marketplaces': 'While the market denotes the abstract mechanisms whereby supply and demand confront each other and adjust themselves in search of a compromise, the marketplace is far closer to ordinary experience and refers to the place in which exchange occurs' (Bourdieu 2005: 1). Marketplaces are spatially and temporally located places where economic transactions occur that are embedded within wider social activities: it is 'a congregation of a public ... a place for political and religious communications ... as well as flows of information and gossip that may be consequential in political, social or commercial terms' (Slater and Tonkiss 2001: 10; see also Slater 2002a).

While economics as a discipline devotes itself to defining the abstract laws of something called the 'market', the economy refers to 'practical activity', yet the two are divorced from one another so that, according to Callon (1998a: 1), 'If economic theory knows little about the marketplace, is it not simply because in striving to abstract and generalise it, it has ended up becoming detached from its object?'. Economics should, he argues (1998b: 1), 'return to its object, the economy, from which it never should have strayed in the first place' and this point is similarly made by Bourdieu (2005: 7), who suggests that to overcome 'a systematic discrepancy [that] exists between theoretical models and actual practices' what is required is 'observation and ethnographic description' (2005: 7) to connect them back again.

What economics as a discipline does achieve, however, is the power to shape and constitute practices—governments, the World Bank and other such powerful agencies talk of the 'market' in this way, and its abstract principles govern much of everyday life of individuals and organizations in ways that make it constituent of subjectivities, such as *homo economicus,* or the rational, economic actor. Sometimes referred to as 'virtualism' (Carrier and Miller 1998), the result of such abstract thinking is that 'economics in the broad sense of the term, performs, shapes and formats the economy, rather than observing how it functions (Latour 1987)' (Callon 1998b: 2). Or, as Bourdieu (2005: 10) puts it, economic theory in 'most formalised form' is 'never neutral' but finds expression in dominant practices: 'Neoliberal economics ... is tending to win out throughout the world thanks to international bodies like the World Bank and International Monetary Fund who 'directly or indirectly, dictate their principles of "governance"'. This understanding of economics challenges the neutrality of the 'economy' as it is spoken of by economists, rendering it an entity that is social and socializing rather than abstract and scientific. Material culture and Science and technology (STS) inspired accounts of markets (Callon 1991, 1998c; Callon, Meadel et al. 2005) have been part of a widespread re-awakening of interest in the economy more broadly within the social sciences (Slater and Tonkiss 2001), challenging the standard account of 'the economy'. This has been an important corrective to the 'cultural turn' following postmodernism in the 1980s which had all but abandoned the 'economic' in favour of 'cultural' practices that seemed especially meaningful. Postmodernism and the later 'cultural turn' were in large part a reaction to earlier, Marxist-inspired accounts, derived largely out of Althusserian analysis, that privileged the economic as the determining factor in social life, denigrating as secondary—or super-structural—all things 'cultural' (Du Gay, Hall et al. 1997). The swing away from structuralist Marxism, inspired by certain branches of feminism and also cultural studies in the 1980s and early 1990s, resulted in a welter of studies paying critical attention to signs, dress, subcultures, the body, cultural products and cultural industries (Du Gay, Hall et al. 1997), and away from dull 'economic' things. In some branches of sociology and cultural studies, 'cultural' things were given the very highest priority, with terms like 'aestheticization of everyday life' (Jameson 1991; Lash and Urry 1993), suggesting that 'culture' really had taken over as the primary location of 'meaning' and activity.

More recent writing 'after the turn' (Ray and Sayer 1999a,b; see also Du Gay and Pryke 2002; Jackson 2002; Amin and Thrift 2004) have challenged this privileging of culture, interrogated the economy/culture dichotomy upon which both Marxist and culturalist approaches depend and which they have participated in constructing as separate domains. Indeed, placed in inverted commas, to designate that these terms do not describe pure entities or distinct areas of life, the arguments made more recently focus on how 'culture' and 'economy' are not separate and distinct entities at all, but hybridized or entwined. This echoes some earlier arguments from within economic anthropology (Polanyi 1957; Granovetter 1983), which consider economic activity already 'cultural', since 'economic' provisioning happens in a context—'embedded'—not a vacuum, and demands meaningful interpretation. One strand within anthropological approaches to the economy, and drawing on other social sciences, is 'material culture' (see Miller 1987, 1997) which looks at the ways in which things—artefacts and commodities—take on meaning in their use and thus how value is generated through everyday practices, relationships and transactions. The idea of an abstract system—the market—with abstract laws is anathema to all these approaches.

From this wide literature we now have numerous academic attempts to connect up activities seen as 'cultural' and 'economic' (Jackson 1999; Slater and Tonkiss 2001; Slater 2002a). One strand of this analysis (Negus 1992, 1999; Scott 1999, 2000; Hesmondhalgh 2002; McRobbie 2002a,b; Pratt 2004a,b) has focused on the 'culture industries', where cultural products and services are examined as businesses, increasingly playing a central role in the economies of cities, regions and nations. The question of how to define these and whether they constitute anything particularly new or challenging to our ideas about culture and economy, I return to below. Related to this work is research on the service industries, where the argument made for this seemingly 'cultural' sector depends upon 'hard' economic materiality—manufacturing and labour—for example. Recent work on business and organizations (Du Gay, Hall et al. 1997; Amin and Cohendet 2004; Thrift 2005), once firmly designated as 'economic', demonstrates how 'soft' 'cultural' concerns inflect the discourse and practices within, with such things as 'management culture', 'meaning' and 'communities of practice' becoming new business 'buzz-words'. Other analyses focus on retailing as a major meeting point between production and consumption (Jackson, Lowe et al. 2000; Wrigley and Lowe 2002) seen to belong to the separate spheres of 'economy' and 'culture' and previously split off to 'plough' two separate paths (Fine and Leopold 1993). Thus, the emergence of retail geography (Gardner and Sheppard 1989; Crewe and Davenport 1992; Wrigley and Lowe 2002; Hughes and Reimer 2004) attempts to reconnect them as intimately linked and merging concerns previously seen as either 'economic' or 'cultural'.

One influential term attempting to capture these concerns and new emphasis on the economy within social science is 'cultural economy' (Amin and Thrift 2004; Du Gay and Pryke 2002; Ray and Sayer 1999b). Du Gay and Pryke (2002: 2) argue for an analysis from the perspective of 'cultural economy' which examines how economic discourses—economics and related ones like marketing, or accounting—'format and frame markets and economic and organizational relations, "making them up" rather than simply observing and describing them from a god's-eye vantage point'. This, they argue, means going much further than simply arguing that the 'economy' is 'embedded' in a cultural context; it seeks to establish how the context is, itself, 'made up'.

This argument therefore goes further than arguments about 'embeddedness' which assume the existence of an *a priori* 'context'—i.e. 'culture'—within which the 'economy' is situated. Whereas embeddedness maintains the distinction between economy and culture as separate realms, cultural economy and STS research challenges the idea that we can designate these as separate activities or spheres. However, to understand this problem we need to first define what we mean by 'culture': can it be said to exist as an idealized realm of activity prior to the 'economy'?

Culture

Just as 'economy' has undergone revised definitions, subject to different sorts of analyses as a result of different disciplines or areas of debate, 'culture' has also been hotly contested. There are definitions that narrowly locate 'culture' as the repository of value and meanings, very often linked to Romantic notions of 'cultivation' and 'civilization' and developed by people like Arnold (1932) to refer to the restricted realm of expression in the 'high' arts. In the twentieth century, broader definitions of culture as 'ordinary' (Williams 1963) emerged, developed most fully in early branches of cultural studies and social sciences from the 1960s, to characterize culture in terms of a 'whole way of life' encompassing everyday activities and signifying practices not restricted to the high arts. What the different approaches share is some sense of culture as bound with intrinsic *meaning* and value: as Ray and Sayer (1999b: 5) put it, 'A crucial feature of many of the goals or goods associated with culture is that they are primarily internal.' They qualify this by saying that the internal qualities of culture are not objective or essential, since all value is 'relational' but, for Ray and Sayer, intrinsic values are non-instrumental, whereas economic activities 'involve a primarily instrumental orientation; they are ultimately a means to an end, satisfying external goals to do with provisioning' (1999b: 6).

Here is where the problems begin since, in practice, this difference between two sorts of activities, each with a different logic, cannot be easily maintained: as Ray and Sayer (1999b) themselves acknowledge, economic life is bound up with social and aesthetic values and, as we have seen, provisioning is always and everywhere culturally specific. However, while they concede that the economy is 'culturally inflected', they still posit a tenable distinction between 'culture' and 'economy' based on some sense that the two have intrinsically different internal value systems and logics. As they put it, 'To speak of a unity does not preclude the possibility that culture and economy may follow separate logics of development' (1999b: 6). In other words, we can talk of intrinsically different spheres of activity because, as they insist, 'despite the inflections, economic and cultural logics remain different and often pull in opposite directions' (1999b: 9).

However, can we speak of 'culture' and 'economy' as different spheres of activity? Is 'culture' a realm of intrinsic, non-instrumental reason and the 'economy' a realm of pure instrumental action? Not so, claim Du Gay and Pryke (2002). They ask, what happens when certain sorts of work are not able to align themselves to 'culture' or 'economy'? They give the example of service work: 'Rather than being solely an "economic" or a "cultural" phenomenon, service work is a contingent assemblage of practices built up from parts that are economic and non-economic (but always already cultural) and forged together in the pursuit of sales and competitive advantage' (Du Gay and Pryke 2002: 4). The same can be said for many other activities: retailing or fashion modelling, which I examine, do not fall easily or readily on one side of the culture/economy divide, and so too marketing (Cochoy in Du Gay and Pryke 2002) and advertising (McFall 2002, 2004).

As with McFall's (2004) claims about advertising and Du Gay's et al. (2002) claims about service work, retailing (Entwistle 2006) and modelling (Entwistle 2002) are 'hybrids', combining things characterized as 'cultural' and 'economic'. Take the idea of 'aesthetic labour' (Entwistle and Wissinger 2006) which is labour demanded of employees, especially those in the service industries, to 'look good and sound right' (Warhurst, Nickson et al. 2000; Nickson, Warhurst et al. 2001; Witz, Warhurst et al. 2002) and is, therefore, part of the production of a service. Workers' bodies, particularly their appearance, is part of the 'hardware' of the service organization, and the productive capacity of the company may depend on the ability of workers to produce the appropriate appearance. Entwistle and Wissinger (2006) extend this concept beyond its usual application in the service industries, to show how freelances in fashion modelling perform essential aesthetic labour to manage their careers, and it is true also of other arenas in high fashion, like retailing, as I will argue.

There are, in effect, many different ways in which things seemingly designated as 'culture' (such as aesthetics) and the 'economy' inflect one another. Aesthetic labour is just one example of how the seemingly nebulous qualities of 'style', 'aesthetics' or a 'look' are important to the 'economic' effectiveness of a firm, organization or individual worker selling themselves to such firms. This has implications for understanding model agencies and a fashion store like Selfridges, as well as other sorts of businesses and firms. These are primarily *businesses* orientated towards profit, to consider them only in terms of economic categories, like profit and loss, would fail to capture the *particular* ways in which they secure economic success and what makes them tick *as* businesses. Aesthetics refers not to some abstract realm of beauty, but the precise ways in which things are inflected, or articulated (Du Gay, Hall et al. 1997) with aesthetic qualities that are important and, in some businesses, essential, to company success. Thus, precisely *how* such aesthetic qualities and associations are made meaningful and generated around products is key to understanding what makes these businesses successful. As I argue throughout this book, these aesthetic qualities have to be *calculated* by agents in such markets and these calculations are not reducible to rational economic calculation, as defined within neo-economics and some branches of economic sociology. In aesthetic markets aesthetic value is *the* value generated around the commodity and the business selling it. Profit and loss are, of course, important, but important to understanding these are the aesthetic qualities and meanings of their products traded, which are seemingly bound up with nebulous, 'non-economic' concerns as well.

It is important to reiterate here that aesthetics are not an essential property of the object, but are *created, accrued, attributed, qualified and requalified* (Callon, Meadel et al. 2005) to the object/commodity over its life course, as discussed in the next chapter. For aesthetic commodities subject to incessant change, the qualities of 'style' or appearance have to be *stabilized,* if only momentarily (for a fashion 'season', for example). The spotlight falls upon the calculations demanded of agents in such a market concerned with seemingly non-economic things; such things as status acquired through valued connections with key actors, the creation of brand identity, the media profile of the product and fluctuations in aesthetic trends, bound up with decisions assumed to be 'economic': is the price right? Can we sell X number of tops in aubergine/this model for £10,000 a day? Are we running out of stock/Do we need to buy more stock?

We are, at this point, some distance from an idealized version of the market as an abstract, impersonal, instrumental mechanism orientated in terms of precise laws of supply and demand; instead we are situated within particular *marketplaces* with their own specificities for making sense in localized and situated encounters of trade. This point is made forcefully by Callon (1998b; Callon, Meadel et al. 2005) as well as by Bourdieu (2005) and is one that I will return to below. Hence we come full circle, back to the questions raised at the beginning of this chapter and the discussion above of markets and marketplaces and how to reconnect 'economy' and 'culture'. With respect to model agencies and Selfridges I ask the question, what kind of a business is this? How does one calculate the aesthetic object within such a business? To answer these questions, it is necessary to examine the ways in which cultural and economic concerns are meshed in the everyday market-making activities of individuals. However, as Jackson (2002: 4) has suggested 'calls to transcend the "great divide" between the cultural and the economic have significantly outnumbered the empirically grounded studies that demonstrate the difference that such a move would make in practice.' That is to say, we still need more analysis that focuses attention on the actual ways in which these two are intertwined in everyday activities. One way to do this is with a 'production of culture' approach which demonstrates how 'an unhelpful conception of the culture–economy relationship maps onto, and underpins, this artificial separation of production and consumption' (Pratt 2004a: 118; see also Du Gay, Hall et al. 1997; Pratt 2004a). The other way to do this is to focus particular attention on the culture industries. However, care must be taken as to what emphasis to place upon them. As Pratt (2008: 95) notes, 'Arguably, the study of the cultural industries presents the best opportunity for a case study in the "eye of the storm" of economic–cultural change.' However, as he continues, the best justification for looking at the cultural industries is not to argue 'that production is becoming more cultural, but what the specificities are of cultural production' (95–6). There may indeed be specific features characterizing cultural production that warrant our attention. As I argue in the later chapters on fashion buying, cultural products may emphasize qualitatively different forms of knowledge—expressive and embodied knowledge that challenges the dominance of cognitive accounts of economic knowledge—and may have its own spatial characteristics.

In other words, empirical studies that do more than simply critique the culture/ economy divide are, therefore, still required to give some sense of the diversity of markets. I want to focus on three approaches that lend themselves to studying markets as cultural entities, each of which propose different spatial metaphors to account for the multiplicity of activities and relationships involved in market-making: 'field' (Bourdieu 1993a,b, 2005), 'network' (Callon 1991; Hughes 2004; Latour 2005) and 'circuit' (Cook and Crang 1996; Du Gay, Hall et al. 1997). Each, in different ways, affords the possibility of delineating the ways in which goods circulate and come to acquire meaning and (cultural/economic) value and provide concepts which attempt to mesh 'culture' and 'economy' together. These approaches are usually presented as mutually exclusive, or, more specifically, field theory and network analysis or ANT are said to be incompatible; whereas the concept of circuit is more in sympathy with that of 'network'. However, rather than choose between them, I suggest how two in particular—field and network—each offer something of value to the analysis of aesthetic markets. In particular, I examine the connections and synergies between Bourdieu's and Callon's work and demonstrate how, to understand an aesthetic market and analyse the particular marketplaces of fashion modelling and fashion clothing, one needs to lift concepts from each of them. As for the 'circuits' metaphor, I take it up in the following chapter when discussing the 'circuits of value' created around aesthetic commodities and so critical to them, and return to this in Part II of this book when examining the relevance of 'commodity circuits' in retail.

Field or Network?

Three Key Differences

Field theory and actor-network theory (ANT) offer two quite different spatial metaphors for grappling with the complex ways in which markets are 'made up'. In terms of understanding how markets are put together, these two different spatial metaphors offer, at least at first glance, two very different, mutually exclusive, approaches to the same problem. Indeed, they are underpinned by two very different ontological assumptions about the nature of the social world. Let me illustrate by setting out some of the basic terms of approach, albeit rather schematically.

Space: Defining the 'Social'. First, the spatial metaphor itself is significant. Fields are bounded spaces of action and interaction for Bourdieu (1993b: 72): they present themselves 'synchronically as structured spaces of positions (or posts) whose properties depend on their position within the spaces and which can be analysed independently of the characteristics of their occupants'. While he allows the possibility that sub-fields may accumulate, there is always a sense in which action takes place within a confined space of possibility, separated or distinguishable from other fields, each operating according to different 'forces', 'players', 'capitals' and 'strategies'. These terms are closely tied to the other metaphor frequently used by Bourdieu to describe the social world, that of the 'game', as discussed below.

In contrast to the idea of enclosed fields of action, the metaphor of the network suggests something relatively open as opposed to being bounded or fixed in some way, and always in process of connecting and flowing. However, following the logic of this spatial metaphor it is obvious that the basic tenets of network theory offer a radical challenge to social sciences, since even the idea of the 'social', 'social space', 'social context', even 'society' itself, are questioned, premised as they are on categories that are themselves social and which 'establish a partition between the natural world' (Latour 1991: 11) and the one designated as social. That is to say, in ANT distinctions between 'social' and 'natural' worlds—as well as the distinctions between 'human' and 'non-human'—are not natural and thus cannot be taken for granted. As a form of network analysis, actor-network theory does not accept the dichotomies established by classical forms of sociology, as exemplified by field theory. As Latour (2005: 5) puts it, where classical sociology assumes the social exists, almost like a 'glue' holding things together, network analysis starts by asking '*what is glued together*'.

Thus, what the first position takes as 'its solution, namely the existence of specific social ties revealing the hidden presence of some specific social forces', the network position takes these ties as 'the major puzzle to be solved' (Latour 2005: 5). Such things as 'social structure' are, therefore, not assumed to exist and then studied by sociologists, who, armed with their social theories, are thought to have the key to understanding things. Instead, these 'structures' are the very stuff of research, open to interrogation to be explained, not taken for granted, with the social theorist no more an expert on the things observed than those who are observed. So, although the social is often assumed to be a 'homogenous thing, it's perfectly acceptable to designate by the same word a trail of associations between heterogeneous elements' (Latour 2005: 5). Thus, social as a fixed thing is replaced by ' "social" as in "associations" ' (2005: 64): the 'social does not designate a thing among other things, like a black sheep among other white sheep, but *a type of connection* between things that are not themselves social' (2005: 5). It is only as and when things are assembled that they become 'social', designated as such, and many of these assemblages invoke or enrol things that might otherwise be consigned to the 'non-social'—chemical, biological, material, etc. In other words, if ' "society" exists at all, *this is achieved by heterogeneous means*. Or, to put it somewhat more radically, that the social is not purely social at all' (Law 1991: 7). It is 'the name of a type of momentary association' (Latour 2005: 65). Thus, the basic tenets of classical social theory—society, social norms and conventions, etc.—are the very things that ANT seeks to unpack, things ordinarily 'black-boxed' (Latour 1987).

The other way to define this difference is in terms of the classic macro/micro division that has been evident in sociology since its inception. Field theory remains committed to the sort of macro-sociology that ANT seeks to debunk. While Bourdieu seeks to identify macro structures and outline a grand theory of the social, ANT seeks to unseat such a macro-theoretical project and focuses its attention on the small-scale ways in which things are made up. These two approaches have obviously different epistemological foundations, as discussed in more detail below. For now, it becomes obvious that if the grand social structures, such as 'society', the 'economy' or 'culture', are said not to exist as stable entities in themselves in network theory, then the other side of the classic sociological dichotomy—agency—is similarly questioned.

Agency, Actors, Actants.   Thus, a second major difference between field theory and ANT is in terms of understandings of actors and agency. Where field theory takes the term *actor* to refer to a human agent, and agency to be the property of such actors, for network theory, an actor can be non-human and agency is said to not reside in any essential characteristics of these actors, but distributed across the network and flows established between different actors. This has implications for a further range of concepts attributed to actors. Field theory assumes that the human agents are endowed with characteristics that are, in effect, the properties of the field they occupy; hence field-specific capitals, dispositions, status, positions take embodied form by agents who enact them. Thus, in field theory, the social world is characterized in terms of underlying 'structures' which are responsible for the conditions under which 'agency' emerges—as the class structure/agency dichotomy assumes. These deep structures—for Bourdieu, class primarily—set the terms under which fields operate, distributing such things as economic, social and cultural resources.

The other metaphor, used frequently by Bourdieu, is the idea of the 'game'. Fields have different 'rules' organizing them, much like games are organized according to different principles: 'In order for field to function, there have to be stakes and people prepared to play the game, endowed with a habitus that implies knowledge and recognition of the imminent laws of the field, the stakes, and so on' (Bourdieu 1993b: 72). Thus, agents, much like players in a game, enter the field aware of the 'rules' of the game within that field and develop different sorts of 'strategies' according to their position in that field and the amount of 'capital' (such as economic, social, cultural, symbolic) they are endowed with. They may be endowed with significant capital and thus occupy a 'dominant' position as an 'established' player, with strategies orientated towards 'conservation' of this position; or they may be a new or young 'contender' or 'challenger', seeking to acquire a more dominant position through challenging of the positions of others (Bourdieu 1993b). Either way, the bounded rules of the field establish the conditions under which these agents face one another and how they operate as a result. Thus, agency is delimited by the conditions of possibility—the deep structure/s—governing the field of action.

However, in network analysis, actors do not have fixed or essential character-istics, but are made up and brought into being by the very ways in which they are networked. Indeed, important to ANT is that it is based 'on no stable theory of the actor; rather it assumes the *radical indeterminacy* of the actor' (Callon 1999: 181). This is an analytical distinction not an ethical one, according to Law and, he points out, the dividing line between people, animals and objects is always shifting. In the process, many 'hybrids' are created that are assemblages of human and non-human elements. As Law (2001: 857) puts it, 'Is an agent an agent primarily because he or she inhabits a body that carries knowledge, skills, values, and all the rest? Or is an agent an agent because he or she inhabits a set of elements (including, of course, a body) that stretches out into the network of materials, somatic and otherwise, that surround the body?'

The answer is, he suggests, that an agent or actor is never solely located in a body 'and bodies alone, but rather that an actor is a patterned network of heterogeneous relations, or an effect produced by such a network' (Law 2001: 4). That is to say, the network and the agents within are always contingent, always in flux, established and re-established, accordingly. Objects, such as molecules, test-tubes, engines, or finan-cial data, can shape the way things are assembled along a network, helping to consti-tute or augment how things are seen, what course of action is taken, or whatever, and are, therefore, agents or actants with efficacy, involved in assembling the social. The opening up of agency to non-human elements challenges most classical ideas of actors as in some way conscious or partly conscious of their action, or at least able to give an account of it: but what of a test-tube or microscope? They cannot adopt a position, embody a habitus, or jostle for position in a field. Even the term itself— ac*tor* as borrowed from the stage—implies that 'it's never clear who and what is acting' (Latour 2005: 46); script, playwright, prompter, etc. Indeed, 'the very word actor directs our attention to a complete dislocation of the action, warning us that it is not a coherent, controlled, well-rounded, and clean-edged affair. By definition, ac-tion is *dislocated.* Action is borrowed, distributed, suggested, influenced, dominated, betrayed, translated' (Latour 2005: 46).

Just as one cannot assume to know and explain something designated as 'social', there cannot be anything certain about what we know of action: we have 'to remain puzzled by the identity of the participants if we are to "assemble them again"' (La-tour 2005: 46). There are, says Latour, too many imponderables, too many 'traces', to ever be certain as to what inspires or 'determines' agency. With no 'structure' imposing itself upon stable actors to delimit their 'agency', the ability to become an actor and act depends upon a whole range of heterogeneous factors that require 'trac-ing' rather than simply left unexplained in terms of 'social forces' or whatever.

Epistemology: Theory/Practice. Third, these ontological assumptions are closely linked to the epistemological positions established by each. This epistemological problem may not, in fact, be so significant, if one adopts particular strands of Bourdieu's work, as I will argue in a moment. However, it is important to distinguish some elements of his theoretical work from the impulses of ANT. In his field theory, theory is often substituted for actual observation, a problem that deepens over time as his work moves further from the anthropological insights of his earliest studies, although he appears to return to fieldwork in his last published work in English (2005). However, during the time he develops his field theory, all too frequently assumptions about the world are made prior to empirical observation: structures and fields are assumed to exist in advance of fieldwork and actors are thought to be endowed with characteristics according to their position in fields, and so on. In contrast, in network analysis, there is a resolute determination to avoid assuming one knows how things operate prior to observation, but simply 'follow the actors' and 'assemble' the social world through observation not theory (Latour 1987, 2005).

One reason the two remain so segregated has to do with the kind of critique that is proposed by ANT. Part of the problem with ANT is that, once inside the actor-network approach, it is very difficult to get outside! This is a strange problem indeed, given that the analogy of a network would seem to make great claims about the possibilities of connections. Once you accept any or all ANT tenets, going back to some early social theory is very difficult indeed; the principles or foundations of these theories have been exposed as shaky to say the least. Moreover, Bourdieu is one particular social theorist singled out as an example of 'bad' social science, and his concepts have been critiqued very directly by Latour (1991, 2005), although some elements of his analysis have been seen as 'compatible with that proposed by social network analysis' (Callon 1998b: 15), a point of convergence I return to below. However, the task of tying these together is not so outrageous if one returns to some of Bourdieu's early and very latest work. Then it is possible to trace connections to ANT impulses with empirical observation, description and analysis.

As I have suggested, the problem with *field theory*, as defined throughout much of Bourdieu's career, is that it gets increasingly hived off from actual fields of practice or *fieldwork* (Entwistle and Rocamora 2006). While Bourdieu claims to be talking about practice, he all too frequently assumes the position of an armchair theorist, assuming to know the world but without getting his hands dirty by actually going and having a look at it! However, the problem of relating Bourdieu's theory to practice is more complex than this. This theory was derived directly out of fieldwork, particularly his early anthropological work on the Berber house (Bourdieu 1973) and in his analysis of taste (1984). These studies, based on extensive fieldwork—observation and data—informed the direction of the theoretical concepts he proposes, such as habitus, although his desire to develop a general theory of field ultimately results in him losing sight of the particularities and complexities of fields *as they are practiced*. He does hint at the importance of empirical observation as when he suggests that fields evolve stakes that are irreducible to other fields and 'which are not perceived by someone who has not been shaped to enter that field' (1993b: 72). And yet, despite this, Bourdieu appears for a time to think that theory can explain practice without needing to have direct contact with it. In acknowledging the specificity of fields but not deigning to study them through fieldwork, Bourdieu's concepts become increasingly abstract, theoretical and further away from the social reality he claims to be explaining. One cannot help but have sympathy with ANT which takes issue with such 'lazy' sociology!

Field and Network: Connecting Them Up

This brings us to the problem of how, given these quite radical differences, one can '(re)assemble the social' (Latour 2005)—the marketplaces in aesthetic commodities, in this instance—drawing from both field theory and ANT, as I intend to do. Bearing the differences in mind, I want to examine some points of connection, some synergies that enable, if not a resolution of these very different perspectives, at least the possibility that elements from each may be 'assembled' in a coherent and logical manner to the analysis of high fashion markets. Why should a study of these marketplaces be forced to choose between these two approaches? Why not assemble the different elements of these approaches to produce an analysis that is heterogeneous—a hybrid even—rather than a homogenous analysis that is ascribed to one or other? But how can any analysis borrow from such radically opposed schools of social science?

I want to suggest that, despite all the appearance of incompatibility, these two approaches can be partly reconciled, with elements borrowed from each in order to understand aesthetic marketplaces (and, perhaps, other things too, though I will restrict my analysis to aesthetic marketplaces). There are, indeed, some obvious connections. As I have already discussed above, Callon and Bourdieu both critique classical economics as being too abstract and divorced from actual marketplace practices and their points of critique are in congruence. Both concede that the idealized version of the market has become something of a 'reality' in the many enactments of it—from global fiscal policies of the World Bank or IMF to the local ways in which markets are put together. They also insist on the necessity of examining the practicalities of marketplace practice and here is where some real synergies can be found. Bourdieu's (2005) very last book in English on the housing market in France comes some distance towards ANT in terms of its insistence on the necessity of empirical observation of markets, and recognizing, therefore, the value of 'following the actors' (though not in so many words) by examining the ways in which they encounter one another. Many such encounters are recorded in minute detail in the transcripts and analysis given throughout the book and together they can be seen to 'trace' how various actors perform and produce the housing market.

Bearing this epistemological meeting point in mind, let me return to the other remaining problems raised above. Firstly, there are the obvious differences between these two as captured in the two spatial metaphors of field and network. These differences I want to examine in terms of the world of high fashion. I then want to examine three further substantive issues. As I will go on to suggest, to understand embodied practices in markets, it is helpful to turn to Bourdieu's concept of habitus, and there are ways in which this can be developed in ways that are not inconsistent with ANT. Two further concerns, which link directly to the issues I am concerned with in this book, also link the work of Callon and Bourdieu; these are the issue of *calculation* and the issue of *mediation*. These two concepts are dealt with in both authors' work in very different ways and, although the tensions between them are not readily resolved, I want to explore the ways in which each describe and define them. I will conclude by suggesting how both Callon and Bourdieu may shed light on the work of actors in my two aesthetic marketplaces.

Fashion Fields or Networks?

Whatever the specific details, even in this last study, Bourdieu remains committed to the idea of a field as a bounded or enclosed space of action with its own inherent rules and properties, and this is fundamentally at odds with the metaphor of an open, always contingent network. This difference cannot be resolved entirely but even here there are ways in which one can accept certain tenets of field theory that are congruent with network analysis. Again, if one takes field as *practiced*, not as theoretical or abstract space, it is possible to describe *how* the world gets bounded *as* a field; that is, how it gets closed off in terms of its own logic of action from the rest of the world (if only momentarily). I will return to this in a moment but first it is worth considering what the different spatial metaphors offer in terms of an analysis of the world of high fashion.

The bounded nature of field is very applicable to high fashion: here is an exclusive world not everyone can participate in and one that requires particular knowledge or competencies and, as I argue, a particular bodily habitus. (The specific details of this world are described at various points in this book.) One problem with the bounded nature of field is that Bourdieu does not adequately explain how fields relate to one another or how actors may be able to participate in more than one field. Yet for example fashion buyers have to move beyond high fashion and are aware of wider trends and tastes that span the world of design (furniture, home interiors), the arts and popular culture. Buyers also draw on their own experiences of taste and, at times, their buying decisions emerge from knowledge they glean as consumers themselves. Fashion buying choices, then, are a heterogeneous assembly of things—drawing on observations of consumers, markets and people they encounter outside the field of fashion. Even tastes in fashion modelling, while seemingly very esoteric, are connected to the world outside fashion. 'Heroin chic' (from the 1990s) for example emerged out of music culture and tastes for particular models are often influenced by the cinema. So far from being a world unto itself, the field of fashion has leaky boundaries and is connected to other spheres of cultural production. The bounded nature of field does not take account of these connections between fields of cultural production.

One way out of this is through the idea of the network. According to Hughes (2004), one of the advantages of network analysis is that it refers to spatial relations between actors. Network analysis is largely a methodological approach: as Hughes (2004: 213) notes, 'the theory dictates that networks are always localized, working in real places and at specific times. As such, they can only be made known by accounts of their workings on the ground, and can only be considered as globalized in terms of their physical extension across space in practice.'

As one 'follows the actors' one inevitably moves with them across space that stretches outwards from the local. The concept of 'network lengthening' allows one to trace the connections further and further outward, as necessary, but always by working from the local actors. Thus, my observations of fashion buyers necessitated following them to studios around London, New York, Paris and Milan, and it is possible to see the connections and relationships they establish with the designers, their agents and others, in the course of their buying. But networks are not unlimited either. Had I had the budget to follow the buyers over a whole year, it is likely that many of these connections would prove to be fairly predictable. Similarly, the 'circuits of value' that are created within the fashion network are fairly predictable, linked to well-established names in the business. While new names appear all the time, there is more continuity in terms of the big-name designers and photographers and journalists than might be implied by the idea of an endless network. Indeed, does there come a point, when, as Strathern (1996) puts it, we need to 'cut the network'? When we reach the outer limits do we not need to ask ourselves whether networks are endless?

Do we need to decide between these two terms? Does one or another decide if fashion is more adequately described as a field or network? One way out of the necessity of choosing between these two is to be site-specific and simply examine how markets get realized or are *materialized*. Taking the idea of field, it may be appropriate to describe fashion as a field as and when it gets enclosed. This idea of a field as practiced rather than a field as some idealized, abstract field of action is detailed in Entwistle and Rocamora (2006). In this article, Entwistle and Rocamora argue for a reconnection of Bourdieu's early fieldwork with his later, abstract and reified notion of field detailed in later field theory, and demonstrate how, in the manifestation of the spaces of London Fashion Week (LFW), the field of fashion is materialized in time and space. Following our observations closely, we detail how the orchestration of space at LFW renders the field visible to itself; that is, to the participants themselves, as well as to the press who represent it to their readers; and examine how various 'positions' or identities of key 'players' in the field of fashion are secured and reproduced. We examine how the 'capitals' of this field, in particular 'fashion capital', are performative of these identities, describing the style and demeanour of the participants as observed in live encounters between actors. Such fashion capital is literally embodied through the acquired fashion 'habitus'. These concepts of 'capital', 'position' and 'habitus' are, therefore, derived from observation. What is pertinent for this discussion is that the field of fashion as rendered at LFW is indeed a hived off, bounded space of action: access is restricted, real gates are erected around the shows and VIP, with the effect of configuring the world of high fashion as a separate, bounded space or field of action. However, to repeat the point one last time, all of this is *observed* in situ rather than *assumed* and, indeed, lasts as long as LFW itself. What is significant in terms of our observations is that the metaphor of field as a bounded space *actually works* in terms of understanding what is going on here; it has an empirical reality. Fields-in-practice really can be enclosed spaces of action; the key is to describe them as they appear, to see *how* they get enclosed rather than abstract them from practice.

Our account is not too dissimilar to studies inspired by, or inspiring ANT; strawberry markets are rendered in similar ways in France (Garcia 1986), financial markets are enclosed spaces of action (Abolafia 1998; Knorr Certina and Bruegger 2004; MacKenzie 2004). While these authors do not use the term *field* to describe what is going on here, this metaphor, and attendant concepts derived from Bourdieu's field theory, are appropriate for describing LFW. This does not preclude the possibility of examining how fashion markets might be rendered in other ways, in other spaces of activity. Indeed, when following the actors at Selfridges around during their fashion buys, I observed other things and can usefully employ concepts from ANT (as discussed in Part II of this book; see also Entwistle 2006). Further, it does not preclude the possibility of analyzing how calculation and forms of knowledge inside markets are networked, as I also do in this book. In other words, field can be used in precise ways to describe particular sorts of *boundary related* activities, while network can be preferred when describing some of the ways in which things inside the constructed boundary or frame are linked or assembled.

Indeed, this way of thinking about fields is not too dissimilar from Callon's idea of 'framing' and he even draws on Bourdieu to describe some of the processes of framing. For Callon (1998c), markets are formatted through the 'framing' of activities. Framing takes many forms. Part of this framing involves the creation of 'externalities', but other, very material frames are also used and he gives the example of the strawberry market in Garcia's work (1986). Here an idealized market was created, constituted in the image of the market in textbooks on political economy. This 'perfect', impersonal market is constituted out of very 'material investments'— warehouses and auction rooms are built and particular sorts of interactions get constituted as a result of this spatial arrangement that ensures the market performs in a very particular way. The main difference between field and network analysis is that, rather than taking the boundaries as an *a priori* (theoretical) given, as Bourdieu does, ANT begins by asking *how* do the boundaries get framed? This is, therefore, one of my initial questions, linking both field theory and ANT.

Indeed, this idea is not so radical when one recalls early studies of cultural production derived from symbolic interactionism. Becker (1982) in his classic *Art Worlds* opens with a quote from Trollope who describes the importance of his groom to his literary success: this groom brings to him his all-important morning coffee at 5:30 a.m. so that he can set to work early in the day. Becker uses the quote to note, in much the same way as Latour (see also Latour and Woolgar 1979; Latour 2005) or Law (1986a,b; 2002) have done elsewhere, all the various small objects, process, regimes critical to any material production. Indeed, much like ANT accounts, he considers a range of cultural objects and agents involved in producing art, from the most seemingly peripheral—such as the people who make the coffee for the artist, or sweep the floor of the stage—through to those who are designated as artists. All, according to him, constitute the making of the art work. He (1982: 35–5) also reminds us that 'One important factor of a sociological analysis of any social world is to see when, where, and how participants draw the line' around their activities, defining what is and isn't art in the process. 'By observing how an art world makes those distinctions rather than trying to make them ourselves we can understand much of what goes on in an art world' (Becker 1982: 35–6).

My point is that one can retain the concept of field to look at the specific ways in which they draw boundaries around their activities and identities, but this concept does not exclude other forms of analysis where they are appropriately derived from observation. My use is precise and only appropriate to the observations I make of the world of high fashion.

Agency: How to Account for Embodied Market Practices?

A further problem with field theory that limits its applicability, as well as strengthening ANT criticisms, concerns the classic agency/structure dichotomy central to sociology in general and to Bourdieu in particular. In assuming the existence of stable structures and clearly designated human agency, Bourdieu is on shaky ground, according ANT. Moreover, numerous other problems come into play as a result of assuming this dichotomy. One criticism levelled at Bourdieu is that his account is mechanistic and deterministic. Structures reproduce themselves endlessly because agency is restricted to the articulation of such structures and, thus, agents become the puppets of the structures that contain them. This problem is a particularly complex one in Bourdieu's work given his stated aim (Bourdieu 1977, 1990) to overcome the classic structure/agency dichotomy. The criticisms levelled at him are fair but this is because he fails to carry through on the promises of his own theory. Certainly, some of his field analysis is stunningly reductive of practice: where he describes how actors move in fields according to their field-specific dispositions, his analysis tends to be mechanistic, reducing agents to mere puppets of the field structures containing them. Thus, while field emerges out of a broader concern to delineate a 'theory of practice' (1977) and describe 'the logic of practice' (1990), all too often his own field analysis errs too much on the side of structure and is as deterministic as it is mechanical. However, if we look beyond his own specific applications—or, rather, his failure to *apply* or *develop* theory in relation to practice—and instead return to the aims of his 'theory of practice', we can, perhaps, move beyond this impasse.

Bourdieu (1990) specifically set out to overcome the tendency in sociology to privilege either objectivisim (as in structuralism) or subjectivism (as exemplified by phenomenology) to generate a productive account of agency and structure. The concept that Bourdieu developed to overcome this problem and bridge the dichotomy between structure/agency is the habitus.

The theory of practice as practice insists, contrary to positivist materialism, that the objects of knowledge are constructed, not passively recorded, and, contrary to intellectualist idealism, that the principle of this construction is the system of structured structuring dispositions, the *habitus*, which is constituted in practice and is always orientated towards practical functions. It is possible to step down from the sovereign viewpoint from which objectivist idealism orders the world—without having to abandon it to the 'active aspect' of apprehension of the world by reducing knowledge to a mere recording. To do this, one has to situate oneself *within* 'real activity as such', that is, in the 'practical relation to the world' (1990: 52).

The point for Bourdieu is that the habitus is both *structuring*, i.e. orientating of practice, as well as *structured*, by field/history, a point which he argues does not reduce habitus to *either* structure *or* agency, but allows us to examine them at one and the same time, as they are manifest in practice. There has been much debate as to whether or not habitus does, indeed, resolve the agency/structure problem but, just as with the concept of field, it all depends on how you apply it. Rather than go over this much trodden ground, I want to suggest how habitus is useful for understanding elements of high fashion practice. It certainly is possible for habitus to become a rather mechanist and even deterministic concept, but the concept still holds the *potential* for a much richer discussion of how bodies move in practice if it remains close to the things observed. For now, I leave my substantive discussion of habitus—with examples from my fieldwork—to Chapters 6 and 7. Let me develop these theoretical points relating to how I am using it.

My reason for borrowing this term is that, for all that ANT acknowledges the body by attending to the very material formations of things (see for example Mol and Law 2004), the language for describing bodies in laboratories or markets is actually impoverished and, all too frequently, bodies are actually passed over rather rapidly in the analysis. Thrift's (2005) discussion of management discourses refers to bodies all over the place but, since his analysis is heavily theoretical and his only empirical evidence drawn from texts and manuals, he tells us little about bodies in practice. MacKenzie (2001) acknowledges how hand signals are important in communicating and performing in financial trading markets but this gets no more than a passing mention. Law (2002) attends to bodily enactments of a more mundane kind in describing how things move or come together in laboratories or offices, but these remain fairly superficial observations. Callon, meanwhile, gives the body no single mention.

Habitus is closely linked to Bourdieu's idea of 'capital' (economic, social, cultural, etc.). These capitals are unequally distributed in any field, according to Bourdieu, and traded by 'players' or market agents to maximize success. Capital and habitus are conceptually distinct in his field theory; capital can take the form of cognitive knowledges (various forms of educational or cultural knowledge, for example) and social ties, links, social network connections; but capital can also be embodied, enacted through the acquired habitus in practice. This is the case with 'fashion capital', the specific knowledge demanded inside high fashion, as discussed by Entwistle and Rocamora (2006). In high fashion markets, fashion knowledge is the combined accumulation of forms of cultural, social, symbolic capital: to be *in fashion*, one has to know particular designers, labels, fabrics, styles. However, knowing is also about being able to demonstrate this knowledge through *bodily enactments and expression.* That is to say, not only does the knowledge orientate the market agent towards particular sorts of distinctions (ones that would not strike the eye of someone positioned in another market, because they would lack the appropriate capital and habitus); critically in this market the knowledge is *worn on the body.*

Thus, Bourdieu's concept of the habitus allows one to describe some of the richness of bodily presentation and performance and the *importance* of such presentations and performances to the actions inside the marketplaces of high fashion. This is important for understanding markets that are *about* the body, as fashion obviously is. As I suggest throughout my analysis, one has to *have* a particular kind of body to even be inside this world in the first place. This may appear an obvious point to make when discussing fashion modelling, where certain standards of bodily shape and size are required, but the same can be said of the bodies observed at Selfridges and in the spaces of fashion buying. Indeed, it is probably true of other markets orientated towards the body or in some way premised upon the styling of the body, as in sex and performance work for the former, and service industry work for the latter, which all demand some degree of aesthetic labour (Entwistle and Wissinger 2006). However, I would hesitate to suggest that bodily appearance is a significant feature of all markets.

Without pre-empting my discussions in other chapters, let me briefly note a few obvious things about the world of high fashion. Markets in high fashion demand particular kinds of appearances and performances. In the spaces where high fashion is made and shared, particular kinds of bodies circulate, dressed in certain sorts of clothing and walking and talking in similar ways. These appearances and performances are striking to the outsider (such as myself) and are heightened in the enclosed spaces, such as LFW, where the fashion market is actively rendered or configured in a confined arena. The habitus captures something of regularity or patterning of these appearances and enable one to describe something of how these bodies are configured because it is sensitive to the importance of bodily enactments specific to the practice observed. Thus, to understand how models, bookers and buyers make sense of their market, it is necessary to grasp the importance of their embodied presentation and sensibility. These points I take up in full in Chapters 6 and 7 when I describe the importance of embodiment in the articulation of 'tacit aesthetic knowledge'—the sense and sensibility that is pre-reflexive and critical to understanding and sense-making in this market. In short, habitus refers to a particular sense and sensibility that enables high fashion actors to make distinctions and calculations between goods—clothes, models—in order to select them.

The habitus is a performative knowledge, signalling that market actors have the appropriate embodied understanding of fashion. Through enactments of fashion habitus, market actors inside high fashion signal their knowledge and show they belong there but, more particularly, they *perform* it. Such individual performances are critical to their success inside this market: in encounters with suppliers and other actors inside and outside the store, Selfridges buyers were conscious that they had to 'look the part' and 'embody' the appropriate high fashion image the store was seeking to establish and maintain.

However, performativity, as distinct from performance, is concerned with the production of the subject in and through discourse, rather than referring to an authentic subject (Butler 1993, 1994). Drawing on Austin (1962) and the notion of performative speech acts, performativity is '*that aspect of discourse that has the capacity to produce what it names*' (Butler 1993). Thus, the endless enactments of fashion habitus—the repeated renditions of it in performances—serve to generate the appearance of 'fashion insider', thus reproducing the subject/market agent in the process. Of course, in reality, as Lloyd (1999) points out in her critique of Butler, one cannot easily distinguish performance from performativity since the latter is premised on the repeated renditions of the former.

However, here we return, yet again, to the old dichotomy of structure/agency conundrum: the problem of 'determination' between individual/agency and generative structure. Rather than attempt to resolve this, I suggest that what matters is to *examine the things as they appear in practice* and trace the links and connections established through performative gestures rather than attempt to resolve this problem at a higher theoretical level. I concur with Latour (2005), that there are too many traces to be reduced to one determining factor, one 'social force', but this does not mean that we cannot describe some of the traces or patterns we see. The fact is that the term *habitus* enables us to examine practice; indeed, it directs us to do so! That is to say, let's look at the business and practice of high fashion: how is this market put in to practice? As a market, it functions largely through enactments of fashion sense and sensibility—that is to say, the fashion habitus. I suggest that, for want of a better term, the concept of habitus affords the possibility of tracing some of the forms of knowledge and kinds of encounters between and amongst agents in this market.

Thinking about habitus in these ways is not inconsistent with the more ANT-inspired accounts of markets and agency. While habitus is an embodied *human* attribute or disposition (it is hard to imagine how molecules or microscopes could be said to have a habitus), drawing on it does not mean *only* seeing agency in terms of human dispositions or capacities. Actors can take other forms too and agency is not delimited to only that which is enacted or embodied by human actors. Habitus represents only one disposition or capacity held by some actors in the market. Indeed, more to the point, since it is not the sole possession of the individual, habitus can be seen in terms of the actor-network as a distributed knowledge that flows between actors.

Calculation: How Are Things Stabilized inside an Aesthetic Marketplace?

My third point is one of connection between field and ANT and closes in on one of my critical questions concerning the logical market activities shaping these commodities and ensuring they acquire value as high fashion. This concerns the issue of calculation. According to Callon (1998b: 32), the question of calculation is a critical one for understanding markets. His definition of a market implies the formatting of calculative agencies. That is to say, the very idea of a market is premised on the notion that agencies—buyers and sellers—can and do meet to agree to prices—and to do this, they need to be able to 'calculate—i.e. to rank—her [*sic*] decisions ... draw up a list of actions that she can undertake, and describe the effects of these actions on the world in which she is situated' (1998b: 4). In other words, they must be able to calculate, often under conditions of radical uncertainty, something of the effect, goals, implications of their actions. If markets presume a logical, calculative agent, he then asks the question: 'Under what conditions is calculativeness possible? Under what conditions do calculative agents emerge?' (1998b: 4). The answers may vary; indeed, the point for Callon is to examine the many forms that markets take, rather than accept the standard accounts in economic textbooks: 'The objective may be to explore the diversity of calculative agencies, forms and distributions, and hence of organized markets' (1998b: 51).

Crucially, for Callon, calculation and calculative agencies are not derived from some essential 'nature' (as *homos economicus* of classical economic theory would have it), but are formatted by the very way in which the market is itself envisaged and put together. Once established, markets tend to become 'path-dependent' or 'lock-in' ways of doing things and ways of being: 'lock-in denotes all the mechanisms through which the evolution of a market or an institution becomes more and more irreversible. Progressively, the range of options narrows down' (1998b: 48). In other words, actors get caught up in the network—'a socio-technical network'—and, through their entanglement inside, the calculative agent is born: the calculative agent 'is formatted, framed and equipped with prostheses which help him [*sic*] in his calculations and which are, for the most part, produced by economics' (1998b: 51).

For Bourdieu the question of calculation is present, albeit framed in terms of 'strategies' of field 'players'. Fields can similarly be seen to 'lock-in' ways of doing things (although he does not use that term). Agents in fields could be seen to have certain 'path-dependent' lines of action open to them, according to the position they hold in that field and the variable amounts of capital they might possess. The very idea of the 'game' implies calculation: 'players' in a field are caught up in a game, whose rules they must by necessity play by, and they do so by calculating how to maximize their position. For example, the players who are dominant in the particular field of haute couture are the designers who possess the highest degree of 'power to define objects as rare by means of their signature, their label' (Bourdieu 1993b: 133). They will be 'opposed in a whole host of ways to the newcomers, the new entrants to the field' (133). Established figures have 'conservation strategies' and newcomers have 'subversion strategies' (Bourdieu 1993b: 73). He cites the debate on television between Balmain and Scherrer and he notes the different styles of speech between them, with Balmain emphasizing 'French quality' while Scherrer speaks 'like a student leader in May 68' (133). While the dominant designer is conservative and will be vague and ineffable (things 'go without saying'), by contrast, the Left Bank designer strategies come down to 'a will to overthrow the very principles of the game—but always in the name of the game, the spirit of the game' (Bourdieu 1993b: 134).

For Bourdieu, the calculative agency is an actor whose ability to calculate and strategize are attributes of the field. Although these are, in one sense, not essential or natural attributes of the actor, there is an implicit assumption in his analysis that humans are always strategizing agents, regardless of the field they occupy. Although a similar point is made in Callon: 'Agents are "de facto calculative"' (1998b: 12), the difference here is how the 'economic' and 'calculativeness' are conceived in both their work. For Bourdieu, there remains a clear sense of separate (though linked) 'culture' and 'economic' logics; indeed, the former, as rendered in terms of strategies, capitals, habitus, and so on, is always, ultimately, an expression of the latter. That is, his analysis tends to place economic maximization at the core of strategizing/calculation, albeit with elaborate devices and seemingly non-economic or 'cultural' violence exerted to conceal this fact. For Bourdieu, then, humans are *de facto* economically calculating. However, for Callon, 'culture' or cultural strategies do not exist, nor does 'economic' calculativeness in any pure sense. If humans are calculating, it is because of the ways in which markets get formatted and because they are open in networks: 'the agent-network is *by construction* calculative, since all action is analysed in terms of combinations, associations, at relationships and strategies of positioning. The agent is calculative because action can only be calculativeness'

(1998b: 12, emphasis added). In other words, there is no essential economic subject in his analysis, as there is in Bourdieu's.

A further difference resides in the way fields are said to operate. The field enables (or closes down) the possibilities for agency, opening up particular sorts of calculations and strategies as a result. However, in Bourdieu's account, the field serves as an *a priori context* in which pre-established and stable identities confront one another. In this way of thinking calculation is presumed to be 'the culturally or socially constructed dimensions of this competence' (Callon 1998b: 5) or takes the form of 'embedding'—actors are 'embedded' in social contexts that equip them to behave the way they do. What is radically different in Callon's actor-network is that there is no context, no social structure or even network 'already there, but a network that configures ontologies' (Callon 1998b: 8). Borrowing from Granovetter (1983) he argues that networks do not link pre-existing and stable identities, 'endowed with a set of fixed interests and stable preferences' and then 'form what would be a rigid social structure constituting the framework in which individual actions are situated' (1998b: 8). Instead, 'Agents' identities, interests and objectives, in short, everything which might stabilize their description and their being, are variable outcomes which fluctuate with the form and dynamics of relations between these agents' (1998b: 8).

In Callon's network analysis, we substitute 'two traditionally separate notions' (an agent) immersed in a structure (network or field), with one single entity, the actor-network. Thus, the dualism of conventional sociological analysis, like Bourdieu's, is replaced by monism of network analysis: and banishes 'any explanation separating the agency from a network' (1998b: 12). Unlike habitus—which presumes a stable distinction between agency/actor and structure—the idea of an always contingent network dispenses with the need to maintain this dichotomy and forces us to examine how things are configured to form an actor-network.

However, despite this difference, and it is a critical ontological one, Callon (1998b: 14) draws on Bourdieu's account of gift-giving as the 'only ... answer' to the questions he asks about framing and how calculation in markets comes about. That is to say, when Bourdieu describes action in time and space (as opposed to describing some idealized and abstracted space), his analysis is useful for explaining how actions get framed in terms of either calculativeness or disinterestedness. Here he is referring to Bourdieu's work on gift-giving. Such a situation requires explanation: 'To explain the emergence of calculativeness agencies we have also to explain the emergence of non-calculative ones too' (Callon 1998b: 13). The key to understanding whether actions are read as disinterested or not depends on two elements: the interval between gift and counter-gift that 'masks' ' "the contradiction between the intended truth of the gift as a generous, free, one-way gesture"' (Bourdieu, in Callon 1998b: 14) and the real truth that it is a moment of exchange. The key element is the time-lag: return a gift too soon and the exchange is deemed interested, while the longer gap enables 'amnesia' and therefore the sense in which the gift is disinterested. According to Callon, by examining the temporal arrangement of this encounter, Bourdieu's analysis allows for a non-essential explanation of the encounter, i.e. it has nothing to do with inherent altruism or selfishness, nor is it about the essential particularities of the relationships (either market or love). For Callon, Bourdieu's analysis rests upon 'the formatting of these relationships which will orientate the agent towards calculativeness or disinterestedness' (Callon 1998b: 15). What is significant in this example is that, when focused on encounters in situ, that is, on practice, Bourdieu's shares some similar features to that proposed by Callon.

Why this focus on formatting of calculativeness? The point here is that in all markets the conditions under which choices and decisions are made depend upon the way in which encounters are formatted. Agents in markets are equipped with competencies located within a particular actor-network (or field in situ) and their ability to act is formatted by the ways in which they encounter one another; I describe some of these encounters in Chapter 8. In sum, both approaches stress the formatting of relationships and encounters within the *particular* ways in which a market, like fashion, is put together. Borrowing the insights from both provides one way to examine the calculativeness of agents inside this market and the creation of value around commodities.

Mediation and Mediators

A final point of connection between Bourdieu and Callon concerns the issue of mediation. This issue is key to examining the work of people like model bookers and fashion buyers, since these workers can be said to mediate between different agents within the fashion market. However, here again there are critical differences between the two, which should, by now, be fairly obvious. Bourdieu (1984, 1993a) has been associated with the concept of 'cultural intermediaries' which he defines in an early quote concerning the 'new' petite bourgeoisie, as journalist-writers and writer-journalists involved in the creation of value around the work of art. He later (1993a) qualifies this and extends his definition to those involved in 'symbolic production' of the work, and thus the term can be extended to those involved in advertising, marketing and the like, who are responsible in generating meanings around things. Models, model bookers and fashion buyers can be called 'cultural intermediaries' as argued in Chapter 1, since their work enables the dissemination of things—goods, aesthetics, tastes—to consumers.

As is probably obvious now, for Callon (1986), an intermediary and mediation can take many forms and should not be limited to particular occupations, or categories of actors (human beings). Whether something mediates something else depends on where one enters the network. 'The division between actors and intermediaries is a purely practical matter. Is a group an actor or an intermediary? ... The answer has nothing to do with the metaphysics, ontology, or rights of "man". Rather it is empirical' (1991: 141). Thus, a nuclear plant can be an actor or an intermediary: the

'Question is where the buck stops—you focus on the group or you go on further and focus on the actor or you pass through it into networks beyond and you have a simple intermediary' (142). The concept of mediation is one that is also developed in his idea of 'translation' since this concept concerns how things are rendered meaningful and sent on particular journeys. Market agents do this work of translating all the time, moving goods from one location to another. This is discussed in Callon's analysis of the translation of the 'good' to a 'commodity' (Callon, Meadel et al. 2005) and is developed in Chapter 8 in this book, when I discuss how goods in studios have particular sorts of qualities that are meaningful in the encounter between a producer or agent and, for example, the fashion buyer. For these goods to be rendered as commodities, sold to consumers, particular qualities have to be translated into something else. Given that high fashion commodities have an aesthetic quality that is entirely arbitrary and therefore not stable, the question—what is going on here?—focuses our attention on how the aesthetic quality of that we might call 'fashion' is *stabilized* long enough to be selected, distributed, sold. The key issue is that agents actively make sense of goods and establish the qualities desired; all of which point back to the importance of *calculation*.

Certainly both concepts of cultural intermediaries (CI) and mediation are useful. To understand the work of fashion buyers, model bookers and models themselves, it is useful to describe how these particular *human* actors mediate things. However, we do not have to limit our discussion of CI and mediation to human agents only. Instead, as in Chapter 8, it is important to examine processes of mediation (McFall 2002, 2004), neglected in Bourdieu's account, and to acknowledge the many, multiple mediations that occur even in a simple encounter between a fashion buyer and a supplier/agent for a supplier. There is, in fact, not one, but many things being mediated in this encounter, something that is overlooked or oversimplified in Bourdieu's analysis and in subsequent studies following this.

Conclusion

This discussion opened with a review of the different ways in which 'culture' and 'economy' have been traditionally defined as separate domains of life and how they have been subsequently connected up in various ways. Instead of envisaging these two as separate domains, it is apparent that no easy distinction can be drawn between them since they are not distinct areas of life with different, moral logics and characteristics. The potential of field theory and network analysis is that they both offer interesting and useful ways to reconnect things designated as 'cultural' and 'economic'.

Although many points of similarity and difference between Bourdieu and Callon have been examined, one particular point is worth reiterating because it sheds some light upon this matter of how to join up 'culture' and 'economy'. In Bourdieu, these are readily connected in everyday practice: strategies and calculativeness are every-where dressed up as 'culture' although, ultimately, they serve 'economic' interests, namely, to reproduce class domination. However, no such distinction between seem-ingly 'cultural' and 'economic' logic is apparent in Callon's application of ANT: instead of such dualisms, we are encouraged to trace the connections along one single entity, the 'actor-network'. This distinction between the dualism of classical social theory and the monoism of ANT—and, thus, their different ways of connecting 'economy' to 'culture'—remains a central distinction in both their work. However, if one stays true to empirical observation, both theorists allow one to examine the practices of marketplaces—calculations and mediations—that automatically 'join up' things often separated into the 'cultural' and 'economic'. Both approaches em-phasize the web of calculations involved in real marketplaces: decisions in markets emerge out of a myriad of seemingly 'economic' and 'cultural' concerns and logics, which are merged rather than independent of one another. Markets, as both suggest, do not break down in this way.

What does all this theoretical discussion add up to? How can these different ap-proaches be applied to understand the work of market agents inside high fashion worlds? If one takes as a starting point something of the shared epistemological foundation—that one should start from observations and practice—then the issue becomes one of how to make sense of the emerging data and what concepts to em-ploy. By staying close to observed encounters, to fieldwork, and thus to some of Bourdieu's earliest and latest work, it is possible to avoid some of the limitations of field theory. Indeed, it may well be that an ANT-inspired analysis can more appro-priately interrogate some of Bourdieu's field theory and concepts than his own, often inadequate applications have done, extending or reworking them. In this respect, the strengths of each can be pooled.

However, when trying to capture something of the ways in which the world of high fashion is 'made up', it is hard to not use Bourdieu. Fashion does indeed operate like a field; it is a world that is maintained through the creation of particular kinds of enclosures and boundaries and a world where different identities are attributed different values and status. Thus, something of the characteristics of high fashion as a highly differentiated, status-orientated marketplace are captured in Bourdieu's concepts of field, capital, position and habitus. His analysis also gives weight to the central role of the body and how critical appearances and embodied performances are to the everyday working in this marketplace, features absent from ANT-inspired accounts of other markets. This latter point I take up in detail in my case study analy-sis of fashion buying in Part II.

It is also true that the insights of ANT are more far-reaching than field theory: they entail a radical critique of classical sociological concepts that characterize Bour-dieu's work. ANT provides a more extensive definition of the 'social'—as associa-tions rather than rigid structure, and made up from supposedly non-social entities. It also provides a more rigorous approach—a clear-sighted empiricism—as to how to 'trace' these associations than field theory. In doing so, ANT provides more routes for *enquiring* into the shaping of markets than Bourdieu's analysis, allowing us to push his observations further, but precisely because it is a methodology, it does not arm us with all the concepts to properly unpack these. As an approach, ANT can and should remain open to, rather than closing down, many possible theoretical concepts for analysis, so long as they are drawn from observation. The point is that, unlike field theory, 'ANT is not a theory' (Callon 1999). Indeed, while field theory builds towards a universal theory of the world, the ANT agenda is quite the reverse.

It is this that gives it both its strength and its adaptability. 'Moreover we never claimed to create a theory. In ANT the T is too much (*'de trop'*) ... We have to be wary of this type of consecration especially when it is the work of our best friends ... I fear our colleagues and their fascination for theory' (1999: 194).

3

The Aesthetic Economy: The Production of Value in the Field of Fashion Modelling

In Chapter 2, I set out some of the terms of a theoretical approach that adopts the insights of both field theory and network analysis and argued that there are advantages to using both *field* and *network* in any analysis of the fashion world. The aim of this chapter is to apply these theoretical insights to give an account of high fashion markets, where the aesthetic commodities traded throw up intriguing questions about value. I take the example of the high fashion modelling, specifically male modelling. The starting question is a simple one: 'what kind of a market is this?' This leads, naturally, to related questions about how this market is put together, which concerns the actors, processes and practices inside the market itself.

Starting with the commodities themselves it is apparent that high fashion commodities throw up many questions as to how value is generated in such a market. Fashion models or fashion clothing have a high aesthetic content and are particularly unstable in that their aesthetic value is subject to constant fluctuations that are temporal—as each fashion 'season' or 'mid-season' brings along a 'new' style/s—and also spatial—while fashions spread globally, they are always to be adapted to local context. Thus, the central feature is changing aesthetics; indeed, the logic of fashion is aesthetic 'change for change's sake' and without 'progress'. This logic of incessant change is centrally bound up with *economic* value: this season's 'hot' denim label or 'exciting "new face"' of fashion modelling can sell at quite a price today. However, by the end of season, the denim jacket might be in the mark-down section of a department store, and the model long forgotten, replaced by another. In other words, economic value is always and everywhere undermined by the systemic momentum of change, as another 'new face' or 'cult' denim label, or 'hot' colour will, inevitably, follow. The temporal dimensions of this incessant aesthetic fluctuation characterize much of the 'risk' in this market, in two significant ways. For one, market decisions, in retail, are taken in advance of goods arriving—fashion buying happens months in advance of the actual season and thus orders are placed that will not reach the consumer for weeks, if not months. In modelling, this risk is minimized, since models are picked up and dropped as and when clients want them. However, bookers still need to decide whose career to invest in and this is an investment of time and effort that they cannot always predict the outcome of. Added to this is the further temporal dimension that fashion commodities are clearly depreciating at a fast rate: once in store, there is a small window of opportunity to sell fashion clothes before they are 'out of fashion', while fashion model careers are notoriously short-lived and have only a few seasons in which to make an impression.

What is going on here? How can something sell at one price one day and be half price the next? What qualities allow a commodity to be 'hot' one day and not the next? Further, how do those *inside* these markets see these qualities? Take the world of fashion modelling which translates 'the look', sometimes called 'beauty' but not always, into a commercial (day or job) rate and raises a number of intriguing questions: how is something so seemingly subjective and 'cultural' as physical appearance or 'beauty' commodified? How does a particular 'look' come to acquire status as the latest one? How do those in the market recognize what looks will sell? In other words, in fields of cultural production, where the generation of an aesthetic is central but where the aesthetic content is always changing, how is the value of any particular object *secured* (long enough) so that value can be extracted from it?

Aesthetics are central to the production of a whole range of different products and services, such as advertising, fashion design, retailing, graphics, Web site design, architecture, interiors and furniture design, to name but a few examples. However, debates about the 'aestheticization' of economics and everyday life (Baudrillard 1981; Lash and Urry 1994) are theoretical and very little empirical analysis of this process has been undertaken. While Bourdieu (1993a) and White (1993) have developed parallel frameworks for the analysis of artistic production, empirical research, vis-à-vis the workings of actual market, is required to test their propositions. Asper's (2001) study of markets in fashion photography in Sweden, Negus's (1992, 1999) account of the cultural production of popular music and White's (2000) study of the development of Italian fashion in the post-war era are some exceptions to this. All are empirically detailed accounts of the market conditions under which cultural artefacts with a high aesthetic content are produced (Berger 1972; Becker 1982).

My analysis builds upon some of this work, as well as extending work on markets in general within economic sociology. Aesthetic markets afford the possibility of understanding the particular ways in which 'cultural' and 'economic' considerations are merged in markets trading in cultural artefacts. This partly addresses the current bias in economic sociology which tends to favour other markets—either basic commodities, like food, technology markets, like cars, or financial markets. However, aesthetic markets demand our attention, not only because they exist and have economic significance, but also because they enable us to 'explore the diversity of calculative agencies, forms and distributions, and hence of organized markets' (Callon 1998b: 51). Thus, analysis of aesthetic markets extends our knowledge of the diversity of ways in which value is generated within different commercial practices.

My case study in this chapter, male fashion modelling, may seem a rather unusual or marginal one. However, it sheds light on how aesthetic values are generated in markets trading aesthetic goods, and the ideas outlined here are developed in relation to fashionable clothing here and in later chapters of this book. I begin with Definitions and Introductions; I want to define and introduce my case study, first by explaining some of the features of fashion modelling as a specific form of work within the cultural economy of particular cites, and then delineating the particular characteristics of aesthetic economies or markets. In Networks and Circuits in the Aesthetic Economy, I examine the specific aesthetics of fashion modelling and the sorts of calculations that are made between 'economic' and 'cultural' value. In Circuits of Value in the Aesthetic Economy of Modelling, I examine the 'circuits of value' that are central to the calculations and journeys of actors inside the fashion network.

Definitions and Introductions

Modelling and the Cultural Economy of Cities

Fashion modelling is situated in what might be called the 'cultural economy' of many cities. That is, in recent years, as more model agencies are established in the major 'fashion cities', they might be said to constitute something of the 'new economy' of cities built upon 'cultural' goods and services. However, defining what is meant by the term *cultural economy* is tricky, as already noted in the previous chapter, as is the task of delineating the relationship between the two terms—*aesthetic economy* and *cultural economy*—as they are used in this chapter. As previously noted, while the term *cultural economy* designates a myriad of different theoretical responses and approaches, one restricted usage is in relation to industries which trade cultural commodities. Further claims have been made as to the increasing significance of these industries to the economy of cities and nations (Scott 1999, 2000; Pratt 2004b). Whatever the problems with these claims, there are many features that distinguish these industries from more traditional, 'harder' industries. Tonkiss (2002: 191) suggests we need to define 'what is distinctly "cultural" about the cultural economy', and argues 'the skilled deployment of technical expertise in tandem with economic nous and cultural knowledge appears as particularly crucial in a setting where demand for products and for labour can shift very rapidly.' This would seem a very pertinent starting point in terms of understanding modelling and some of its specifically 'cultural' elements. As a commercial practice, fashion modelling shares all these characteristics of the (more restricted) understanding of the 'cultural economy': it is highly dependent upon cultural knowledge and other categories of culture, such as prestige or kudos. Further, dependent as it is on novelty, there is a rapid turnover in product and labour force, as models' looks come in and out of fashion. In terms of specifying the relationship between these two terms, then, *cultural economy* refers to some of these broad features of modelling as a market that is shared by all industries trading cultural commodities. As discussed in more detail below, I use the idea of 'aesthetic economy' to refer to those industries concerned with trading a specifically aesthetic quality. In other words, not all markets designated as 'cultural' are centrally bound up with 'aesthetic' qualities. Film-making is not, primarily, about selling an aesthetic, although in some instances it might be and aesthetics are *part* of film-making. Modelling is, however, primarily about selling an aesthetic look.

The importance of cultural knowledge ensures that fashion modelling is a metropolitan phenomenon. Fashion modelling is primarily located in major cities across the world associated with fashion: London, Milan, New York, Paris being the ones most noted and setting the agenda in terms of their regular 'fashion weeks', with many also asserting themselves, inserting themselves, within the 'fashion week' system, such as Tokyo, Los Angeles, Miami and Stockholm, which have smaller markets in fashion (see for example Aspers 2001). Thus, while modelling is global work *par excellence*, with models travelling constantly for work and their images globally transmitted, it is also very much situated within the local economy of these cities. This insertion of the local within the context of globalization is a common feature of what Sassen (1991) calls 'global cities', a feature which is also detailed by Scott (2000). In his discussion of the cultural economy of cities, Scott (2000) notes that cultural production is rooted in the unique communities of workers embedded in particular localities. This is certainly true of modelling: model agencies work to build up close institutional and social relations with clients in the city; indeed its survival depends upon building up these relations. A large part of a booker's time is spent meeting and negotiating with clients in the city, waxing lyrical to them about models and setting up 'go-sees' (meetings between models and potential clients) in the city. While a model can be booked directly for work anywhere in the world on the basis of his or her reputation, as a result of previous work which has reached clients abroad, by the Fed-Exing of his or her model 'book', or via the Web, most models spend their time (especially early on) at castings and 'go-sees' meeting clients (more on this below). In this respect, models, like agencies, must be based in the big cities where the major clients are located and where most of the creative work is produced.

These different cities are often referred to by bookers as constituting different 'markets', testimony to the local character of modelling, despite its global reach. Since fashion depends upon constantly changing aesthetics in its search for the 'new', a 'hot' model, booking lots of jobs with clients in their home city one season may mean being 'old' and out of work the next, as they are superseded by *new faces* (an industry term often used by agencies to distinguish new models from the rest). Experienced models, having seen all the major clients in their home city, sometimes find their careers stagnating as a result. As one London head booker, Gwyneth put it, 'You can do really well in your first 3 months then do nothing for 6 months; you can do 3 campaigns in a row then no-one will touch you'. Thus, to invigorate a model's career, it is sometimes necessary to, 'ship them off to another market—you send them to Japan, Germany, the States, you get them out of town, shuffle them around; you say to them "Well you've been seen by everyone here, so you need to go to Milan or Germany"'.

The socio-physical specificities of this industry are even more localized. *Within* the major fashion cities there are particular regions/territories that are associated with fashion and modelling. This is a business that depends upon building informal and cultural connections within particular localities. Wissinger's study (2007b) of fashion models in New York demonstrates this, and so too does Aspers (2001) in his analysis of the fashion photography market in Sweden. He notes (2001: 89–90) how, in Stockholm, particular restaurants, bars and a whole area of the city, Soder, or 'the South', are the locations of those in the fashion business. Fashion model agencies are thus located in particular parts of the city: SoHo, TriBeCa and the Flat Iron district in New York are closely associated with the fashion industry and are densely packed with model agencies; while Hoxton/Shorditch has, in recent years, taken over from the older locations for agencies in Covent Garden and the Kings Road in London where most model agencies were located. This is evidence of the high importance of culture to the business of fashion and fashion modelling: in such an industry, success depends upon the interweaving of social/cultural and work activities in order to 'do business' (Neff et al. 2005). Describing the 'entrepreneurial labour of fashion models' and 'new media workers', Neff et al. (2005: 322) note, 'A fluid boundary between work-time and playtime is shaped by compulsory "schmoozing," "face-time" or socializing within the industry after the workday.' For models, this may mean having to go out on dinner dates and to parties regularly to meet clients: ' "Half my job [is] taking out models and clients four nights a week," says a male model agent' (2005: 322). They conclude by noting that the 'cool' nature of these 'creative' occupations makes such work highly desirable, even while the realities of the job are not always so attractive: a high degree of job insecurity, long hours and often low pay (especially for those at the beginning or on the lower echelons of the career ladder). Indeed, as they note, 'Culturally desirable jobs bring, paradoxically, lowered expectations of economic stability' (2005: 331).

Having described some features of modelling work within the 'cultural economy' of cities, let me now define what I mean by 'aesthetic economy'.

Defining the Aesthetic Economy

An aesthetic economy is one in which aesthetics is a key component in the production of particular goods and services within a particular industry, organization or firm, and one in which aesthetics are central to the economic calculations of that setting. In other words, in aesthetic economies, aesthetics *are the product/s* and, as such, are at the centre of the economic calculations of the practice. As I have previously argued (Entwistle 2002) aesthetic commodities are more nebulous than other sorts of products, such as vegetables or garden implements, since they are concerned with properties of 'beauty', 'style' or 'design', which are effervescent categories that change over time and across different social spaces. This is not to say that design is not a feature of other markets—even the humdrum vegetable markets have aesthetics as part of their calculation, with vegetables increasingly selected by supermarkets for their supposed 'beauty' (misshapen ones rejected in the process). Rather, aesthetic markets exist at one end of the continuum where calculating aesthetics is critical: trouser lengths and colours come rapidly in and out of fashion, the aesthetics of Brussels sprouts or green peppers do not keep changing season on season, but remain relatively stable over time.

I use the term *aesthetic market* rather than other, more widely used terms such as 'aestheticization' or 'dematerialization' of the economy, quite deliberately. I am doing so in order to argue explicitly with the radical strands of postmodernism that suggest that the economy has been reduced to signs and symbols; to de-material 'floating signifiers'. Marxist analysis suggests we can attend to the material and immaterial (cultural) elements of a commodity as if they were separate qualities or 'moments'. For Haug (1986), the capitalist system seeks to create 'aesthetic illusion' that embellishes the physical content of the commodity by creating perceptions—cultural meanings—around it, and she focuses analysis upon the practices of advertising to weave meanings and desires around commodities. However, as Fine (2002) demonstrates, this distinction between the material content of goods and their cultural meanings is too simplistic. He (2002: 93) argues that 'the aesthetic illusion is inevitably more deeply rooted than a form of deceit at the point of sale and purchase. Advertising and design are inextricably linked ... as are design and production. These are all cultural as well as material activities.' Similarly, for Slater and Tonkiss (2001: 180), 'Aestheticization features in all stages of a commodity's life cycle and indeed draws together processual moments—production, circulation and consumption—which have been regarded as separate by earlier economic and social thought.' The approach that comes closest to understanding this is that proposed in Du Gay and Hall et al. (1997) in their case study of the Sony Walkman, discussed in more detail in Chapter 5.

Aesthetic marketplace calculations have their own particularity or 'local rationality' (Abolafia 1998). That is to say, aesthetic values do not come out of nowhere but are generated *internally* to the market itself, by the routine actions and practices of individuals and institutions. In the world of modelling, the models' looks are constantly changing in response to the fluctuations of the fashion system and the differing needs of clients. The question becomes, how then do those in the field stabilize the product—a model's look—they are selling? The fluctuations and instabilities within aesthetic markets are routinely dealt with through particular strategies, calculations and negotiations that are entirely meaningful and 'rational' to them. As Slater (2002b) argues, for an economy to exist at all, objects must be stabilized through what he calls, 'processes of materialization'. In other words, the object is rendered calculable and meaningful by actors at a given moment in time. His analysis extends to even the most seemingly 'immaterial' commodities, such as aesthetic objects, as part of a persuasive critique of theories about 'dematerialization' or 'aestheticization' which, he argues, are based upon a dubious distinction between the material (i.e. physical) and the immaterial (i.e. signs). Thus, he contends, *all* commodities are calculated and materialized within economic action and markets.

Hence, rather than focus on signs themselves, disembodied from producers and consumers, and thus from markets and practices, I examine how aesthetic values are generated *within economic action* by actors and increasingly essential to carrying out economic practices. While images of models are one feature of these practices, I do not offer a semiotic reading of them but examine the way particular signs (text or images) generate meanings and values around the commodity form (model or clothing). In other words, by using the term *aesthetic economy/market* I assert the necessity of examining precisely *how* aesthetic values are generated as part of the calculations inside these markets. As I suggest, modelling provides an example of the ways in which a peculiarly unstable commodity—the style or look of the body—is 'materialized' within a particular economic field. I now want to examine the specific aesthetics of fashion modelling and the sorts of calculations that are made between 'economic' and 'cultural' value.

Networks and Circuits in the Aesthetic Economy

While the inherent instabilities within this aesthetic economy, described above, are something of a problem to both models and bookers who, when asked to define the qualities of fashion model looks in interviews, struggle to define what they look for, it is also an accepted aspect of their work, routinely dealt with through strategies entirely meaningful and rational to them. In other words, practices within this market stabilize the quality, rendering it a calculable object whose meaning and value is 'fixed', if perhaps only temporarily. To understand how things acquire commodity value we need to examine two main dimensions of market practice: the *calculations* actors in markets make and how they make sense of—stabilize and 'translate' (Callon, Meadel et al. 2005)—objects to render them commodities; and second, the circuitous *journey* of the commodities themselves, in their life course, to trace how value is secured. In a moment, we begin our journey at the model agency.

These two concerns—with calculations and journeys—are linked: the calculations demanded of agents in a fashion market are heterogeneous, concerned, of course, with matters of price, but arrived at also by the object's entanglement and journey along a network of seemingly non-economic or 'cultural' factors. The nebulous and hard to define aspects of work in fashion modelling are described by Wissinger (2007a: 15) as 'immaterial labour'. Drawing on Lazzarato, she notes that immaterial labour is labour which 'produces the informational and cultural content of the commodity (Lazzarato, 1996: 133)', the latter involving a 'series of activities that are not normally recognized as "work"—in other words, the kinds of activities involved in defining and fixing cultural and artistic standards, fashions, tastes, consumer norms, and, more strategically, public opinion (1996: 133)' (Wissinger 2007a: 251–52). This labour 'also involves processes of "codification and de-codification" in which personality and subjectivity become involved in the production of value (Lazzarato, 1996: 135)' (Wissinger 2007a: 252). While I do not take up these arguments about immateriality, these points resonate in terms of my own interviews with male models, as I discuss below. I also agree with her description of how modelling work is organized on a project-by-project basis into

> "small and sometimes very small 'productive units' (often consisting of only one individual) are organized for specific ad-hoc projects, and may exist only for the duration of those particular jobs," which Lazzarato claims are typical of immaterial production (1996: 137). This complex web of relations is not readily evident in the typical image of a fashion model; models are usually depicted as if they are alone, staring out of a magazine page in a solitary moment of fashionable repose. (2007a: 252)

She then instructs us to 'take a step back, outside of the frame' (2007a: 252) to consider the people working on a shoot—photographers, stylist(s), make-up artist, hairstylist and all their various assistants, along with personnel from the client and possibly also the people at the venue where the shoot is taking place, adding, 'These are just the people in the room' (2007a: 252), since a host of others work around the model but not specifically on shoots—the model's agent or publicist, for one.

It is to the collective aspects of modelling work that I focus on in this chapter in order to understand the ways in which an array of actors and processes create model value. As the above description of modelling project work suggests, the aesthetic object—in this case the model himself or herself—is networked; that is, a model's value lies not in anything intrinsic to the model, but is generated around the model, through many different engagements and processes. As I argue in this chapter, aesthetic value is *created, accrued* and *attributed* along the network in which the object/model becomes entangled. In other words, aesthetic value is not an essential quality of the object, but something assigned to it over its life course. The usefulness of the network metaphor has, according to Hughes (2004: 212), not been applied to commodities and yet is useful to apply it to 'the economic in order to describe how different kinds of nodes (people, firms, states, organizations, etc.) are connected to one another in complex and multi-stranded ways'. Summarizing Thrift and Olds's argument, Hughes (2004: 212) goes on to note how the concept has been applied 'to represent the organization of social and cultural ties in economic linkages' and to suggest that 'at the most general level ... it captures the patterns of webs of interdependence existing between different sets of actors in the economy.' In an aesthetic market these webs of interdependence accrue *status,* that is to say, through associations of cultural prestige from valued connections to established or important actors, like designers or photographers, the creation of brand identity, the media profile etc., as I now want to demonstrate.

The model's journey almost inevitably begins in a model agency, since prospective models are likely to have little access to the sources of value and status independently. Much like the laboratories described in Science and Technology Studies (STS) (Latour and Woolgar 1979; Latour 1987), the model agency generates its own alchemy, selecting a few bodies and turning them to 'gold'; that is, into special creatures of desire for their clients and, ultimately, the consumers of the images they appear in. It is alchemy that also depends upon a multitude of other actors and processes—photographers, stylists, make-up artists, digital retouchers, and the like. These actors and relations are materially significant to creating model value, inflecting calculations ordinarily assumed to be economic: Is the price right? Can we sell X number of tops in aubergine/this model for £10,000 a day? Are we running out of stock/Do we need to buy more stock? That is, high value of 'the look'—the (male) fashion model or the high fashion garment label—is collectively produced— *valorized*—by the actions of those inside this marketplace. For this reason, the work of Bourdieu (1993a,b) and Blumer (1969) is particularly useful as they point to the features, of status, relationships and 'collective selection' that constitute the world of fashion production.

To understand these processes I want to first introduce the fashion model aesthetic. While the content of this aesthetic fluctuates, there are some particular aspects to the fashion model aesthetic that set it apart from other sorts of body aesthetics, such as the 'everyday' 'good looks' of commercial modelling or 'glamour' modelling.

That 'Certain Something': The Aesthetics of Fashion Modelling

The high fashion model 'look' is by no means self-evident. Although it is true that many male and female models are considered 'beautiful', recognized and celebrated as such in popular culture, modelling looks are not *necessarily* about 'beauty' and models do not always correspond to popular aesthetic tastes in faces and bodies. The best way to illustrate the intriguing nature of aesthetics in high fashion is to go inside the model agency itself. Prior to starting my research, I had assumed that fashion modelling was about the commodification of something called 'beauty' and that I shared the same ideas about beauty as those within the field of modelling. However, I sometimes found that what model agents (or 'bookers' as they are known) described to me as 'fantastic', or 'amazing' looking models appeared to me as either quite odd or merely unexceptional. One model, a teenage boy with a successful career in modelling developing, was described in hyperbolic terms by his London booker Gwyneth as stunningly 'beautiful', and she told of how everyone in the office was mesmerized when he first came into the agency. He had been introduced to them by a stylist who 'discovered' him boarding a plane with his father at Rome airport. However, I could not have been more surprised when I met the boy, who was 16 at the time: instead of a stunning Adonis, here was a very fragile looking boy, with a body unusually small for someone his age and with a face that I can only describe as 'strange' or 'unusual'. Moreover, I would never have picked him out from a crowd as having modelling potential, as had the stylist who discovered him. It was only once he opened his 'book' (or portfolio) that I could see what his booker and others had seen in him: in photographs he had an ethereal appearance that was quite striking.

On another occasion, just as I was ending my fieldwork, I was asked to take a young woman around to some model agencies. Helen (not her real name) had been told frequently that she had 'model potential' and, for this reason, she was passed to me as someone with some (limited) knowledge of the modelling industry. This young woman, 17 at the time, bore a striking resemblance to the actor Julia Roberts. Having met her, I too was confident that she had model potential and agreed to spend a morning cold-calling some agencies with her. What happened to her is character-istic of many initial encounters between young hopefuls and a model agency. At the first agency we were told to wait, along with another two hopefuls, in the lobby area until the head booker was available. When he first arrived he instantly dismissed the other women with the line—'You're not right for us, but here is a list of reputable model agencies, go and introduce yourself to them'—before turning to us. At first glance he seemed interested in Helen. He asked her to take down her long hair which was in a ponytail. As she shook her thick brown curls free he set about examining her face, staring intently, but, just as I was feeling confident, she was dismissed with the same face-saving refusal. She didn't even warrant a Polaroid, which is the next step in 'testing' (Callon, Meadel et al. 2005) model potential. I will return to this jour-ney through the agency in Circuits of Value in the Aesthetic Economy of Modelling below, when I examine what happens to those who pass the initial inspection.

For now, it is important to note that these two incidents impressed upon me the very different aesthetics 'inside' fashion modelling, as opposed to 'outside'. It also points to the ability of those 'on the inside' to see at a glance some quality which es-capes 'outsider' perception. Bourdieu's (1993a) idea of the 'cycle of belief' seems apt here. Referring to the art world, Bourdieu uses the analogy of magic to describe the value that accrues around particular art works by their very selection and promotion by art dealers. Drawing on Mauss, Bourdieu (1993a: 80–1) suggests that magic is not so much concerned with the specific properties of the magician, or even of the magi-cal operations, but to discover the bases of the collective belief or *'collective misrec-ognition'*, within the 'magic group' which is the source of the power of the magician. It would seem that the successful model's career is similarly about the generation of belief that, like magic, is produced through 'collective misrecognition' within the group. A model's career progress requires the initial selection by a reputable agency whose belief sends the model to meet potentially influential clients. The more a model is selected for work, especially work for prestigious clients, the more belief is gener-ated and a model's career is secured. Not belonging to this 'magic group' I did not always understand their belief and throughout the fieldwork I continued to be puzzled by the bodies held in esteem in modelling and made aware that the aesthetics of this field had their own specificity.

Defining the Aesthetic of Fashion Modelling

Although the actual aesthetic content of the high fashion model look is not the focus of my attention, it is worth trying to define this look since it is quite distinct from 'beauty' as defined outside, or indeed, within the world of commercial modelling:

> Being attractive is not quite the same thing as being a model ... we're talking about a *strange genetic ideal* here. The principle of 'model beauty' is not the same thing as 'next-door beauty' or as [one magazine editor puts it] "There is '*industry beauty*' and there is '*street beauty*'" (www.models.com, emphasis added).
>
> At the moment, I'm looking for something *a little different*. A big nose, a beard or a tattoo—it's not about being gorgeous; *a lot of them are actually quite strange-looking.* (Corner 2001: 8, emphasis added)

In the *Sunday Telegraph* article in April 2008 the male model look is described in terms of different clients/fashion houses: 'There are definitely two main looks at the moment: edgy boys such as Eddie Klint and Nick Schnider who work for Prada and a more classically handsome guy like Matt Gordon who is more Gucci' (Webb 2008).

That *fashion* modelling has its own particular body aesthetics is demonstrated by the fact that not just any look can make it in this arena, since not everyone can become a *fashion model*: agencies exist for 'ordinary' people (like Uglies in London) but for commercial, not fashion, clients. Indeed, fashion model agencies are very exclusive, rejecting many more people who walk through their doors than they accept. Characterizing the fashion look is quite difficult—even models and bookers themselves often find it hard to define. So, while on the one hand, bookers talk about certain physical requirements of bone and flesh, these characteristics have to be 'translated' and 'qualified' by bookers; that is to say, these qualities are not self-evident, but rendered meaningful through their actions of selection and calculation. Indeed, the very qualities said to be 'essential' are also always re-calculated or qualified, as with models who 'break the mould' and establish a new look (Kate Moss is 'short' at 5′ 7″ and Sophie Dahl was a 'large' size 14–16 when she first started modelling). The age range is also very young: fashion models range in age from 15–25, with only a few 'celebrity' fashion models extending their careers much beyond that.

There are industry standards which impose themselves on the calculations of bookers, such as 'sample size', (the size of samples in studios). These play an important role in setting the physical parameters of model size—US size 4 or UK 8 is usual sample size for women, while in men's modelling, as head booker Gwyneth in London put it to me, a man must 'have the right proportions: 40 regular, 34 inside leg and height. There's about two inches in that height, maybe you can go down to 5′ 11″, maybe up to 6' 3", but most of them are 6' to 6' 2".' She summed up these physical qualities as being about 'facial symmetry and body proportion'. Beyond the strictures of these standards, model looks are described as having a mysterious quality, a certain *je ne sais quoi* which is undefinable, even though it is apparent to their 'eye'. As Joan, the head of an agency in London put it to me, 'Obviously it is ingredient X that makes it work and is quite difficult to put your finger on and say what are you looking for, but I can say that *when I see it, I usually know it*' (emphasis added).

In contrast to hand, feet and leg models, a clearly defined sub-division of modelling which falls outside this study, the fashion model 'look' is made up of the entire model's body—hair, face and body—and, critically, how these features translate in a photograph. However, the look is also *more* than the sum of the parts of the body. The look is also built up through the work the model does: as I discuss below, a model's look can be defined as 'commercial' or 'editorial' and these categories are reinforced through the work the model does. Very few fashion models make a living from runway or catwalk work alone and therefore models must be 'photogenic' to shoot 'editorial' (fashion magazine) work. For this reason, the model's look becomes increasingly codified through the images they appear in and develops an objectified character over the course of their career, in the form of jobs, contracts and images, which are materialized in the model 'book', and by their accumulated 'reputation'. These images are almost an extension of the model's body, since how the model looks in person has only a small part to play in their success in securing work: how they photograph is at least as crucial. This discrepancy between the physical and the photographic body of the model was sometimes referred to by models and bookers in interviews, with many of them commenting on the fact that most models look nothing like the images they appear in. Indeed, the first thing an agent does if they spot someone with potential is photograph them with a Polaroid. This tests instantly whether they are photogenic, after which they are sent to photographers to shoot some 'tests' to see how they perform for the camera and produce images for their 'book' (portfolio).

The fashion model look is often referred to as an 'editorial' look, referring to the importance of editorial work for fashion magazines within this market. Frequently this editorial look is described as 'edgy', a word that is difficult to define but which refers to the unusual, odd or 'quirky' nature of these looks. At one of the top agencies in London Martin, head booker for men, described it as follows, 'the current look is defined as *quirky*. About a year or two years ago now it was *very extreme*. What's happening now is extending to be, still quite young, still 16 to 21 or 22, but more young and beautiful, quite fresh again, but *not square jawed*. So *pretty*, without being too feminine, maybe have a slight *edge*.'

According to Martin and other bookers in London, the 'grunge' look associated with what also became known as 'heroin chic' of the 1990s popularized such extreme looks as a reaction to the overly glossy and perfect bodies of the female and male models of the 1980s (the Amazonian supermodel, such as Linda Evangelista, and the square-jawed hunk of Calvin Klein commercials). This look has become particularly associated with a London market. Martin notes that this extreme aesthetic would appear to change (more 'beautiful', 'fresh' or 'pretty') but it is apparent from these terms that this aesthetic is still quite different from conventional ideas of masculine good looks; different too from the looks found within commercial male modelling, both of which demand a more 'manly' or 'hunky' look. As these quotes suggest, the looks appropriate to fashion modelling are very often less connected to popular taste than to the esoteric and rarefied world of high fashion, and this makes it less accessible to the outsider's eye and the mainstream public. In this way, the aesthetics of fashion modelling have much in common with the avant-garde within the field of art, promoting looks that at first may seem ugly or strange. Like the avant-garde, fashion modelling seeks out that which is 'strange-looking' as part of a relentless search for something new, or 'different'. These are looks that demand 'cultural capital' (Bourdieu 1984) in the form of cultural competency, knowledge and an acquired aesthetic sensibility, to be intelligible.

The 'extreme' or 'edgy' aesthetics of fashion modelling can be contrasted to the looks required for other sorts of modelling. 'Glamour' modelling demands a quite different aesthetic. Sometimes referred to as 'topless' modelling, because the work involves nude or semi-nude posing, this market favours larger or 'curvier' bodies than fashion, along with 'girl-next-door' good looks. It also sells to different clients, usually men's products (e.g. men's weekly and monthly magazines, tabloid newspapers, cars). Closer but still distinct from fashion modelling is commercial modelling. The editorial look is often defined in relation to commercial work, where 'good looks' in the shape of the square-jawed handsome faces found in catalogues or toothpaste advertisements for example are favoured. Commercial modelling favours models with a broader appeal ('next-door-beauty'). Since the market orientation for catalogues and lifestyle products is older, commercial modelling generally favours older male models (25+). Some young fashion models are versatile enough to do commercial work, but most usually grow into this work as they age. However, while fashion models may cross-over into commercial work, older commercial and lifestyle models do not shoot high fashion.

Fashion and commercial modelling serve as important co-ordinates within modelling, orientating models and bookers to particular clients. The differences can mean a separation *between* agencies: commercial agencies, found in many cities, serve local clients, while fashion agencies are only based in major fashion capitals. The main difference between them can be summarized in this way: commercial agencies do not do fashion but fashion agencies usually have to combine fashion and commercial modelling; indeed, as I argue below, their survival depends upon combining the two. Thus, as I discuss in more detail below, there are different circuits of value *across* the range of modelling practices and also *within* the fashion modelling. 'Editorial' and 'commercial' are therefore more than aesthetic categories: they serve to shape or direct a model's career and the overall profile of an agency. A model defined as 'edgy' will book mostly editorial work, while a model with a 'commercial' look will book catalogue or TV commercials. This has a bearing on their earning potential and longevity; as Aspers (2001: 85) puts it, 'the agency "directs" the model. If the model's appearance is considered suitable for catalogues, her career may be orientated to catalogue customers. Others, who have a stronger "character," have more potential, though their career is less predictable than in markets where customers preferences are more "stable" (like mail-order companies).'

As this quote suggests, the aesthetics of fashion modelling, while having more 'potential', are inherently unstable and 'less predictable', dependent upon the constantly fluctuating aesthetics of fashion and changing needs of clients. This makes fashion aesthetics a more unstable commodity than commercial aesthetics which need to be stabilized, temporarily, to allow models and their agents to do business, as discussed in the final section of this chapter.

Models themselves have little control over these unstable aesthetics and may remain puzzled as to why they book or fail to book a job. They may, however, try to effect some control through various forms of 'aesthetic labour' (Warhurst, Nickson et al. 2000; Witz, Warhurst et al. 2002) that aim to 'second guess' what clients might be looking for, although market fluctuations and the often hazy requirements of clients ensure that there is no clear criteria or guaranteed strategy (Entwistle and Wissinger 2006). This labour takes many forms: dieting, exercising, styling one's hair frequently, and other such grooming techniques. However, the degree to which male models engage in such studied attempts to control their bodies depends on the market itself. The New York models were much more likely to lift weights to achieve a 'cut' body or consciously style their hair than the London models, since the market in the States is often orientated towards sports and leisure wear and calls for a much more toned and muscular physique than that demanded in the London market. In London, I observed that male models effect something akin to a 'slouchy' 'laddish' attitude, which means they tended to distance themselves from bodily work, effecting a 'don't care' and 'casual' demeanour. One of the more successful male models I interviewed in London had perfected this attitude and claimed not to care how he looked, preferring to spend more time tuning his guitar (which he played frequently in his spare time) than his body. This itself is not entirely without aesthetic quality: indeed, the 'slouchy' look and generally 'uncared for' appearance evident in how the London models styled themselves—in loose trousers, baggy T-shirts and trainers and with long and unkempt hair—very much fits the London editorial model look favoured by niche fashion magazines in the city at the time.

Circuits of Value in the Aesthetic Economy of Modelling

Fashion and Commercial Modelling: Calculating Cultural and Economic Value

Not only are the aesthetics of fashion modelling different from commercial modelling, but the economic and cultural value of each differs considerably. It may come as a surprise to anyone outside the industry that some of the most prestigious and high profile work is editorials (fashion stories in magazines and newspapers) and covers for magazines such as *Vogue, L'Uomo Vogue, Arena Homme,* which pays little or nothing and has no immediate economic value to a model. Regardless of whether you are a 'new face' or a famous one, editorial work pays very little—£100–200. Indeed, the economics of this kind of fashion production are peculiar, as Aspers (2001) notes, with photographers, stylists and models even *losing* money after they've paid the costs of getting to the shoot. In contrast, commercial work brings in big money on a regular basis: a day rate for a commercial model might be around £2,000 which, on a catalogue shoot, can last days or weeks. Fees rise considerably for large campaigns by major clients, where day rates are high and sums of money for usage and distribution built in. A campaign for Pepsi Cola in Europe may pay around £35,000, while a worldwide contract pays around £60,000.[1] However, while commercial work is far more lucrative than fashion, it is also far less prestigious and is certainly not valuable in establishing a *fashion* model's career, as will be discussed.

Given the considerable difference in economics, why would models shoot for *Vogue, The Face,* or *L'Uomo,* perhaps even turning down a commercial job booked the same day? The answer lies in the high *cultural value* attached to such work, which is invaluable in lending status or kudos to a model. However, the value of high fashion work may not always be immediate: models might spend months shooting only editorial and earning no money and some may never graduate beyond this work. The successful few hope these editorials will give them enough 'tear sheets' (images in their book) to increase their profile and chances of landing a fashion campaign with a major fashion house (such as Gucci or Calvin Klein). Even commercial clients look for editorial work: as one booker put it, 'Clients like to see lots of tear-sheets, it helps to up the commercial rate'. In other words, high status fashion work, for which there is no immediate economic gain, lends *symbolic capital,* in the form of prestige and celebrity, which can, potentially at least, translate into *economic capital* at some future date. The converse is not true, however: commercial work does not lend any cultural value. A Pepsi-Cola commercial or toothpaste ad are worth no more than their monetary value and may, indeed, diminish a model's overall cultural kudos: cultural kudos, once gained, can also be lost if a model 'sells out' and becomes too 'down-market'. This explains why even famous models continue to clock up a proportion of covers and editorials with major fashion magazines throughout their career for tiny sums of money, and why they may turn down lucrative commercial work which will be detrimental to their image and overall career trajectory (Neff, Wissinger et al. 2005). Thus, calculations of the long-term cultural value of particular work often out-weigh short-term commercial gains when it comes to developing a model's career. These calculations are usually made by the model booker directing and advising the model.

Bookers calculate models' careers, careful to balance commercial to editorial work. This balancing act between fashion and commercial work was described to me by John, a New York booker, as 'a bit of a seesaw. You have to convince them [the models] that it is important to do that $5,000 job and to make $125 because this is for your book. But most of them get that, they understand.' Simon, an experienced, London-based model put it this way: 'High fashion is where everyone wants to be, yet catalogue has the money. So you have catalogue models wanting to do high fashion and you've got high fashion models wanting to do catalogue because they want the money!'

Models who manage to book both sorts of work have to ensure that the economic value of one does not diminish the cultural value of the other. Hence, a clear separation is maintained, with the commercial images never making it into the model book. When questioned about whether they want to do catalogue or not, two London models said they both sought this work but Robbie noted it can't go in their book: 'No! Alongside Italian *Vogue* and Burberrys?!' Simon explained: 'No, you need a book full of tear-sheets, decent things in your book from magazines to get jobs with.' Thus, a model's career, materialized in the form of his book, must be carefully calculated, in relation to questions about both the relative cultural and economic value of the work he books.

Even *within* fashion editorial, distinctions are drawn between quality jobs, which accrue cultural value for the model, and those which are down-market and thus may diminish it. These two have to be carefully calculated as Gwyneth, a head booker in a large London agency, put it:

> There is such a thing as image. All better agencies try to protect the image of their models. If he was shot for *L'Uomo Vogue* we would never allow him to also shoot *Cosmopolitan* magazine at the same time. Or if he started doing *Arena* he couldn't go and do a beach story for *Just 17*, even if he was 16. If they start at a level, they stay there. They can start out on teen magazines but once they break, they must not go back.

Not only does the agency have to carefully calculate the balance of models' work, it must also carefully balance its own profile, between the two forms of modelling, accruing a reputation as high fashion or 'cutting edge' as well as 'commercial', if they are to survive. Hence, bookers described the need to maintain a balanced 'Board' (the line-up of models on its roster), recruiting and developing models with a range of looks that span from the more 'extreme' aesthetics of fashion to the 'handsome' good looks of commercial modelling. This is how one industry Web site, www.models.com, describes this balancing act:

> Every modelling agency has two elements it must master ... the first is the Y axis 'profitability'. This is where commercials, catalogues and campaigns (of a mass market nature), come into play ... the second, the X axis is 'fabulousness'. This is where the edgy, editorial, runway [fashion shows] and campaign jobs that make fashion ... come into play ... The best agencies for your career are the ones that can plot a straight line between the two axes.

Thus, to continue the mathematical analogy,

> When an agency swings too closely to X, it runs the risk of being fabulous today, bankrupt tomorrow. If it veers too closely towards Y, an agency's image suffers and it ends up on the sidelines excluded from fashion's VIP sanctum.

In other words, in high fashion modelling, aesthetic and cultural values are central to economic value. Similar calculations of value can be found at Selfridges, as discussed in Part II of this book, where the need for commercial profit and for big selling labels that sell in volume is carefully balanced alongside the need to sell 'edgier' high fashion labels, consistent with the store's image of itself as 'high fashion' and 'cutting edge'. Similarly, in the market for fashion photography in Sweden, Aspers (2001) describes how nebulous cultural concerns are critical to the market, since cultural prestige helps shape careers in fashion photography. A similar hierarchy of work, between commercial and fashion, is evident here as well.

The Fashion Network and the Circuits of Value

As I argue, therefore, considerations of status or prestige are central to the calculations inside fashion modelling, since a fashion model's career depends upon accruing maximum cultural value that may translate, at some indefinite point in time, in economic terms into contracts for prestigious work. I now want to examine these calculations further and investigate how a successful model is 'qualified and re-qualified' *as* a model (Callon, Meadel et al. 2005) in the process. As discussed in detail in Chapter 8, 'qualification' describes the process by which things are defined, examined, shaped, acted upon by actors in order to make sense of and render them calculable. This requires investigating the patterning, or 'morphology' (Hughes 2004) of the fashion network and the ways in which the aesthetic commodity—the fashion model—becomes entangled within it. Calculations in this market are centrally bound up with managing the journey the model must make across this network; that is, how their value is generated or accrued across 'circuits of value' within this network. This value is close to my earlier point about 'circle of belief'. To explore this further, let us continue the journey the model must make, following their selection by the model agency and examine the calculations that attempt to secure maximum value.

While competitions and 'open call' are used in the industry to 'find' models, and some 'cold call', as did Helen and the two young women I described above, the majority are 'found' or 'discovered' on the street by fashion industry insiders. These might be freelance 'model scouts' or paid agency staff who source their commodity by roaming the streets of major cities in search of the next 'big' thing or 'hot' look. This initial selection is, however, only the starting point of a model's journey. Once 'found', potential must be 'tested' (Callon, Meadel et al. 2005) by the model agency and some of this testing has already been described above: bodies are scrutinized—in the flesh and in Polaroids—they may be measured, possibly even weighed. In other words, in various activities, the model body is 'qualified' by the booker. Through this qualification process model agents act upon markets, their selections resulting in the particular assemblage of, in this case, models in the agency. The process of qualification is continuous, as commodities are constantly examined, always open to interpretation and transformation as they move from one actor to another in a market. In modelling, qualification does not stop at the agency: clients, such as photographers and designers, act upon the model—selecting and styling them—and bookers monitor the effects of these selections and decisions to calculate and re-calculate a model. Bookings and contracts are secured and feedback from clients is monitored, digested and translated into the knowledge that will form the basis of further calculations of the model's value.

Returning to the agency and the first contact between a potential model and booker, we find that a number of things inform the qualification process in this encounter. After examining the features of the prospective model, as described when I introduced Helen to an agency, the next stage is the Polaroid. This test is critical, for the reasons noted above: a model must be photogenic and the Polaroid will allow examination of how the physical properties of flesh and bone translate in a static image. The picture is not set up: the camera itself is hardly professional standard, there are no lights or make-up or hair styling. Hence, the quality sought is the ability to photograph well without these trappings and be 'natural' (Wissinger 2007b). The qualities of the truly photogenic body often mean that the 'raw material' converts into something ineffable; that is, something almost 'magical' is translated from the physical to the photographic body that is beyond conscious control of the subject. Bookers talk of that 'certain something' or special 'charisma' that is communicated in the photograph. If this ineffable quality is found in the Polaroid, then the relationship with the agency begins with the signing of a basic 'terms and conditions' which enable the agency to act on behalf of the model. Models remain freelance, however, this is not a contract of employment.

The newly signed model is then featured on what is known as the 'new faces board'—that is the roster of new models that the agency is promoting. When models have worked for a while they will move from this board to the main men's or women's board. A 'new face' is, however, still untested, or rather, the testing and qualification process is carried outside the agency. Newly signed models have to impress clients and book jobs. Often a new face is sent out immediately—sometimes the same day—on 'go-sees', castings, or to photographers to shoot some 'tests'. The process from untested 'new face' to jobbing model can be very swift if the qualities seen in the agency are re-qualified quickly by significant others. For example a really strong set of Polaroids may be enough to secure a booking with a major client, and some of the bookers described model careers that took off the very day the model walked into the agency. If the model gets booked for a job in their first few days this re-qualification confirms them as having model looks: they are marketable. If a model lands an editorial shoot for a major fashion magazine then their career appears to take off more quickly. A couple of London models interviewed told of how, days after their selection by the agency, they were booked for a shoot for *L'Umo Vogue* without realizing that this exclusive magazine offers a hallowed entry into the sacred world of high fashion. This particularly valuable editorial work might be shot by a major photographer, such as Mario Testino, and in some especially fortunate cases, might lead to prestigious and lucrative campaign work, since Testino is responsible for some of the most prominent campaigns for major fashion houses and has a powerful say in the models he shoots for these campaigns.

Fashion shows are also a critical part of this value system. Milan is often the city where new models break into the industry, especially during the fashion week collections attended by big names in the industry who are on the look-out for the next 'new face'. For this reason agencies will often send models straight out to the city to meet clients on 'go-sees' and hopefully book to appear in some of the big shows for a major label, such as Dolce and Gabbana or Versace, giving them exposure to a whole range of influential people who sit in the front row beneath the runway. Almost all the models in London and New York described how they were sent to Milan early on in their career and this important market was frequently described, in unflattering terms, as a 'cattle market', with so many hopefuls chasing too few jobs and the attention of big clients. It is not unheard of for a new model to be chosen for a campaign, by a major photographer, on the basis of an appearance in a big show for a major Italian fashion house.

However, not all models secure such prestigious work immediately but still need to develop a series of images for their 'book'. For this reason, they are sent to particular photographers to shoot 'tests'. These are non-commercial jobs where everyone involved—model, photographer, stylist, hair and make-up—works for nothing to generate some images for their respective portfolios. Often a 'new face' may shoot many such 'tests' to put in their model 'book' before landing their first job. These 'tests' are also important in the qualification and testing process, establishing whether the model has the qualities and abilities demanded of work on a shoot: models not only need to look good in different clothes, they must be 'versatile' and show different 'looks' if they are to work for different clients. They must also possess other personal skills and qualities, such as good communication skills, manners, discipline and the like (Entwistle and Wissinger 2006). Together these qualities will increase the chances that a model gets booked and re-booked. Critically, the model's success and longevity rest upon the acquisition of a good reputation, which means not only securing prestigious work but the ability to be nice and pleasing to work with. A bad attitude, poor interpersonal skills or rudeness mean a model will only see a client or photographer once and, as word spreads, will not secure work with others either. (For a fuller discussion of 'reputation' see Entwistle and Wissinger 2006; see also Wissinger 2007b.)

Another way to test the qualities is to send the new model out on 'go-sees'. These are basically quick meetings with potential clients or influential people in the city and who the model 'go-sees' will depend on what 'look' they have that the booker feels it will appeal to. For example a guy with a 'good body'—i.e. muscular, sporty—may be sent to meet photographers known to shoot underwear campaigns or clients, such as the designer Calvin Klein, who are known to select models on the basis of this criteria. Usually 'go-sees' do not mean a direct booking, but are a way of introducing a 'new face' to potential clients. Significantly, if a new model is chosen by any of these influential actors, their careers get off to a significant start, much like the model who books a prestigious editorial shoot in their first few days or weeks.

Thus, the ways in which a model's qualities *as a model*—i.e. a commodity selling a 'look'—are tested are wide-ranging: commercial success is not unknown in the first few days (booking a major editorial job leading to a major campaign), although such cases are less common than the usual experience of shooting 'tests' and trudging around town on 'go-sees'. What happens at any of these tests will ultimately determine whether the potential seen in the Polaroid is confirmed—re-qualified—by selection along the network of other, key actors. While bookers make the initial selection, and lend their value and 'belief' to the model—bookers often described how they 'talk up' their new models to potential clients, spending inordinate amounts of time waxing lyrical to clients about the particular models they hope to push— success depends on others (designers, stylists, photographers, etc.) selecting them and adding their value to the model. It is in this way that reputations and careers are made, with each actor qualifying the model and participating in the construction of collective 'belief'.

The key players, such as famous photographers (Mario Testino or Bruce Weber, for example) and, in recent years, certain fashion stylists (Katie Grand or Katie England in the United Kingdom, for example), play an important role within this network of belief; they have the power to 'consecrate' a model through their selection. As one booker in London put it, 'It is fantastic if a stylist likes a boy (because) he will use him. [Also] Mario Testino is good for using people again and for using new people, so is Bruce Weber.' However, despite the importance of particular names, players' power to define the aesthetics of fashion modelling *is activated by their place within the fashion network—or field*. To say this is, of course, to challenge the charisma of the creative individual, precisely what Bourdieu intends with his field analysis. He (1993a) notes how the power of particular individuals in fields, such as art and fashion, depends upon their mythical status within the field. He addresses this issue particularly closely when he examines the problem of 'succession' within artistic or creative fields. He (1993: 136–7) notes that the field of fashion is interesting since it

> occupies an intermediate position ... between a field that is designed to organise succession, like the field of bureaucratic administration, where the agents must by definition be interchangeable, and the field in which people are radically irreplaceable, such as

the field of artistic and literary creation ... Here, we have a field where there is both affirmation of the charismatic power of their creator and affirmation of the possibility of replacing the irreplaceable.

His example (1993: 136), drawn from haute couture, examines the question (asked in an edition of French *Marie Clare*) 'Can anyone replace Chanel?' but is equally applicable to the individual status of particular photographers. The charismatic power of major photographers, such as Testino, cannot be denied, but, like the designer Chanel (who was, indeed, ultimately replaced), his retirement tomorrow would not bring about the end of the position he occupies, since another major photographer would step into place and perform the same function. Likewise, other key players within this field are also replaceable: most models recognize this early on in their career and are aware that they have a short 'shelf life' and even top models are ultimately superseded. Individual names are important, of course, but in due time their power diminishes as new individuals emerge to occupy the positions they vacate. Thus, one of the features of the fashion modelling, as with other cultural industries and communities is that, as Scott (2000: 33) puts it, 'They are less constituted as miscellaneous jumbles of individuals following many different and disconnected pursuits, than they are comparatively homogenous collective ... whose members are caught up in mutually complementary and socially co-ordinated careers.'

The 'mutually complementary' nature of careers in fashion and the circuitry nature of value in this kind of economy can be demonstrated very clearly in the Sarah Doukas/Kate Moss story. Doukas, the head of the London model agency, Storm, claims to have changed the face of fashion modelling when she discovered Kate Moss at an airport in the early 1990s. Moss's look was in complete contrast to the Amazonian supermodels of the late 1980s: shorter by several inches, ultra-thin, with awkward teeth and short legs, she was the first of the so-called superwaifs. However, Doukas did not so much as single-handedly change the body aesthetic at the time; rather, she read and interpreted the times so that she produced the right model at the right time. To use Blumer's suggestive term, Doukas's position in the fashion network gave her some grasp of 'incipient taste'. However, the look has to be picked up within the industry and carried beyond: in the case of Moss, the photographer Corinne Day played a further influential role in shaping her career and the aesthetic of the time, which became known as 'grunge'. Day was one of the first and foremost 'grunge' photographers, living and working in London where the aesthetic emerged. However, even she did not act alone in promoting this aesthetic: her work captured the 'incipient taste' for an alternative look to the supermodels of the 1980s and rose to prominence when the influential magazine, *The Face,* used her photograph of the then-unknown Moss in an editorial story in March 1990 and later that year, on the 'Summer of Love' front cover. These iconic images lent crucial cultural capital to both model and photographer, establishing both Moss and Day as the 'cutting edge' model and photographer of the 1990s.

As this example demonstrates, the *network* of relations between agency, model, photographer and magazine confer cultural value on the model, but it has to be the *right* agency, the *right* body/look, the *right* photographer, capable of delivering the *right* images, and the *right magazine* for the *right* exposure. In the case of Doukas/Moss/Day/*The Face*, all elements in the chain conferred high cultural value: replace one or more element, Day with a commercial photographer shooting Moss for *Sugar* or *J17* (low-value teen mags) not *The Face*, and the story might have been a different one. When asked how important being in the right publications is to a model's career, Joan, head of a smaller agency in London said, 'Oh, it's really important. It is an absolute minefield if you don't know about it.' The Doukas/Moss/Day/*The Face* story illustrates the critical importance of cultural valorization in the production of an aesthetic commodity: mutually enforcing circuits within the field produce cultural value. Each element in the circuit lends 'cutting edge' value to the other. As a result of all the right ingredients being in place, Moss's career as a model took off and so too the careers of Day and Doukas, whose agency, Storm, became well established thereafter. As noted, the qualification process never stops. When, much later in her career, Moss was accused of drug-taking, it looked as if her model career was over, as many of the influential players who supported her dropped away and contracts were cancelled (with for example H&M in the United Kingdom). However, with characteristic canniness, and a stint in a re-hab facility, Moss managed to regain—indeed *increase*—her cultural value and, ultimately her economic value as well (she was estimated to be worth much more in contracts after this debacle than before).

In recent years, a new wave of cutting-edge magazines (*Dazed and Confused, Sleaze Nation Nylon, Wallpaper, Pop, Dansk*) have joined the ranks of similar, more established publications, such as *ID*, and are now important within the fashion network in terms of conferring cultural value. Bookers frequently acknowledged the importance of this band of select magazines and rising photographers and stylists in establishing trends in modelling and, while work in this particular niche of the industry pays models nothing at all, the cultural kudos of such magazines is so great that they are happy to book models for these publications. Such magazines promote 'edgier', 'extreme' looking models which fashion agencies now increasingly represent. That such magazines prefer to use 'edgy' models, rather than the latest top models, is not surprising given their avant-garde taste, which often borders on an anti-aesthetic. In turn, the avant-garde taste of such publications is reinforced by the quirkiness of its models, ensuring their 'difference' from the mainstream fashion and celebrity magazines, which tend to use the same few top models.

Conclusion

There is always an element of the unknown in terms of what defines the aesthetic/s of the day within fashion markets. As one London booker put it, 'It is so random, you can never tell what a designer will want for his next campaign. You have to try to please everyone at the same time.' The fluctuations and instabilities in this market demand particular strategies on the part of models and their bookers for coping with this work. Understanding where trends are moving, helping models develop their look and portfolio to keep them 'fresh', knowing the effervescent tastes of clients and photographers, moving models around to different 'markets', are some of the strategies used to promote a model's career. Since they are internal to this world, bookers are better placed to interpret trends in body styles than are the rest of us, aware of what was booking last week/month and what clients are calling up and asking for today. They also work to manage the randomness by strategies aimed at managing the model's career through calculations of who to send them to—what photographers, clients and stylists—who might like them and, in their selection, se-cure some valuable work, which the booker may use to 'talk up' the model to the next client.

Bookers seeking prestige for a model must have the right cultural capital, in the form of a stock of knowledge about trends, which stylists and photographers are 'in' and what publications and clients are valued, to make informed decisions. They em-ploy this knowledge to good effect, asking several questions before booking a model on a job: they always ask which photographer is shooting the story and insist that as London booker Martin put it 'If it is editorial, it's got to be something they can use in their book to get them campaigns.' Thus, who is on the job, what publication, as well as the quality, size and placement of images, are all of critical importance and play their part in the decisions made as to whether or not a model will be booked.

As I argue, therefore, aesthetics, not just in fashion modelling, are the outcome of social processes, relationships and networks, built upon categories of culture rather than some abstract quality of 'beauty' (Bourdieu 1993b; White 2002). Indeed, the success of any particular model is only partly to do with his or her individual physical characteristics or qualities; the quality or the aesthetic is the outcome of processes, *added on or attributed to* the model. As already discussed, this is a market which depends upon the procurement of value in the form of status or prestige which is se-cured through selection by significant actors and thus by association. In other words, here is a commercial practice concerned primarily with an aesthetic commodity and, as such, depends upon cultural calculations as much as it does upon economic ones. The model's value is built upon categories of culture which are built into the every-day commercial decisions within the field of production itself, rather than featuring as mere by-products after production. Thus, while basic economic calculations of value have to be made about such things as price, fee, day rate or contract, these cal-culations are inextricably bound to more nebulous concerns to do with cultural value. The latter is required in order to build up the day/job rate for the model.

One further point; to be a player in this field of production, one must be fully em-bedded within the particular culture of the field. While other commodities demand forms of economic and cultural knowledge (about, say, the market and consumer demands) they generally do not entail such a finely tuned aesthetic sensibility, de-tailed cultural capital and place within a social and cultural network. Thus, while you or I might need some training as to the specific features of the household app-liances market, or the seasonal and consumer constraints in vegetable retail, such knowledge could be quickly gained and does not demand much cultural knowledge or investment in the field. However, you and I would be at a loss to spot, promote and sell such commodities as a model's look, a young British artist, the next big fashion trend, a fashion photograph, or the latest style in graphic design, to name but a few aesthetic commodities. The aesthetic sensibilities and cultural capital, as well as the social, cultural and institutional connections and relationships which sustain them, are critical to the commercial transaction of such commodities, generated internally within the field of cultural production itself. Economic calculations in aesthetic eco-nomies are always, by definition, cultural ones.

Part II
Fashion Buying: A Case Study

–4–

Introduction to Case Study

In the following four chapters in Part II of this book, I examine the organization of fashion buying at Selfridges. This chapter builds upon the theoretical discussions in Part I to examine, in detail, how a market in high fashion clothing is made up. My analysis begins with an overview of fashion retailing in the United Kingdom in Chapter 5. This enables me to contextualize my analysis within broader research on fashion retailing and situating my case study, Selfridges department store on Oxford Street, London, within the wider fashion retail landscape in the United Kingdom. It is here that I also introduce the women's wear department itself and examine how it is organized in terms of different 'buyerships'. As I demonstrate, these buyerships give shape to, and actively produce, markets and marketplaces for high fashion women's clothing in the store, producing internal boundaries between products and consumers that shape the retail environment of designer clothing in the store.

In essence, the basic question, running through this case study and across all the subsequent chapters, can be boiled down to 'How do fashion buyers buy?' However, this question involves also asking, 'How do they *know* what to buy?' and specifically 'What forms of *calculation* do they employ?' In other words, understanding how this market works involves examining the sorts of knowledge employed to calculate high fashion, as well as examining the material forms and practices that shape this knowledge to enable calculation. The next four chapters are therefore concerned with the *epistemologies* of knowledge within fashion buying, the *materialities* or forms this knowledge takes and how they translate into *practice*, along with the *spatialities* of knowledge, that is how this knowledge is situated and how it circulates. Thus, I am not so much concerned with *what* buyers buy—although something of the content of the selections is interesting—but *how* they buy. In sum, I am concerned with the *processes and practices* of buying and with the forms of knowledge and calculation employed by the buying team.

To take the first point, by epistemologies, I examine the different forms of economic knowledge and what particular forms of knowledge are valued within Selfridges. This point is examined in detail in Chapters 6 and 7 where I take issue with the tendency to define economic knowledge in narrow terms as rational and cognitive (Allen 2000). Such a focus may have something to do with the sorts of firms and markets routinely examined within economic sociology and business studies. These literatures tend to focus on particular commodity markets in fruit or food

(Hughes and Reimer 2004), financial markets (Knorr Certina and Bruegger 2004; MacKenzie 2004) and so-called research intensive firms (Swart and Kinnie 2003) or manufacturing, which relies on intensive scientific knowledge for restructuring and automation (Callon 1986). In other words, in the wide literature on economic markets and businesses, there is a bias towards 'hard' markets in basic commodities, finance or science. In contrast, aesthetic markets, like fashion or art, have been paid far less attention and what little literature exists demands further explication, either because these accounts are too theoretical and not empirically grounded (Bourdieu 1993a; White 2002), in need of further explication and testing (Aspers 2001) or, quite simply, rather old and in need of updating (Blumer 1969; Becker 1982).

As already argued in Chapter 3, I do not propose that such markets are radically different from markets in vegetables or cars; indeed, they share many similar features. Rather, aesthetic markets exist on a continuum, along which can be charted a whole range of markets where aesthetics feature as part of the product—car design or vegetables even. However, I am concerned with aesthetic markets where the aesthetic value is highly variable and unstable—as it is in fashion modelling or designer clothing—and where aesthetic value is *the* quality central to calculations of agents (Weller 2007). Since these markets tend to be neglected, we know little about the knowledge demanded in them, which I argue is *expressive* and *embodied*. These ways of knowing are central to economic calculus inside Selfridges and the model agencies, yet fall outside conventional understandings of economic knowledge. To develop my analysis of knowledge, I draw on the work of Allen (2000) and also Bourdieu (1984, 1993a,b) and Blumer (1969), as well as more studies within economic sociology, such as Callon (1998b,c), where relevant.

Second, across all these chapters, I examine the *materialities* of aesthetic knowledge, i.e. the specific forms knowledge takes in companies, as well as the everyday *practices* of calculation which render the knowledge practicable, since the material forms of knowledge cannot be separated from the ways in which knowledge is put to work in a company. In other words, knowledge circulates and is made tangible in its various guises in an organization like Selfridges and this cannot be divorced from practice, since fashion buyers put this knowledge to use in embodied practices. The materialities of knowledge are examined in detail in Chapter 6 where we go inside the company and the Buying Office itself to analyse some of the main ways in which fashion buying is organized in the store. The concern here is with some of the ways in which knowledge about fashion emerges and circulates at Selfridges and how it shapes the way in which fashion markets are imagined and put together in the store. Knowledge circulates in many material forms within a fashion buying department—through spreadsheets, merchandising statistics, planning documents, trend forecasting projections, for example. These all constitute some of the formal and codified ways in which knowledge is generated and circulated in a fashion clothing company like Selfridges. However, codified knowledge is only one part of the story. Hence, as I argue in Chapter 7, tacit knowledge is a critical dimension and very much an embodied knowledge. Here I take up debates about the nature of economic knowledge generally, and delineate the specific dimensions of 'tacit aesthetic knowledge' as expressive and embodied knowledge which inevitably challenges conventional notions of economic knowledge as cognitive and rational. Something of this knowledge is always intangible, but it is important in my account to capture the embodied realities in fashion; those of dressing, sensing and being in the market.

In Chapter 8, I move in closer to this buyers' knowledge and practice to consider actual buying encounters and the micro practices involved in selecting and mediating fashionable dress. All the various knowledges and ways of making sense are brought together on the fashion 'buy', where the buyer selects and purchases garments. Here I specifically focus attention on the constant 'qualification and re-qualification' (Callon, Meadel et al. 2005) of goods, as they are examined and rendered into meaningful products that will sell within the store. I also examine the complexities of mediation in these encounters, as buyers might be said to mediate many things and the processes of mediation are multi-directional rather than linear. Buyers don't simply mediate clothes from showroom to store, nor from producer to consumer; instead, there are multiple mediations occurring in this interaction, as I detail in this chapter.

The final dimension to my analysis involves examining the *spatialities* of knowledge and this point is taken up in various ways in the different chapters, beginning with examination of the theoretical frameworks for thinking about product flows and distribution in Chapter 5. In this chapter I examine the different metaphors for analysing the production, distribution and circulation of commodities—'systems of provision', 'commodity chains' and 'commodity networks'. I then move on in Chapters 6 and 7 to consider practical examinations of knowledge location and circulation within Selfridges itself, and within the wider fashion network. The critical point here is that knowledge is always situated, and how it circulates—within a firm and locality and globally—has become a matter of some considerable debate amongst academics in economic sociology, geography and business studies.

Much debate on space and knowledge maps out a codified/tacit dichotomy onto the global/local spatial axis. As I suggest, the spatialities of fashion knowledge are rather more dynamic and complex than this, since fashion knowledge is both dependent upon highly networked connections and relations, and is therefore global, but always locally situated or translated in particular settings. I shall argue that static, spatially fixed notions of 'local' and 'global' are inadequate to capture the dynamic spatial dimensions of fashion's tacit knowledge. Hence, it is important to consider how the unique positioning of the Selfridges flagship store on Oxford Street and the ways in which travelling and connections to other places shape the overall identity of the store. Further, space is important within the store as well, both in terms of understanding the different locations of knowledge across the office and shop floor, and how the positioning of goods on the shop floor helps to create and sustain the various identities of designers/brands, consumers and the store itself. These dimensions are examined in Chapters 5 and 6. Finally, the actual spaces of travel (to studios, global cities, international fashion shows) and encounters with goods that take place in these spaces are considered in both Chapters 6 and 8.

A Brief Introduction to the Fieldwork and Selfridges

The fieldwork upon which this book is based was conducted in the Buying Office at Selfridges department store on London's Oxford Street over a 6-month period from March 2002, with a few follow-up interviews in early 2003. Funded by the Economic and Social Research Council, the project began life as an ethnographic study concerned with the way in which fashion buyers might be said to be 'cultural intermediaries' (Bourdieu 1984), said to mediate between production and consumption. In terms of the fieldwork, my observations covered a whole range of activities buyers are involved in.

Over the course of the fieldwork I followed three head fashion buyers around the office, located adjacent to the store in Davis Street. As noted in the main Introduction I observed them in weekly and monthly sales meetings, on 'floor walks' with the shop floor staff, and in meetings with suppliers. I also followed them on their buying trips around London, New York, Milan and Paris. Throughout the longer buying trips I was in a position to chat informally about their work and pick up issues from my observations as they arose. Since so much of the fashion buying season is organized around 'fashion week', I also observed the Autumn/Winter collections at London Fashion Week (LFW) just prior to my fieldwork starting in February 2002 and followed the buyers around at the Spring/Summer collections during September and October 2002 in London, Milan and Paris. The length of the fieldwork time allowed me to follow buyers through the full range of buying activities, from planning, to buying and selection, and the entry of the goods to the store. I therefore gained a sense of the spatial and temporal patterning of their work over the fashion season.

In addition to interviews and observations with the three head buyers, I also conducted formal interviews with key people within the department: the head of women's wear, all the head merchandisers, the head of the Fashion Office which co-ordinates the overall store trend directions (more on this in Chapter 6), as well as the Marketing Director and the Managing Director. Access was first negotiated through the Managing Director who supported the project. From there, I met with the two heads of departments—women's wear and the Fashion Office—who had some reservations at first, but ultimately provided me with excellent support and access to their two departments.

For those readers not familiar with Selfridges, let me say a few words about the store, as I found it at the time of fieldwork. Selfridges is a very large department store, first opened in 1909. Part of what makes Selfridges unique is its colourful and auspicious history within UK retailing. Opened by American businessman Harry Gordon Selfridge, it began as a great emporium, renowned as much for selling spectacle as it is for selling distinctive products (Honeycombe 1984). This original ethos of Mr Selfridge remains true for today's Selfridges. However, there were years in which the store fell out of favour and became something of a dinosaur. One buyer described how, when she first started working there, there was a strict dress code for staff and the overall feel of the place was dated. At the time of my fieldwork, this old identity was just a memory and the store was enjoying new-found success as a lively and exciting retail environment. This identity was constructed over the late 1990s after the appointment of charismatic Italian businessman Vittorio Radice as Chief Executive. Radice effectively turned around the fortunes of Selfridges from old-fashioned store selling middle-of-the-road products to a 'high fashion' department store, promoting 'fashion-forward' designers and brands and seeing itself at the 'cutting-edge' of retailing.

As I followed the buyers I became interested in the role they played in the shaping and fashioning of this new identity. This identity depended upon securing the 'right'—i.e. fashion-forward—commodities for the new Selfridges. Since buyers are important conduits through which commodities, by necessity, flow, their ability to identify and secure contracts with appropriate suppliers—high-end designer labels—is critical to operationalizing the new Selfridges. This is one way in which buyers can be seen as 'cultural intermediaries' (Bourdieu 1984), acting as critical mediators or 'middlemen' (Fine and Leopold 1993, [*sic*]) between store and supplier and between store and (virtual) customer. I take up these points in the following chapters as I examine the knowledge, practices and mediations involved in buying work.

I offer these chapters as both a case study into a hitherto 'black-boxed' practice of fashion retailing in particular, and as a case study of an aesthetic market more generally. My analysis is an important corollary to much of the recent work on retailing practice within the social sciences, which, despite a burgeoning of literature within human geography on retailing (Moore 2000; Wrigley and Lowe 2002; Gregson and Crewe 2003; Dwyer and Jackson 2003; Crewe 2004; Jackson, Thomas et al. 2007; Crewe 2008), has overlooked buyers and buying practices. There are a few exceptions to this: an early article by Crewe and Davenport (1992) has examined some aspects of buying power among retailers, and further work by Hughes and Reimer (2004b) has focused on furniture distribution, while Hughes (2004) has provided a detailed account of networks of distribution within the cut-flower trade. My analysis therefore adds to this body of work on retailing, as well as to the scarcity of work on aesthetic markets, noted above, within business and knowledge literature and economic sociology. Analysis of fashion buying provides evidence of how one aesthetic market is constituted and how an aesthetic commodity is calculated, selected, mediated within it, that will hopefully suggest to other researchers possibilities for future research.

–5–

Understanding High Fashion: Retailing and Buying

As many academics have argued, fashion has played a considerable role in industrial and post-industrial economic development (Crewe and Forester 1993; Fine and Leopold 1993). Fine and Leopold's early sociological work in this area argues convincingly that fashion and associated industries, such as textile production, have been at the heart of industrial developments, both in the United Kingdom during the nineteenth century and in developing nations today (in countries like Korea, India or China). More recently, Crewe (2008: 26) notes, 'The fashion industry is an important creative component in the making of economy and has made a major contribution to the contemporary proliferation of material culture'. Thus, fashion has become central to claims about modernity and, more recently, the 'new economy' and debates about post-Fordist production, 'flexible specialization', and the significance of consumption in contemporary economies. As part of this, a burgeoning retail geography now addresses the importance of retailing practices and processes (Crewe and Forester 1993; Jackson, Lowe et al. 2000; Wrigley and Lowe 2002; Coe and Wrigley 2007). However, with a few exceptions (Crewe and Davenport 1992; Crewe and Forester 1993; Gereffi 1999; Moore 2000; Winship 2000; Pettinger 2004; Crewe 2008), there is little research on fashion retailing and distribution and as yet no detailed analysis of buying practices. There are, of course, numerous practical textbooks on fashion buying (see for example Jackson 2001; Goworek 2007) aimed at aspirant fashion buyers, but the practices of buyers, within the context of their role in framing and acting on fashion markets and critical input into the economic performance of the retail practice, have still to be unpacked. Retail geography and economic geography have been strangely silent on these issues.

This book does not attempt to understand all aspects of fashion buying but to understand fashion buying within the designer clothing market. In order to do so, it is necessary to first define and contextualize high fashion within the broader landscape of fashion retailing in the United Kingdom, as I do in the following section. Then, in Systems, Chains, Circuits, Networks: Untangling the Different Metaphors, I examine the theoretical frameworks that metaphorically describe and analyse how commodities are produced, distributed and consumed—'chains', 'circuits' or 'networks'. Although I tend to favour the term *network,* I want to summarize the relative merits of the different terms. Finally, in Organizing Fashion in Selfridges, I introduce my case study, Selfridges department store, beginning by noting the store's unique historical location and identity in the United Kingdom before introducing the women's wear department. I then examine how high fashion is organized *inside* Selfridges through the construction of 'buyerships'. As I will argue, the organization of the women's wear department into buyerships shapes how markets for high fashion are made up, enabling the establishment and positioning of goods, brands and 'virtual' consumers. Each buyership is situated in relation to the others in the department and is given shape in terms of a budget, resources and an organizing concept or theme, as I will discuss. In this way, as I shall demonstrate, the buyership constitutes a 'space of calculation' within the store.

Fashion Retailing in the United Kingdom

Defining high fashion clothing and describing the UK fashion retailing arena is far from easy. As Crewe and Davenport (1992: 183) describe it, 'the clothing retail sector is by no means a homogenous entity ... since it is dissected across a variety of dimensions, including size, ownership, and market segment. Marks and Spencer is clearly a very different creature to a small independent designer store.' As they point out, there are further conditions that make it difficult to study this sector: it is fast changing, with newcomers often gaining market share very rapidly, and it is characterized by diverse arrangements for production, marketing and sales. Further, they note that the relationship between the two sectors—multiple and independent designer—is 'neither direct, simple or stable' (1992: 183). All these points are still true today, perhaps even more so.

Fashion clothing markets in the United Kingdom are highly differentiated, broken down into many different levels; in effect different markets. These levels are defined partly by *price-points,* which is the term buyers use for the price level at which particular consumers are prepared to pay for particular items of clothing. The entry of low-priced retailers in the United Kingdom, such as New Look, Primark and Matalan, as well as the growth of supermarket fashion brands, such as 'Florence and Fred' for Tesco and 'George' for Asda, have taken the fashion retailing world by storm and the strength of these retailers continues unabated (Mintel 2002a,b). Besides the obvious appeal of low price, it is the success of these retailers in fast meeting trends that ensures their continued success. Indeed, the term *fast fashion* is often used to describe how stores, like Primark and other more expensive but equally popular high street stores like Zara and Topshop, can meet trends in season.

The significance of fast fashion has been accompanied by the continued charisma of individual designers and designer clothing at the other end of the market. Indeed, one characteristic in recent years, described by Crewe and Forester (1993), is the polarization of fashion retailing in the United Kingdom over the 1990s between discounting outlets and an emerging designer sector, a polarity hinged upon cheap, mass-produced clothes on the one hand and unique, high-quality fashion clothing on the other. These arguments still resonant today, perhaps even more so. The contemporary UK high street remains highly polarized between cut-price outlets, such as Primark, and high fashion stores, blending 'own ranges' and 'designer', i.e. branded clothing, such as Whistles or Joseph. As part of this polarization, the UK clothing sector has become concentrated in the hands of a small number of large multiples. Unlike other European countries, multiples make up larger proportion of the market in the United Kingdom with independents stores constituting a smaller percentage (Mintel 2002a,b).

The buyers I followed in Selfridges are firmly located at the 'high' end of women's clothing, what is also referred to as 'designer' clothing. The size of the UK designer fashion economy alone was estimated at £600 million in 1996 (DCMS 1998, 2001), and more recently, as £800 million in 2006 by Mintel (in Roodhouse 2003). However, despite its apparent obviousness, the term *designer* clothing is surprisingly vague. Mintel (2002a) defines it very broadly to refer to four things: 'couture', dominated by French-based international brands like Dior or Chanel; 'international designers', referring to a label usually dominated by one name: Donna Karan or CK; 'diffusion designers' who produce 'high-street' ranges for stores, such as Jasper Conran at Debenhams; and 'high fashion', referring to new designers often endorsed by celebrities. However, when I pressed Julia the head buyer for Designer wear to define this term she noted, 'It's not a terribly specific term any more', and went on to say,

> I might buy something which is very specifically designed; for example the Alexander McQueen collection is very much him, he is the designer and, you know, he is very much a person who you think of, whereas MaxMara, you don't think of anybody, it's just a brand name. So it's a bit misleading.

However, she qualified this by noting that the term

> does really indicate a certain level in the market, sort of the higher level of the market, which includes ... some of the big lifestyle brands, when I say "lifestyle", you know, I mean like DKNY where they sell everything from leisure wear, smart formal wear, evening wear, sleep wear, you know, they do the whole thing, that you could live your life in DKNY if you wanted to. So it encompasses that, but at the same time it does encompass the smallest designers as well. So don't get confused by the title, it doesn't mean anything!

Thus, designer fashion for her, and all the buyers at Selfridges, sits within the 'higher level' range identified by Mintel in 2002a, encompassing only the first two definitions, although we must set aside couture, as its market is economically insignificant (though symbolically important). Designer clothing at Selfridges refers to a number of things. Firstly, prêt-a-porter 'Collections' of individual designers that retail at considerable prices, are made to order and are therefore quite exclusive. The most elite designers do both prêt-a-porter and couture, such as Givenchy or Yves Saint Laurent. Prêt-a-porter has its own spatial and temporal arrangements, 'showing' at the international 'collections', or 'fashion weeks' in London, New York, Milan and Paris. This involves the physical movement of the world's fashion players—journalists, buyers, designers, models, etc.—around the globe at the same time, with some shows also taking place in cities peripheral to this historic configuration of fashion cities but who now organize their own fashion weeks (Breward and Gilbert 2006). These cosmopolitan hubs are not only where the design houses are located; they are the location for all the machinery of styling, photographing and marketing. As I describe below, the collections set a temporal rhythm to designer fashion. These shows are bi-annual and this structures the flow of such clothing, with buying cycles geared to two main seasonal deliveries.

The temporal dimensions of female fashion at this level are also very particular. Prêt-a-porter is produced to order in smaller batches, unlike high street female clothing made in bulk, with a longer time lag between order and delivery. It is organized into two seasons, Autumn/Winter in January/February, and Spring/Summer in September/October. This means that the clothes are shown and purchased four to six months ahead of the actual (real-time) season, making for a rather slower fashion cycle than the contemporary high street which meets trends closer to real season. To address this, big brands and major designers now show 'mid-season' or 'pre-season' collections, such as the 'Cruise' collection in October/November. Indeed, those brands that do pre-season collections account for 65 to 70 per cent of sales at Selfridges,[1] hence greater even than mainline collections. However, most small to medium-sized designers do not have the capability (investment, manufacturing and time) to produce pre-season collections so the bi-annual buying cycle remains significant and sets the overall pace of fashion for the majority of designers.

This generates greater risk, as I argue below, because trends are shown further ahead of the season. The contractual arrangements between the store and suppliers mean that, except for very late deliveries, once placed, orders cannot be cancelled, while re-orders for more stock are highly unlikely. This contractual arrangement adds to a high degree of risk as to what to buy that must be met and managed within the everyday calculations of economic actors. These very particular organizational structures set the terms within which agents have to calculate and manage fashion.

While prêt-a-porter is expensive and exclusive, other designer brands, or 'lifestyle' brands as Julia, above, put it (CK and Armani or DKNY), are less exclusive. These labels may do shows during fashion week but have 'diffusion' lines with wider appeal that are less expensive as they are made in bulk and not to order.

This pattern is becoming more common even among designers known for prêt-a-porter, and 'diffusion' ranges with lower price-points and wider appeal are now widely available, such as 'Marc by Marc Jacobs', or Alexander McQueen's McQ line. Other famous designers have diversified further designing for multiples, such as Matthew Williamson or Jasper Conran for UK store Debenhams, or the one-off ranges by designers, such as Stella McCartney, for H&M. While these ranges trade on the designer's name, they are mass produced, not 'designer' fashion.

While 'designer' fashion retailing is differentiated into markets, I focus my attention on the more exclusive, high-end of the market. In their analysis of the conditions determining the high fashion independents in the Nottingham Lace Market (NLM), Crewe and Forester (1993) draw out the significant features of the market, notably, the focus on quality garments produced largely out of local linkages or networks between buyers and designers, often dependent upon 'word of mouth' and 'reputation'. The result is a market with local character and identity: 'The distinguishing feature of the area is a sense of individuality and uniqueness, which is far removed from the controlled, placeless tone of the two indoor centres which form the traditional retail core. Thus is very much a space with a unique local identity' (1993: 224).

While this description may seem far removed from a large department store like Selfridges, some similarities can be drawn between them. Selfridges has established a 'unique' identity and it is a very particular kind of retailing space or 'unique experience', as the Marketing Director put it. In particular, its identity in recent years has moved in the direction of high fashion, but it also prides itself on being a 'spectacular' retailing environment. Thus, unlike a large multiple like M&S or a department store like Debenhams, Selfridges is not a 'placeless place' but retains a unique local identity, even while expanding, slowly, out of its historical location on Oxford Street in London. Through such things as the design of the buildings, interior shop floor layout and unique blend of 'own-bought', or specially selected collections by fashion buyers, as well as concession ranges, Selfridges asserts a distinctive identity which trades quite strongly on the distinctive history of the flagship store on Oxford Street. It is also firmly located within a global fashion network that depends upon flows of knowledge circulating locally and globally, and seeks to build on its own reputation by developing a unique blend of designers. New designers, showing at London Fashion Week for example form a small part of the 'own-bought' budget. Finding and securing arrangements with new designers is the responsibility of the buyers and, like those in the Lace Market, this depends upon networks of reputation and 'circuits of value', with buyers and designers working along the same networks of showing and selling.

Having arrived at some definition and context within which to place Selfridges designer fashion, I now want to examine how we might understand the circulation of designer clothing, examining different frameworks to untangle the routes of commodity provision.

Systems, Chains, Circuits, Networks: Untangling the Different Metaphors

I have described some of the pertinent characteristics of designer fashion in the United Kingdom and Selfridges, but understanding how this market is put together requires us to analyse where fashion commodities, images, ideas and knowledge are located, and how they are distributed. To capture the spatial dimensions of these journeys of commodities one can turn to a number of spatial metaphors that have become widely discussed in recent years. Concepts such as 'systems of provision' (Fine and Leopold 1993; Fine 2002), 'commodity chains' (Gereffi, Korzeniewicz et al. 1994), 'circuits of culture' (Du Gay, Hall et al. 1997) and 'networks' (Hughes 2004) are all metaphors for analysing the circulation of commodities from production to distribution and consumption. The actual spatial configuration each metaphor invokes differs and so too does the analysis of 'vertical' relationships between parts *within* a 'system' or 'commodity chain', as does the attention paid to 'horizontal' dimensions, such as the relationship between markets and commodities, where factors such as gender might be considered along with the links *across* commodity markets. While there is not the space to discuss these in great depth (and Hughes and Reimer (2004a) provide a comprehensive overview of these various approaches), I want to summarize how these different metaphors/frameworks work to inform my case study of Selfridges buyers. I begin with the idea of a commodity chain and examine, in particular, the strengths of the system of provision approach which emphasizes integration within any commodity chain. I then examine the circuits and networks approaches which address some of the weakness of systems of provision.

Commodity Chains

Hughes and Reimer (2004b: 2) begin by noting that 'the notion of a commodity chain is one of the most pervasive metaphors for thinking about the links between production, distribution and consumption of goods'. Raghuran (2004: 123) succinctly summarizes the commodity chain approach as follows: 'The notion of a commodity chain traces the entire trajectory of the product, usually within a political economy of development perspective derived from world systems theory'. In fact, as Hughes and Reimer demonstrate, two particular strands of analysis, within a broadly political economy perspective, can be discerned within this concept. The first, 'world systems theory' (Hopkins and Wallerstein 1986; Gereffi, Korzeniewicz et al. 1994; Gereffi 1999), traces 'the linear connections of the global commodity chain (GCC)' (Hughes and Reimer 2004b: 2) from consumption in 'peripheral' regions (where there is cheap labour) to 'core' or Western retail and consumption. This literature overlaps with studies of 'filieres' within France and, like GCC, tracks journeys of commodities from raw materials to final product and the transformations in value that occur along the way. The problems with this analysis, as Hughes and Reimer note, are similar to all macro studies in that the analysis is often reductive, over-generalizing and simplifying of complex processes, and, further, assumes the journeys of commodities are unidirectional—from production to consumption.

The second literature within commodity chain analysis, the systems of provision approach, also traces the 'vertical' connections between production and consumption but 'promote[s] a more dialectical understanding of the producer–consumer relations, recognizing the importance of the cultural meanings attached to commodities and appreciates that the producer–consumer dynamic can be different for contrasting industries' (Hughes and Reimer 2004a: 3; see also Leslie and Reimer 1999). Such analysis, developed by Fine and Leopold (1993), sets out to counter simplistic models of markets, both liberal 'free market' accounts of the consumer sovereignty said to drive markets, and Marxist accounts of production which downgrade consumption. The 'systems' approach 'sets the role of consumer choice ... as determined both historically ... and jointly with variable within separate systems of provision (Fine 2002: 83). Abandoning 'horizontal' approaches which examine general themes for example 'emulation', Fine argues that a systems of provision approach is more sensitive to the particularities and historical contingencies of different chains and such an approach also recognizes the critical importance of distribution systems and 'middlemen' [*sic*] as 'linch-pins' within systems of provision (Fine and Leopold 1993). My own project started life as a way of fleshing out Fine and Leopold's systems of provision approach and set out to attend to the gap in our knowledge as to the critical role of 'middlemen' as distributing agents between production and consumption (Entwistle 2005). My analysis has since departed in many respects from the systems of provision approach for reasons I now discuss, but remains broadly in sympathy with many of its aims.

While for Hughes and Reimer, the 'systems' approach goes some way to addressing the limitations of global commodity chain analysis, there are general problems with commodity chain analysis. For one, it tends to emphasize production more than consumption, with the ultimate aim to 'unveil' the conditions of production. For example, although she criticizes the over-emphasis on production in this literature and calls for a 'materialist semiotic analysis' of consumption signs, Hartwick's (1998: 425) analysis has similar ambitions to 'unveil' production relations by attending to the 'radiating effects of the commodity at the consumption node' in order to 'bring home to consumers the results of consumption'. This kind of 'unveiling' is prevalent across much of the literature and has been criticized for patronizing consumers who are more reflexive than academics assume (Jackson 2002). However, for Hughes and Reimer, this idea of 'unveiling' lends itself to a rather simplistic assumption of a linear commodity chain—from production to consumption—that 'may overlook the complex practices through which production and consumption are linked and often fail to consider precisely how buyers may control and condition the economic fortunes of "the periphery"' (Hughes and Reimer 2004: 3).

Commodity Circuits

More recent work on commodity flows has tended to move away from the notion of a linear 'chain' to develop metaphors that emphasize the non-linear, complex way in which goods circulate. Literature on commodity 'circuits' or 'circuits of culture' (Cook and Crang 1996; Jackson 1999) capture the non-linear way in which commodities circulate, with phases of production, distribution and consumption seen not as separate 'moments' occurring sequentially, but as phases which inflect one another. Du Gay, Hall et al.'s (1997) study of the Sony Walkman is a good example of this, as it demonstrates how the production of the Walkman was crucially informed by understandings of their target consumer group and they show how the meanings and usages of the machine by consumers formed part of the development and re-workings of the machine. So, instead of a concern with 'beginning and end points in a chain', the focus shifts 'towards the culturally inflected dynamics of relationships between moments of production, circulation and consumption ... to arrive at a more contextual understanding of meanings attached to goods in different times, places and phases of commodity circulation' (Hughes and Reimer 2004b: 3–4). This spatially informed 'production of culture' approach is also evident in Pratt's (2004: 117) analysis of creative industries which argues for 'a more holistic perspective of the interlinked processes of production and consumption'.

More recently, the concept of 'network' has begun to be applied to the analysis of commodity flows (Hughes 2004; Jackson 2002). The value of network analysis is that, 'connections between actors are seen as complex webs of interdependence rather than fixed, vertical and unidirectional relationships' (Hughes and Reimer 2004b: 5). The advantage with this is that it avoids privileging one site in the circulation of commodities over any other, 'as the network metaphor is extended to include, for e.g., sites of design, research and development' (2004: 5). In her analysis of the international cut-flower trade (ICFT), Hughes (2004) applies both the idea of network and circuit. According to Hughes, network analysis directs attention to the 'morphology' of relationships in a market, while 'flows (or circuits) are the most useful metaphor for thinking about the movement of *knowledge* between nodes in this network' (Hughes 2004: 215, emphasis added). Her study is similar, in methodological respects, to my own, although the actual configurations of relationships and knowledge are different. She demonstrates the power of retailers in this market to shape the relations and channel particular forms of knowledge, but this is not always the case in high fashion markets. This pattern has been described within clothing (Crewe and Davenport 1992; Gereffi 1999). However, Tokatli (2007: 68) warns against taking this asymmetry at face value when the picture might be more complex: 'The business ties between the lead clothing firms and their suppliers are indeed asymmetrical. However, this does not necessarily mean that buyers have automatic power over their suppliers.' Whereas the cut-flower trade is 'buyer-driven'—

that is driven by the demands of suppliers, particularly the big supermarkets in the United Kingdom, with one eye on aesthetic trends that drive the production cycle—in fashion, model bookers and fashion buyers are not the only important nodes in the flow of commodities and knowledge across the markets, and these networks aren't driven by them. Buyers and bookers must 'translate' the looks shown on the catwalks of Paris and New York and the different fluctuations in model looks, but do not have the power to assert particular aesthetics, as do UK supermarkets in their dealings with Kenyan or other flower growers. Thus, as Hughes demonstrates, these two metaphors—circuit and network—are not inconsistent. According to her, both are preferable to the idea of 'commodity chains' which tend to emphasise uni-linear flows that privilege particular points in the life cycle of goods.

It is important to note, however, that these two metaphors are not without their own problems. Raghuran (2004: 123) is critical of ANT-inspired accounts because, 'in focusing primarily on the agency of human and non-human entities, ANT is in danger of reducing complex production and consumption systems into a mechanistic framework. Concentrating on agents operating at nodes within the network and focusing solely on the links between them can disembed these systems from social frameworks and process within which these links are set.'

She counters this by reinstating the agency of workers through personal biography, in this case, of one particular company producing dress for Indian women, which emerged out of the particular frustrations of one woman with existing garment suppliers. Similarly, Leslie and Reimer (1999: 407) admit that while they are 'drawn to the notion of a nonlinear circuit, there remain important reasons for tracing the changing lines of power, precisely because it never remains fixed in one site.' Adopting a circuit or network approach runs the risk of losing a grip on the political and exploitation which makes Hughes and Reimer (2004b: 7) 'hesitant to abandon the concept of the chain altogether'.

While commodity chain approaches stress the need to examine vertically integrated relationships between production and consumption, Hughes and Reimer (2004b) and Leslie and Reimer (1999) also argue for consideration of 'horizontal' features, which might relate different commodity chains. Indeed, they ask, 'Is there a vertical uniqueness to individual commodity chains? Does a vertical approach neglect the interconnections between different systems of provision?' (Leslie and Reimer 1999: 407). Miller (1997) agues there might not be any vertical logic to chains and even while retail links manufacturing to consumption, retailers may treat the two as quite distinct, separating manufacturing from symbolic meanings by for example inflecting mass-produced goods with ideas of 'quality' or craft. For Leslie and Reimer (1999) commodity chains are not just structured by competitive demands and linkages from production to consumption, but other things like class or gender are important to account for the 'multiple and shifting connections between sites' (1999: 403) and between different 'systems'. In their own analysis of home furnishings, gender is 'central to the logic of the commodity chain'. Taking an approach that is both 'vertical' and 'horizontal', they stress the need to attend to the linkages across chains, or to what they refer to as the 'leakiness' of chains. Thus, while broadly in sympathy with the 'systems' approach, they recognize the sign value and symbolic meaning of goods as well, to attend to discourses and not just commodities themselves and to understand the 'geographical contingency of systems of provision' (1999: 405).

Indeed, when examining current work on design-led or aesthetic markets one can see a number of horizontal consistencies that cut across different, vertically integrated systems of provision. 'Fashion', as in regular stylistic change, may be becoming more common across a range of markets for aesthetic goods. Weller (2007) argues that 'Fashion ideas [permeate] multiple 'culturally' oriented commodities, creating complex co-dependencies between the otherwise disparate production sectors ... As a result, commodities with quite different material systems of provision often share common aesthetic sensitivities.' Indeed, as Leslie and Reimer (1999: 414) argue, fashion seems to have become a significant issue in the home furnishings market in both Canada and the United Kingdom where there are

> emergent connections between home furnishings consumption, fashion consumption and identity formation. In the same way that fashion designers and retailers encourage the continual restyling of clothes, furniture advertisements and magazine editorials now often emphasise the pleasure of redecorating with shifts in identity. There was a relatively strong consensus amongst retailers that changes in the furniture industry reflect a shift towards practices in the fashion industry. This crossover often is seen in terms of a merging of the two sectors at both ad/marketing and retail sites.

As their analysis demonstrates, regular changes—especially 'seasonal colour changes'—promote 'strengthening linkages between fashion and furniture chains ... illustrating the "leakiness" of systems of provision' (Leslie and Reimer 1999: 414). Similarities can also be found between designer clothing and cut flowers despite their very evidently different 'systems of provision'. The cut flowers market is, according to Hughes (2004), design intensive; that is to say, it is one where aesthetics and design are central to market calculations. It is also knowledge intensive, depending upon agents sharing and disseminating knowledge of design trends, with such things as design and/or fashion magazines or design 'gurus' playing a part in the circulation of knowledge along the network. In the designer fashion arena, knowledge is more diffuse and spread along the network. It may sometimes be encoded in part, through particular niche magazines and it is filtered through 'guru'-like characters, such as cutting-edge designers, photographers or stylists.

Other horizontal connections can also be traced. McRobbie (1998) suggests that ' "[fashion] retail workers might recognise themselves to have more in common with other workers in the fashion industry than those employed in selling food or furniture" ' (McRobbie, cited in Leslie and Reimer 1999: 408). While all retail workers may share similar conditions, 'aspects of performance and presentation involved in the work are specific to fashion retail and relate to a "fashion" chain logic' (Leslie and Reimer 1999: 408). This 'fashion chain logic' can also be found by comparing other sorts of specifically fashion markets, such as fashion modelling (Entwistle 2002) or fashion photography (Aspers 2001). Despite the obvious differences in commodities (photographic and modelling 'look' or 'style', respectively), as well as different cultural and historical circumstances, Aspers's account of how markets in fashion photography operate in Sweden illustrates similar features to markets in fashion modelling in the United Kingdom. As discussed in Chapter 3, both markets depend considerably on the creation of an 'editorial' look or style which is clearly distinguished from a more 'commercial' aesthetic for corporate clients or mass markets. Further, in terms of the morphology of relationships in both markets and the flows of fashion knowledge through particular channels or nodes (magazines, editors, designers, stylists, photographers, models), these markets are quite similar and indeed the careers for workers in both markets are critically linked. Thus while there are differences across these markets there are also some shared horizontal features, with connections between different aesthetic commodities and labour markets apparent but largely obscured if one only takes a purely vertical approach.

Fashion Buying and Retailing Practices

If this case study was following a purely systems of provision approach, I would be seeking to integrate all practices in high fashion clothing, not just buying. Instead, I focus attention on buyers and, by following them, I 'trace' the connections that spread out from here. A few details about fashion buying need to be noted from the outset. Fashion buying is not organized the same way in all sections of clothing retail. It is important to note that 'the production presuppositions (such as lead times, minimum production runs and rhythms) associated with fast fashion are different from those associated with *haute couture* or designer ready-to-wear' (Tokatli 2008: 24). In addition, even within high street fashion there are significant variations among what are sometimes referred to as 'fast fashion' stores. According to Tokatli (2008: 24):

> Fast fashion retailers can be divided into two categories: while some are retailers, in the true sense of the term, with no manufacturing competencies of their own (represented by Gap, H&M and Mango), others (represented by Benetton and Zara) are 'retailers with factories'. Retailers without factories obviously do not manufacture their own clothes, but instead outsource them to other firms from partially industrialized countries.

In the United Kingdom, large multiples, like Marks and Spencer, design everything under their own label in much the same way as dedicated fashion stores, like Zara or Gap. In these cases, the store co-ordinates design and production, albeit through a sub-contracting chain. Similarly, department stores are varied: some are concessions only, merely renting space to a range of brands while others, like Selfridges or Harvey Nichols, have a concessions business alongside 'own-bought' stock, as discussed below. These different buying arrangements create different sorts of relationships and encounters between retailers and suppliers. In Crewe and Davenport's (1992) analysis of large fashion retailers 'preferred supplier' model, the retailer co-ordinates the production very tightly, while more recent work on sub-contracting chains (Ross 1997), demonstrates a more 'hands off' relationship between retailer and producer that in recent years has been criticized for encouraging 'sweated' labour. However, the micro-relations of buying *within* retail practice remain 'black-boxed' (Latour 1987) because they have been largely neglected.

In taking a network approach I draw attention to 'the complexities of sites other than production and consumption "ends" of the chain' (Hughes and Reimer 2004b: 7). This provides a significant vantage point from which to see how markets in high fashion are put together, the relationships established by buying activities and the sorts of market knowledge required to calculate this aesthetic commodity. Buying is itself a complex location, a nexus where production and consumption 'meet' and are mediated and translated rather than existing as a site somewhere 'in the middle' between these two supposedly fixed 'end' points. Thus, as I argue in more detail in Chapter 8, rather than a simple movement of goods from one to the other, buyers are involved in more complex mediations and translations that are not uni-linear. However, before my analysis can take place, it is necessary to introduce fashion buying and buyers at Selfridges: who are these agents and what does their work involve? I then want to examine how buying is organized in the store and how the high fashion market is thus assembled.

Organizing Fashion in Selfridges

The Fashion Buyer as Calculating Agent

It is an obvious point but worth mentioning from the outset that fashion buyers cannot buy 'on impulse'; their choices are carefully framed by a range of institutional mechanisms and activities that structure what they buy and in what quantity, size and colour. This points to a basic concern, namely, that central to markets is the question of *calculation*, a point I keep returning to: how is a marketplace/s in designer clothing made an object of calculation and what are the conditions of calculation in this marketplace that shape the buyers' buying?

Miller (2004: 179) in his analysis of accountancy practices argues forcefully that the technologies of accountancy powerfully shape the conditions of calculation and 'make the economy visible and measurable'. In Chapter 6, I examine the tools of calculation at Selfridges. However, here it is necessary to consider the basic conditions that bring the fashion buyer, as a particular kind of calculating actor, into being. According to Miller (2004: 180), modern accountancy has 'freed' individuals in companies, bringing into being 'the responsible and calculating individual' who is able to make his or her own decisions. While his examples relate to investment and finance, this ethos of 'freedom' is very evident at Selfridges, where buyers are made responsible for a particular budget and, while given a target and other indicators, told to make their own judgement as to what to buy. Thus, as a 'technology of govern-ment' (2004: 179), this kind of accountancy constructs particular kinds of subjects. As Miller (2004: 180) puts it,

> Rather than confront individuals daily over the allocation of resources, why not provide the funds to an individual who will have both the responsibility and freedom to spend the money as they see fit? Why not, in other words, seek to produce an individual who comes to act as a self-regulating calculating person, albeit one located within asymmetrical networks of influence and control?

This is reflected in the ethos and identity of the buyers at Selfridges who describe themselves, and are described by others, as 'knowing their market' and given rela-tive freedom in terms of calculating what to buy. My analysis focused entirely on the women's wear 'own-bought' ranges which are selected by the buyers. In contrast to concessions businesses, own-bought ranges are owned by Selfridges, constitut-ing vital assets and, potentially, liabilities if they do not sell. A number of things are worth noting about own-bought: firstly, it demands *selection* by buyers who have budgets of millions of pounds, and; secondly, demands careful *calculation* of the market; thirdly, it is more *valuable*, as the margins are greater than in concessions; but fourthly, the stakes are higher too, as the *risk* is carried entirely by the store. These features—selection, calculation, risk and value—make own-bought interesting for an analysis of aesthetic calculation. Critical to the creation of such a 'freed' calculating agent in the store is the formal organization of women's wear into 'buyerships'.

The Buyership

The buyership serves as a mechanism or 'space of calculation' since it forms the basis of 'a boundary within which interactions take place' (Callon 1998c: 249). In order to define a buyership, the best place to start is to examine these boundaries. A buyer-ship consists of seven main components but the best place to start is to think of it as a financial 'decision tool'. 'Decision tools' are defined as 'scripts created by decision makers for coping with the uncertainty and ambiguity of their environment' (Abo-lafia 1998: 74). The buyership therefore serves as a good place to begin to answer the basic question, 'How do buyers buy?' and to examine how the marketplace/s of women's designer fashions are put together or assembled within the store.

Let me describe these seven inter-related components of the buyership further, beginning with the *budget*. The buyership is a designated area of spending. I followed three of the main buyerships in the entire women's wear department, known by the following names—'Designer', 'Contemporary' and 'Casual and Updated'.[2] These named areas of spending are further broken down into smaller areas of spending: as the head of one buyership described it, 'First you have your global figure then your breakdown figure'. A buyership can therefore be seen as a financial resource in which investment in the form of a *budget* is made. Once established, other major resource investments flow from this. It is apparent that a buyership is also defined in terms of designated *staff*, since the budget only comes into being through the activities of the staff who manage and spend it. Thus, a buyership exists through the activities of staff designated to spend it. Principally, all buyerships comprise a head buyer and buying assistants—senior buyer, assistant buyer—as well as designated merchandisers—senior merchandiser and sometimes an assistant merchandiser. While the head buyer looks after the 'global figure', the assistant buyers are allocated smaller pots of money and will be responsible for buying in particular categories of product within the buyership. Other resource investments follow: software/inventory systems, office space, tables and chairs, etc. That said, the buyership is not simply a financial mechanism either, but an institutional means by which the products, sellers and consumers 'out there'—beyond the store—are managed; that is, identified, bought and sold, assessed, evaluated and measured.

In other words, these financial resources—budget and staff—are orientated towards identifying and assembling the other main components of the buyership. In no order or priority, since these elements are thoroughly inter-linked, these components consist of *products* 'out there' and thus involve identifying particular *suppliers*— designers and design houses (usually represented by distributing agents rather than directly). These products and suppliers are often firmly established within the buyership over a long period of time, many of them are big brands which have been bought by the store for years and some even have their own branded space. These products are given an allocation of *space* on the shop floor and this space is important to the materialization of the buyership. The space designated to each buyership tends to be fairly constant. Buyers know what square meterage they have to fill and all products are calculated in terms of how they will look and where they will fit on the shop floor, meaningfully arranged vis-à-vis the other products in the area. Buyers will think about their space when on buys, considering how particular garments will look on the shop floor and how well they will 'sit' next to other products in areas nearby. They will also think through this space on a regular basis when viewing their area on 'floor walks', as discussed in Chapter 7.

The ordering of floor space does not, therefore, happen randomly. Ways of imagining products and their spatial location are aided by an *organizing 'concept'* which renders a 'theme' or 'feel' for the area, and guides the buyer in terms of their buying decisions since products are selected by virtue of their fit with the 'concept'. Thus, the assemblage of products and sellers is not random, but the outcome of a careful rationale, based, in the first instance, on product categories—lingerie or accessories for example and, within the buyership, upon an idea or theme—'contemporary' meaning something quite different to 'designer' and 'casual and updated'. Within each of these three main buyerships, there are further breakdowns in terms of space and 'concepts'.

The buyership's organizing 'concept' apparently stands in contrast to the 'hard' reality of the budget, as a 'soft' kind of knowledge, rather than something based on certain figures/statistics. Nonetheless, the concept is critical to the way in which the budget is allocated because it provides a way of viewing the products bought for that area—a way of making sense of products in order for them to be bought and brought together in meaningful ways. Thus, products are rendered meaningful in terms of an overarching theme which organizes buying choices and is materialized in terms of the eventual assemblage on the shop floor. Last but by no means least, all buyerships operate with an idea of 'imagined' or 'virtual' customers who buy there. Buyers never meet customers directly, but they take on a 'reality' of sorts, albeit through highly mediated encounters with the sales team on the shop floor, as discussed in more detail in Chapters 6 and 8.

Through these visualizations and spatializations the 'market' in high fashion is both assembled through products and suppliers 'out on the market'—an *external* global geography or market of products and suppliers constituted in the process— and actively translated or configured in spatial terms *internally*, since all products are destined to sit in a particular area on the shop floor, existing in spatial relationships to one another. Thus, the buyership enables a picture of the fashion world to be built up in terms of two different spatial registers: global fashion markets and the internal retail geography on the shop floor. It is a mechanism for calculating fashion within the store, assembling and materializing high fashion commodities by making markets visible, meaningful and calculable. Indeed, the buyership enables internal demarcations between different sorts of 'markets' in high fashion to be visible. However, these demarcations and internal market boundaries are not unproblematic. As I illustrate below, in the case of 'designer denim', the internal boundaries between buyerships and markets can and do blur, making it difficult to make clear distinctions between them and rendering a problem for buyers in terms of what and how to buy. However, first, let me introduce the three buyerships observed: 'Designer', 'Contemporary' and 'Casual and Updated'.

Markets in High Fashion I: 'Designer'

Designer wear is described by Julia[1] the head buyer as being 'at the top level of the business', by which she means the labels are the most expensive and exclusive, but also the most high profile, as these designers and brands carry a lot of status. This buyership includes big-name designers, many showing at the prêt-a-porter collections and their status makes for certain 'constraints'. As Julia put it, 'Some of these suppliers can be ... the most difficult, the most demanding'. Celia, the head of department, put it even more strongly, describing how relations at this level of the business can be 'very political' and negotiations to stock (or not), re-fit or create a branded area 'can take months' or longer, as was the case with the 'super-brands' area that was planned and built over months of protracted negotiations during fieldwork. (Too political, indeed, for me to observe.) Julia described these businesses as follows,

> When we're talking about these types of businesses, they have an international profile that they need to maintain, and so they can be very precise with the way they want their brand to be displayed, shown, reflected, whatever, so they may demand very large spaces, they may demand their own image in the shop-fit, they may demand that we pay for it rather than they pay for it—those sorts of things. Also, I mean, there's lots of issues around their distribution, in that they're very specific about which outlets they want to be in, and there are certain brands that we can't necessarily have, because they feel they're over-distributed in other stores. But at the same time, we have some brands here and they don't sell them to the other stores. So there can be some quite complex negotiations around things that are very difficult for us to control.

While the 'older' Selfridges had problems securing relationships at this end of the market, the 'fashion forward' Selfridges Radice set out to develop in the late 1990s depended upon securing arrangements with as many of these companies as possible. Thus, this level of the market is symbolically significant, even if the price range is beyond that of most consumers. These designers are the ones that are looked to for new trends and inspiration by the world's press and so are symbolically very important to the store.

Critically, prêt-a-porter collections are made to order prior to the season starting rather than being made and sold in quantity during the season. This involves greater degrees of risk as money is committed by retailers prior to the season, and thus calculations of what will be 'in fashion' have to be made well in advance of actual goods arriving and customers purchasing them. Once showcased on the international runways, trends are firmly established with little alternation in product design once the season gets under way. In Designer wear, garments are produced to order in much smaller batches than in mainstream fashion retailing and the time lag is the longest. According to Julia upwards of 80 per cent of the budget is committed within the 'own-bought' ranges across the different buyerships before the season starts, but in Designer wear the figure is even higher, close to 100 per cent. Cancellations and re-orders are almost impossible as items are made strictly to order and, therefore, there is little room for manoeuvre once placed. The contractual arrangements between the store and suppliers at this end of the market mean that Selfridges is committed to receiving the stock after the orders are purchased (except in cases of very late deliveries) while re-orders for more stock are not always possible. In this way, designer fashion, unlike the 'fast fashion' of the high street, involves a greater degree of risk because designers commit to designs ahead of season, while

> fast fashion retailers do not directly invest in design but instead are inspired by the most attractive and promising trends spotted at fashion shows and by cues taken from mainstream consumers (Agins 1999; Reinach 2005). They then transform these trends into products that can be put on the market almost immediately, freeing themselves and the consumers from the 'seasonal collection trap,' and in the process changing the conditions surrounding production. (Tokatli 2008: 22–23)

Put another way, according to Tokatli (2008): 'A designer dress photographed on a model during fashion week does not arrive in department stores for months—but something very like it can be spotted hanging in Zara in a couple of weeks'. Given the long delays, ready-to-wear demands more careful calculations than markets that respond to consumer demands in-season. So, while calculating fashion is always an uncertain business, it is perhaps more so than in the high end. As Julia put it, 'they make to order ... So there is no warehouse full of stock that I can take from during the season. Because it's high fashion stock, people only want it in the season that it's in. So we do have to take the risk. But then, selling at that level is a big risk.'

A small portion of a buyer's budget is held back for in-season purchases, adding an element of flexibility, but this does not significantly change the overall seasonal stock on the shop floor. These conditions add to a high degree of uncertainty as to what to buy at this level of the market that must be met and managed within the everyday calculations of economic actors as discussed in Chapters 6 and 7.

Designer wear also includes more mainstream, less exclusive big-brand designers, such as MaxMara, who are not noted for their high fashion creations, but maintain a much more regular flow of staples—products that sell season on season, such as classic skirts and trousers. Rather than 'high fashion', these brands are more 'commercial' than the prêt-a-porter designers. This distinction between 'fashion-forward' and 'commercial' designers in this buyership is a key one, and is significant also in the Contemporary buyership as well, where a similar balancing act between 'edgier' fashions and more mainstream and affordable items is precariously maintained. Indeed, a concern to balance profitable products with riskier, high fashion ones that have cultural kudos is important in Designer wear as well as the Contemporary area. So, Julia identifies her 'signature brands', supplying the 'absolutely must-have' of the season, that will probably make no money, but will be in the magazines and 'the slightly cheaper priced, big turnover' brands that make good profits for the store. In order to maintain the profile of her area, it is important to keep the balance between both the culturally valued but riskier products and the brands with big turnover.

This point is one I return to when discussing the 'Contemporary' buyership, but for now it is worth noting that high fashion markets in the store are concerned to balance 'economic' and 'cultural' value. That is to say, there is a need to be both 'commercial' and 'edgy' or 'fashion-forward' which requires a careful balance between 'commodity purchases' that deliver healthy profits, and riskier, fashion commodities that carry greater risk and make less money, but maintain the market position of the store as 'cutting-edge'.

There is, therefore, a clear similarity between high fashion clothing and other high fashion markets, such as fashion photography (Aspers 2001) and fashion modelling, where a similar equilibrium must be maintained between 'commercial' and 'edgy' work. As I have argued in Chapter 3 and elsewhere (Entwistle 2002) in fashion modelling this balancing act is important for both the individual models themselves, with agents physically separating the two sorts of work into different portfolios for the models, and also the agency, which needs to maintain a balance between commercial models earning big commercial contracts and fashion models whose earnings are often much lower but who secure the highly valued editorial work that maintains the agency's profile *as* a fashion agency. These riskier calculations may not lend immediate profit but add incalculable value in the form of kudos, reputation and status that ultimately supports the market position of the business. This balancing act is a difficult one but during the time of the fieldwork Selfridges maintained an equilibrium between creativity and risk-taking and sales and profit. I will return to this when discussing the remaining buyerships—'Contemporary' and 'Casual and Updated'.

Space plays a crucial role in sustaining these categories and distinctions of 'edgy' and 'commercial'. Model books are physically separated so different clients see different examples of a model's look, and in a fashion store like Selfridges separations maintain differences between brands *within* the buyership and *between* different buyerships. As Callon, Meadel et al. (2005) have noted, and as I discuss in Chapter 8, product placement is a critical part of sustaining identities between products, brands and individual designers/labels. In Designer wear, the high status of the designers is established and maintained by housing them in a separate room—the 'super-brands' room—where the very top end designers are displayed together. This physical proximity reinforces the exclusive identities of each designer. Indeed, so important is this placement that, according to the head of women's wear, Celia, the design of the super-brands room involved complex negotiations between store and designers who were concerned to negotiate the best possible space vis-à-vis their neighbours.

Julia described Designer wear as 'very much led by the press and press exposure, and what people see in magazines'. She describes her markets in terms of big-name designers and brands with very established identities and a 'loyal customer base'. She also described different shopping habits of her imagined customers, who are very 'brand loyal', probably do not shop in the other parts of the women's wear floor, but come in specifically to shop for particular designers/brands. This is in contrast to the other main buyerships, where the buyers there imagine their customers 'moving' across the different products, areas, and designers, including the concessions area on the ground floor, to generate a more 'eclectic' look rather than being dressed in one designer head-to-toe.

In these ways, the market for Designer wear is more clearly demarcated than the other two main buyerships for women's outer wear, both in spatial terms, and also by means of a clearly differentiated customer base. The demarcations between the other two buyerships—'Contemporary' and 'Casual and Updated'—are subject to a degree of slippage, as products, brands/designers and customers sold in the two buyerships are not so clearly differentiated. This poses something of a problem for these buyerships because the lack of clear demarcations means it is not as easy to maintain a distinctive identity or organizing 'concept' for each. This has the effect of making these two buyerships less easily calculable as a result, as I discuss below in terms of the fashion for denim products in 2002. For now, let me introduce these two buyerships in terms of their boundaries of product, supplier, space, concept and customer/s.

Markets in High Fashion II: 'Contemporary'

The Contemporary buyership is the one in which the balancing act between 'cultural' and 'economic' value is most critical. This area of the store was prominent in establishing a range of 'edgier' designers central to the establishment of the 'fashion-forward' identity of Selfridges. As with all the buyers, the descriptions of this area involved defining both product categories and/or 'concepts' and (virtual) customers. The head buyer maria described her area as consisting of three main 'product categories'. At the 'cutting-edge' is the concept 'test-tube', which consists of new, up-and-coming designers, often from London, New York or Paris fashion weeks. According to Maria, this area is 'high on impact,' 'very visual', but 'low on density', since it does not sell in volume, relative to its floor space. While this area does not generate high turnover, it is important because it is 'all about kudos and having the right brands ... So you buy certain labels from just pure image' not for the income they generate. The area's 'impact' is supported by its position alongside one of the main escalators, so that it provides a dramatic entry point into the women's wear department. Its highly visible location is no accident: in placing this area so prominently in the shop floor, it makes visible Selfridges's commitment to high fashion. This creates a high level of 'footfall' (the passage of customers through the store) in the area, promoting the store's overall strategy to be 'fashion-forward' to the widest possible number of consumers who may pass through the area even if they pass through without buying.

The remaining two concept/product areas described by Maria are 'West-end girl', consisting of 'the sort of product that's always in the magazines' and worn by celebrities, and the profitable 'Contemporary lab' made up of big-brand leaders that sell in greater volume and thus help ensure healthy sales and profit for the buyership. Thus, the equilibrium between economic and cultural value is maintained across the buyership by a careful balancing of 'cutting-edge' and 'commercial' product ranges. While 'test-tube' is riskier, it is bought on the principle that it will promote the 'right' (i.e. 'fashion-forward') image for the store and thus promote the overall image to be 'cutting-edge'. Higher density, profit-making brands, on the other hand, help maintain sales volume and profit making for the buyership.

Maria described how this area has to maintain its identity vis-à-vis a range of other areas (buyerships), internally and in relation to markets perceived to be external to the store. When evaluating the relatively poor performance it had suffered in 2002, Maria explained how the area sometimes struggles to define itself: as she describes it,

> Contemporary sits in the middle, you know, it has two areas that it competes against. On the bottom level, it's got the high street, which is extremely strong, and then it's got Designer that's above it, and it competes against those two factors all the time, and sometimes it's really difficult, you've got to get the product just right, you've got to pick the right brand, you've got to get the sizing right and everything.

This concern to maintain an identity, clearly distinguishable from the very vibrant high street and its 'fast fashion' ability to meet fashion trends and the Designer fashions sold in the store, underpins many of her buying decisions. Her buying strategy within the 'test-tube' concept reflects these concerns. For example when buying a collection shown by a young fashion week designer she may buy only a few items, maybe as few as ten or twelve pieces in a few (invariably small) sizes, not buying the whole range, since it would be 'too risky' if the designer is not known. With better-known designers, she will buy 'wide' not 'deep' (buying across the range but only in a few—again invariably small—sizes). Since the mix of designers is entirely 'own-bought' it creates a unique blend of products/designers/brands that help to promote Selfridges's claims to be 'different'. The 'exciting' 'edginess' of the area is also reflected in the arrangement of products, which are given a lot of space, displayed for maximum 'impact'. Loud music, often played by a DJ, helps give the area a young and 'hip' feel. The identity of the buyership therefore appears to support the newly acquired 'fashion-forward' identity of the store itself.

Markets in High Fashion III: 'Casual and Updated'

The descriptions of the two buyerships above show clearly that identities in marketplaces are created and actively maintained by buyers through their identification of particular product categories and virtual consumers. However, these identities are not stable but are constantly calculated. The instability of identities in the high fashion marketplace can be illustrated by examining a third buyership at Selfridges, 'Casual and Updated' (or Casual wear for short).

This buyership includes three main areas within it, described by Jane the head buyer, as follows: a 'classics' area of smart, classic clothes, including evening wear, 'the 'zone', an area aimed at the younger professional woman, and 'designer denim', which covers casual dressing, from T-shirts to jeans, and includes big-brand denim labels. The year prior to the fieldwork this area had been entirely refurbished to create what became known as the 'denim room'. According to Jane, refurbishment changed the look of the area dramatically, attracting newer, 'fashion-forward' 'designer denim' labels. Indeed, refurbishment coincided with a major 'denim trend' in 2001 and 2002 that troubled the boundaries of the Contemporary and Casual wear buyerships. It is therefore worth considering how the 'denim story' put the identities and categories into some confusion at Selfridges in order to illustrate how markets are never guaranteed but always contingent.

The Denim Story

As a product category, denim had previously been clearly demarcated and co-ordinated within the Casual wear buyership until a number of developments saw its identity reconfigured. In 2001 and 2002 denim (predominantly jeans) were 'on trend'—indeed, it would not be inaccurate to say that denim was *the* major trend in women's wear over this period. This altered the identity of denim significantly: while jeans had previously been seen as a 'basic' or 'staple' product, and a relatively inexpensive one, during 2001 and 2002 denim was repositioned as a high fashion commodity. That is, it became a fashion-led commodity, with different colours, styles, cuts and brands coming in and out of fashion over the seasons. This change in its identity came about for two reasons. First, denim appeared in all the prêt-a-porter collections at the time. Second and paralleling this trend, a market in specialist 'designer denim' saw the emergence of new denim brands that, in fashion parlance, gained 'cult' status. The first wave of designer denim brands came from the United States (e.g. Earl, Paper Denim and Cloth, Seven, For all Mankind) with Los Angeles a significant 'hub', although subsequent 'cult' brands have come from Sweden (Acne) and Australia (Sass and Bide and 18th Amendment). As the price-points for these ranges are well above £140, with many of them retailing above £200, these jeans are 'smart' and 'stylish' and have an exclusive caché. 'Designer denim'—both from new denim labels and prêt-a-porter designers—thus challenge the traditional definitions of denim as casual wear.

Alongside these external developments, the other major factor within Selfridges, noted above, was the 'denim room' refurbishment, which generated a lot of interest and 'buzz' about the store and drove considerable sales and profit for the buyership. While a positive thing initially, this later impacted negatively on the Casual wear buyership. These three developments—the trend for denim, the emergence of designer denim and the denim room refurbishment—posed something of a problem to the buyers at Selfridges responsible for Contemporary and Casual areas as I now describe.

With denim redefined as a fashion commodity as opposed to a basic commodity, it challenged previously held ideas about denim within the store and brought to the fore competing definitions within the business. As the head buyer for Casual Jane, wear explains, since 'everyone wears jeans', denim was perceived by some in the store as a commodity purchase, that is, as a 'basic' commodity selling at high volume. This was particularly the case with the financial people—or 'suits' as she referred to them—who have little understanding of fashion and this resulted in a clash of definitions. Thus, while the suits saw denim as a 'commodity business'—that is a relatively low-risk, highly profitable product that should sell in volume—Jane challenged this, arguing, 'We don't do the Gap market, we do high fashion.'

The effect had both positive and negative impacts on the Casual buyership. As Jane summarizes, the 'refocusing of the product, and the refurbishment, and the denim explosion all at once' meant that 'our figures went through the roof', but had a negative knock-on effect in terms of planning for the following season. The perception of denim as a 'basic', coupled with good sales, meant in subsequent seasons her area is 'expected to drive commodity figures' and therefore 'planned very aggressively', that is planned for continued high sales and profit that were unsustainable. The role of financial planning in driving the figures and evaluations of stores will be discussed in the next chapter, but suffice it to say here, 'aggressive' plans in this case set unrealistic targets for future sales that could not be met subsequently. Thus, after strong growth, the area appeared to 'fail' or 'not make plan' as by now the denim trend had plateaued and the refurbishment was no longer a novelty.

Thus, while in real terms denim profits were still quite good, in relation to the department's 'plan' they were actually down. This story illustrates three things in particular. First, products, even seemingly staple ones, like denim, are constantly redefined, recalibrated and demand constant requalification. Secondly, product changes—such as the denim trend and newly emerging designer denim market—challenge other, long-established definitions and identities within and between markets, in this case, between the different buyerships within the store. As a result of the trend in denim, Designer wear was awash with indigo—consisting of many denim products—although its market, price range and customer base, noted above, remained more clearly distinct. More problematic was how the rise of denim troubled the boundaries between the Contemporary and the Casual wear buyerships. This throws light on the contingent nature of markets, market boundaries and identities. Being 'on trend', denim transgressed the boundaries of the Casual wear (in the Casual and Updated buyership), spilling out into the other areas of the store, Designer wear and, more problematically, into Contemporary. This meant that the distinctive market identities of the three buyerships were, to some extent, blurred. This merging posed particular problems for the Contemporary buyer Maria, whose area struggled to maintain its difference. As noted above, she perceives her area to be 'in the middle' between high-end designer clothing and the high street, and with the high street showing denim—picking up catwalk trends—her identity vis-à-vis these two was in some crisis, as it was in relation to Casual wear.

Maria described how her area was less easily distinguished from the Casual wear, which traditionally sold denim. As the two buyerships were both buying substantial quantities of denim and the boundaries between them in terms of product profile diminished, they looked increasingly similar or, rather, Contemporary looked increasingly like Casual wear. Her summary of the poor performance of her area reflects this problem: 'Probably the main factor ... is the content of denim in some of those collections [prêt-a-porter collections in 2002].'

A third and final point this story illustrates is how strategies for managing products—such as financial plans—are not merely passive tools of calculation; they are performative, producing that which they appear to reflect or map. The fashion trend meant denim was put centre stage in the store as a fashion not a commodity purchase, supporting buyers' definitions of the product; but while the exceptional profits could not be sustained, they artificially inflated the figures expected to drive the area. Thus, while planning is one way to calculate the risks inherent in the female fashion market, even 'the best-laid plans' of fashion buyers and merchandisers cannot always get it exactly right.

As is evident here, products are not fixed, hermeneutically sealed entities. While they come into the store with identities, meanings and associations, they are, in turn, rendered meaningful by retail practice, in their positioning, display and promotion. The contingent and fluctuating nature of identities was thrown into sharp relief with the arrival into the store of a newly acquired 'cult' jeans brand from the United States ('Seven, For all Mankind') in spring 2002. This label had become the 'hottest' jean during the Spring/Summer of 2002, when, initially because of a licensing problem in Europe, they were only available in the United States and were only known to fashion 'insiders', such as the buyers I followed and other such fashion workers (journalists, stylists, fashion editors) who meet during the fashion week shows. The redefinition of jeans as a fashion item, and the supposed 'cult' status of this particular label meant that while the 'denim room' would have been the obvious place to locate Seven, For all Mankind, the decision was taken to locate them on one of the 'mats' in the Contemporary area. This decision was, according to the head buyer for Contemporary, under review. She recognized that, if and when its identity as a 'hot', new label diminishes, as it would inevitably do, then these jeans would migrate to the denim room, as they indeed did a couple of years later. Thus, as markets are constantly moving, product identities are also mobile. This story illustrates not only how the products associated with different markets in the store are not fixed, but also how retailing involves the interpretation of products and their meaningful translation.

Conclusion

In this chapter I have outlined the broader context of women's fashionable cloth-ing markets in the United Kingdom through a summary of retailing literature, as well as introduced some of the mechanisms for understanding and linking the many different spaces and moments of 'production' and 'consumption' within 'systems', 'chains', 'circuits' or 'networks' of provision. I have then moved closer to my own case study, examining how Selfridges assembles high fashion markets through the idea of the 'buyership' and how this involves the active configuration of markets in financial, spatial and conceptual terms. I have thus argued that while fashion mar-kets are described by buyers as having an external 'reality', said to exist in terms of external actors (designers/suppliers/consumers, for example), and located within a hierarchical structure ('designer', 'high-street' for example as noted above), these external market conditions still require active interpretation, translation and qualifi-cation inside the business if they are to be meaningfully assembled. Indeed, in order to act within the market, agents have to make sense of a plethora of things 'out there' and it is through the formal organizational structure of the women's wear department into distinct buyerships that such a translation can be made. Such translations have to be made not only because fashion markets 'outside' are in constant flux—as fashion always will be—but also because markets do not have self-evident structures to them but are always and everywhere actively configured in actor-networks.

A second related point to note is that markets depend upon clear demarcations between products, customers and, in the case of Selfridges, concepts or themes that creatively make sense of things. Here the mechanism of the buyership helps create demarcations between different 'markets' within the store, giving shape to markets said to exist 'beyond' or 'outside' the store. However, with no essential qualities, markets are always in motion, never quite fixed or guaranteed, as the case of denim illustrates. When distinct product identities appear to merge, as they did for denim during 2002, the internal mechanisms for creating boundaries between markets—products/customers/concepts—are called into question. While the buyership is one major, formal device for understanding and translating fashion markets, other devices and routine practices shape the calculations within each buyership. These devices and practices form the basis of the formal and informal knowledge that underpins or enables calculations of fashion. It is this knowledge, manifested through particular devices and practices, to which I now turn my attention.

–6–

Markets in Motion: Fashion Temporality and Materiality

Fashion buyers at Selfridges draw on a wide-ranging knowledge. Their knowledge is, of course, partly economic, but making sense in this market requires assembling a vast range of elements; knowledge of past, present and future tastes; previous and emerging cultural trends in music, art, film, lifestyle; shopping habits and retailing trends; imagined customer body shapes, psychologies and preferences; the strategies of competitors, as well as the impact of environment, like the weather, upon shopping habits. These various knowledges are intricately tied together in a seamless web as part of the analysis and calculations of fashionable clothing, so that discussions of weekly sales at a meeting which examines merchandising statistics might include discussion on how the wet weather is 'dampening' spending, the comments of one particular customer to the shop floor staff, a buyer's mother-in-law's feelings about the particular designer brands on offer for older customers in the store, the skilful way in which customers try to circumvent the Selfridges policy on returns, bringing back clothes already worn (a problem in evening wear especially) and the ineffective or poorly marked shop floor signage.

Thus, buying is a complex process, a 'network of materially heterogeneous elements' (Law and Hetherington 2000: 37). I want to describe these elements by delineating some of the routine activities and processes of the Buying Office. Understanding this 'material heterogeneity' (see also Law 2002) involves looking at the different tools and devices used to 'see' and calculate fashion. Likewise, 'following the actors' (Latour 1987) involved in seeing fashion means following them around the spaces of their everyday working life, examining how the Buying Office itself is put together and investigating the tools of calculation themselves, including spreadsheets, statistics and plans produced by the Finance Department, promotional material, trend forecasting and sales meetings. These various tools, devices and practices are the materials through which knowledge of markets is assembled in all its diversity: 'For STS [science and technology studies] analysis, the relations that produce knowing locations, information, are endless. We're saying, then, that knowing is a relational "effect"' (Law and Hetherington 2000: 38). I suggest that knowledge is distributed across a range of materials and locations, with fashion buyers important nodes in the knowledge flow. We begin our tour by first looking at the way in which space is organized within the Buying Office. My analysis then focuses upon three particular strategies for organizing knowledge at Selfridges—the Fashion Office, routine 'floor walks' and the financial plan—all of which are used, in different ways, to make sense, calculate and evaluate women's wear fashion.

This ANT approach challenges some of the conventional wisdom concerning knowledge within business, management and 'knowledge transfer' literature, which defines it in terms of fixed properties and locations. This chapter is divided into two sections. In Defining Economic Knowledge, I challenge some conventional definitions of economic knowledge that assume it to have definite properties of 'rationality and cognition' and certain stable locations in 'research and design' departments—for example often located within 'knowledge-intensive' firms and sectors, such as science, engineering or chemical based. In these accounts, knowledge tends to be defined as an abstract 'thing' or set of properties that can be 'managed' or 'transferred'. There is, therefore, a tendency to privilege some skills, abilities and locations over others and to privilege particular sectors, industries and companies. In Materialities and Localities of Knowledge at Selfridges, I focus in on the actual materialities of knowledge within the Selfridges Buying Office, examining how knowledge is located, circulated and disseminated across a range of practices and materials.

Thus, my account challenges understandings of knowledge that define it as an abstract 'thing'. Bearing these points in mind, I argue two things in particular.

First, instead of defining knowledge in advance of fieldwork, for example developing precise definitions about its content and drawing a fixed binary between codified and tacit knowledge, I follow knowledge-in-use, examining how knowledge is assembled and how, in content, it is multifaceted, residing across a range of actors, tools, objects and locations. Thus, rather than assuming knowledge as a solid and stable property or 'thing', I focus on the relations *between* things and the assemblages produced as a result. I adopt an ANT view that insists upon observing and following actors and practices and expands on some aspects of Amin and Cohendet's (2004: 2) work on the relationship between knowledge and knowing, and agree with their contention that knowedge should be 'viewed fundamentally as a heterogeneous resource that firms value in different manifestations.' My approach also shares something in common with the 'communities of practice' idea (Wenger 1998), which considers how practice is put together. Indeed, the thing that links all these approaches is a concern with knowing as *practice* and as *process*. Knowledge is assembled within organizations out of a range of formal tools, procedures, mechanisms, as well as informal practice and conversations, which challenge any attempt to clearly distinguish between formal and informal, tacit and codified regimes.

Second, I challenge the view of knowledge as cognitive by demonstrating how knowledge is embodied; that is, worn and performed on the body. Indeed in fashion markets in particular (and possibly other markets too) the body is one important knowing location. This discussion is developed in Chapter 7 as a critique of knowledge literature, especially that focusing on tacit knowledge, which tends to disembody knowledge, despite repeated references to practices and '*being* there' (Gertler 2003). I examine how the aesthetic knowledge demanded in the high fashion market is embodied in the style adopted by the fashion buyers at Selfridges.

Thus, my case study of fashion buying attends to the long-standing bias in social science studies of knowledge and the economy which tend to favour some kinds of knowledge and particular sorts of markets in such things as basic commodities (Garcia 1986), financial markets (Knorr Certina and Bruegger 2004; MacKenzie 2004; Tsing 2004), science-based markets (e.g. Latour and Woolgar 1979; Law 1986; Latour 1987), engineering (Callon, Law et al. 1986; Law and Callon 1988; Malecki 2000) or firms defined as 'knowledge intensive' (Swart and Kinnie 2003). However, 'there remain substantial gaps in our understanding of the mobilisation of different modalities of knowledge—their diffusion, transmission or translation across space and time' (Weller 2007: 42). In other words, 'soft' markets trading cultural and aesthetic commodities have been neglected in this focus on 'hard' markets and knowledge. This neglect is evident in academic, business and policy literature so that, as Rooney, Hearn et al. (2007), taking the latter, argue, 'Policy prescriptions ... focus on science, technology and engineering to the effective exclusion of non-technical knowledge. Knowledge embodied in culture, the arts and humanities ... are not currently considered central knowledge policy concerns.' Similarly, as Allen (2002a: 39) puts it, 'Many insightful accounts of economic knowledge remain trapped within a formal, codified script of knowledge that, often unintentionally, marginalizes the expressive and prioritizes the cognitive.'

My study of the neglected area of fashion buying adds to a small collection of similar studies of creative businesses and markets (Negus 1992, 1999; Scott 1999, 2000; Aspers 2001; Weller 2007) to extend knowledge on markets beyond the obvious and well-attended markets favoured by economic sociology. There are very good reasons to focus attention on fashion: as Weller (2007: 40) puts it, 'The meaningful and knowledge-rich nature of fashionable objects ... has barely been acknowledged'. Companies trading 'cultural' or 'aesthetic' products demand our attention, not only because these are important economically as increasingly profitable and highly visible markets in contemporary Western (and increasingly, non-Western) economies. Evidence of this is the increasing attention paid to the 'creative industries' by governments. They also allow us to extend our understanding of the complexity of marketplace calculations. As I hope to demonstrate in this chapter and the next, this case study of fashion retailing forces us to expand definitions of economic knowledge by recognizing how sensual, aesthetic and embodied capacities are important in the fashion marketplace/s' calculations. Fashion is defined in terms of an 'unstable and constantly changing form of knowledge that promotes incessant change without progress' (Weller 2007: 42). Before turning to examine this knowledge, it is worth examining how knowledge, particularly economic knowledge, is normally defined.

Defining Economic Knowledge

Within institutional economics, business studies and economic geography there is a growing interest in 'knowledge management', 'transfer' and 'spill-over' with knowledge seen as an 'asset' key to managing 'risk' and securing 'competitive advantage' (Nonaka and Takeuchi 1995; Boisot 1998; Maskell and Malmberg 1999; Malecki 2000; Nonaka, Toyama et al. 2000). Much of this literature sets out to define knowledge and, referencing Michael Polanyi's work (1967), maintains a distinction between tacit and codified knowledge, with the former considered to be more valuable in setting a firm apart (Howells 2002; Gertler 2003; Howells 2004). One thing that tends to unite this literature is that knowledge is formulated as if it were a separate variable—an 'asset' (Boisot 1998) to be 'harnessed' by the firm; that is, a separate object, variously defined, with different qualities that circulate (or not) within the company. Thus, knowledge is assumed to have certain stable and objective properties. Various attempts to delineate its 'thinginess' shape the dimensions in the debates about knowledge, including the codified/tacit debate, with different qualities of the 'thinginess' identified in the process. For this reason, it is necessary to examine, briefly, some of the conventional forms knowledge is said to take, and the types of knowledge said to be circulating in firms. From there, I want to suggest how my own analysis differs from these accounts.

While Allen (2000) suggests there is actually an 'ambiguity' when it comes to defining knowledge, not least when trying to find and measure it, he suggests there is also an 'obviousness' to definitions as well and there are, indeed, a few characteristics which can be set out. For one thing, knowledge is distinct from information, since it involves translating information and formal data and applying it to practice: thus, knowledge is 'a dynamic framework or structure from which information can be stored, processed and understood' (Howells 2002: 872). Howells goes on to point out that all knowledge involves a 'knowing self and an event or entity' (2002: 871) and emphasizes how 'knowing is an active process that is mediated, situated, provisional, pragmatic and contested' (2002: 872). Similarly, as Allen (2000: 15, emphasis added) puts it, when pressed to define knowledge there is a tendency to fall back on a narrower definitions; 'what are prized above all, are cognitive abilities rather than those relating to *aesthetics and expressive character, for instance.*' Thus, Howells (2002: 872, emphasis added) goes on note how 'Knowledge is ... associated with a process that involves *cognitive structures* which can assimilate information and put it into a wider context, allowing actions to be undertaken from it.'

The narrowness that Allen identifies in definitions of economic knowledge is evident everywhere. In a recent UK Department of Trade and Industry Report (DTI) on knowledge in firms, Barber (2006) identifies different types of knowledge including scientific and technical knowledge, market knowledge, customer knowledge, and the knowledge and skills of employees. Thus, knowledge in firms can take many forms, although there is a fairly predictable, limited range of skills, specifically cognitive ones, that are generally valued as knowledge. Knowledge is recognized as being held or possessed by people, as in the notion of 'human capital' (Swart and Kinnie 2003) although it can also become codified into scientific, technical or market data. When defining 'knowledge-intensive' firms Swart and Kinnie (2003: 3) note that knowledge in such firms involves the employment of 'highly skilled individuals [who] create market value through their knowledge (an *intangible* asset)'.

The valuing of cognitive activities is problematic because of the way it directs attention to a limited range of activities within companies, such as those demanding cognitive skills, like research and design (R&D), and on a narrow range of firms or industries labelled 'knowledge-intensive'. This limitation is recognized by Swart and Kinnie (2003) in their own study of 'knowledge-intensive' companies. They note how 'Reference is often made to a particular industry as being knowledge-intensive: for example biotechnology or management consultancy' (2003: 60). However, they advise 'that it is unwise to define a particular industry as knowledge-intensive' and their definition of 'knowledge-intensive' can be applied to any organization 'that employs highly skilled individuals and therefore creates market value through the application of knowledge to novel, complex client demands' (2003: 62). Their definition is therefore applicable to many organizations and firms, like Selfridges, whose knowledge is not scientific or technological, but aesthetic in content, and yet no less dependent on highly skilled, knowledgeable agents. Fashion buyers' knowledge is critical to Selfridges's success and has to be constantly applied to the ever-changing, dynamic world of fashion and frequently 'novel' situations, as when designers present radically different collections each season.

Something of the contradiction between 'ambiguity' and 'obviousness', which Allen refers to, can be seen in these different definitions: knowledge is both defined as 'intangible' (when referring to knowledge 'held' by individuals), but is thought to take some 'obvious' forms (technical data, for example). This tension remains evident in debates concerning tacit/codified knowledge: knowledge seems to be something solid, material, thing-like when it becomes codified, and yet, on the other hand, it is hard to actually pin down important elements that constitute knowledge possessed by individuals. Embodiment, a central, material feature of knowledge, is, indeed, poorly theorized even in the literature on tacit knowledge (Gertler 2003) where one would expect to find some recognition of it, since tacit 'know-how' is very much embodied in everyday practices. The problem is, in fact, captured cogently by Allen's (2000) critique and call for an expanded, 'expressive' knowledge to be developed. He argues that 'expressive' and sensual ways of knowing fall outside economic knowledge as it is narrowly defined as purely cognitive. Drawing on Foucault's idea of power/knowledge, he argues that a ring of truth attaches itself to the idea that economic knowledge is broadly cognitive, which is to say, repeated statements and analyses reproduce this definition. This comes to have real implications for how economic actors make sense and what comes to count as knowledge.

I concur with Allen and also suggest that conventional understandings of knowledge tend to abstract and fossilize it, treating knowledge as if it were an abstract 'thing'—a property or capacity that can be objectively 'held' or 'harnessed'. Coming at the problem of knowledge in firms rather differently by examining 'communities of practice' Wenger, McDermott et al. (2002: 11) put forward the view that

> What makes managing knowledge a challenge is that it is not an object that can be stored, owned, and moved around like a piece of equipment or a document. It resides in the skills, understanding, and relationships of its members as well as in the tools, documents, and processes that embody aspects of this knowledge. Companies must mange their knowledge in ways that do not merely reduce it to an object.

This view is shared by Amin and Cohendet (2004: 2) who similarly see knowledge not as the 'possession' of individuals or groups but 'a heterogeneous resource that firms value in different manifestations'. In seeking to reconcile knowledge and knowing, they stress 'knowledge as a *process and practice,* rather than a possession', emphasizing 'the pragmatics of everyday learning in situated contexts of embodied and encultured practice' (2004: 8, emphasis added).

Along with Allen (2000, 2002a,b), I suggest that definitions of economic knowledge need to be more varied and expansive, beyond rationality and cognitive abilities, to take into account non-cognitive ways of knowing. Rather than defining knowledge in advance of the actors, following them affords the opportunity to see where they go, what they do, what they think counts as knowledge, and examining how different sorts of information are assembled and interpreted by them in order to make sense of the fashion marketplace/s in the store. Following *knowledge-in-use* affords the opportunity to examine the naturally occurring ways in which knowledge is defined and used and how it is constituted out of different actors, tools and locations, that is to say, different materialities. Knowledge is, therefore, not a fixed property or object 'held' in any particular location or by any particular individual or group, although fashion buyers are important nodes in the knowledge flows in the store. It 'flows' across actors and locations, and is heterogeneous rather than stable in form, assembled out of a miscellaneous range of materials. Again, this is not dissimilar from a 'communities of practice' approach, where practice is taken to refer to the miscellaneous and inventive ways of doing things within organizations. As Wenger (1998: 47) puts it:

> A concept of practice includes both the explicit and the tacit. It includes what is said and what is left unsaid; what is represented and what is assumed. It includes the language, the tools, the documents, the images, the symbols, well-defined roles, specified criteria, codified procedures, regulations, and contacts that various practices make explicit ... it also includes all the implicit relations, tacit conventions, subtle cues, untold rules of thumb, recognizable intuitions, specific perceptions, well-tuned sensitivities, embodied understandings, underlying assumptions, shared worldviews. Most of these may never be articulated, yet they are unmistakable signs of membership in communities of practice.

As this quote suggests, practice involves the heterogeneous assemblage of different kinds of objects, processes, understandings, assumptions, etc. This way of thinking about practice and knowledge in organizations denies any clear distinction between tacit and codified knowledge. Following this more expansive and inclusive way of envisaging practice and knowledge in organizations, I now consider some of the materialities and localities of fashion buying knowledge, beginning by first describing the space of the fashion Buying Office as one location of knowledge, then examining some of the routine and everyday ways in which fashion buying knowledge is organized within it, the tools and practices used, and how these various elements are combined as part of the everyday sense-making in a high fashion marketplace.

Materialities and Localities of Knowledge at Selfridges

The Buying Office at Selfridges

In its organization, design and management structure, the Buying Office embodies what Thrift (1997, 2005) refers to as the management ethos of 'soft capitalism'. This has arisen in recent years to account for 'soft capitalism' (Ray and Sayer 1999a; Heelas 2002) and owes a debt to the growth and extension, since the 1960s, of 'soft skills' like intuition within the business and management worlds (Thrift 2005: 118), partly as a reaction to the authoritarianism of Taylorism. Thrift notes various mechanisms—'organizational', 'inspirational', 'ideological'—that craft particular ways of working and help to engineer a 'soft' management ethos. While these claims are not empirically demonstrated by Thrift, and it is therefore not possible to say whether this management style is ubiquitous or not, I would suggest that some features he describes have particular resonance in a firm like Selfridges which values 'creativity' and 'innovation', precisely because these are the necessary 'soft' skills demanded by a company in an aesthetic market like fashion. It is certainly the case that this management ethos is embodied in the Buying Office observed. Much like the laboratories and offices in science and knowledge production that Latour (1987) and Law and Hetherington (2000: 37; see also Law 2002) describe, I want to examine how the Selfridges Buying Office helps to craft particular ways of being and knowing and how it 'performs', 'that is ... act[s]' and participates 'in the generation of power relations, of subjectivities and objectivities' (Hetherington and Law 2000: 37).

Selfridges's Head Office and buying departments are situated on Davies Street, immediately adjacent to Oxford Street where the flagship store is located. Closed to the general public, visitors enter strictly by appointment and must sign in at the security desk. Beyond this desk lies a bright meeting area, a glossy sunflower yellow space (yellow being the store's brand colour) where, on brightly coloured plastic chairs, buyers sometimes meet other staff to discuss store business and receive outside visitors. The style of this space, yellow, glossy, shiny and modern, certainly 'performs' the company's brand image as creative and 'funky', as do the glossy customer and staff magazines, much like fashion magazines, scattered around the sitting area.

Behind this meeting area are the secure offices of senior management and the buying teams, located on separate corridors. My first port of call, on my way to discuss access with the Managing Director, was the corridor designated for senior management. These offices are all private and to arrive at them one must navigate a deep, plush carpet. Indeed, one of my first and very much embodied observations was of sinking deep into this soft pile, noting how difficult it was to walk on wearing high heels and how it seemed to herald the importance of the people immediately located on the corridor in much the same way a deep red carpet works to signal royalty or celebrity. In contrast, the Buying Office is not lushly carpeted and is open plan in design (with the exception of the head of department). This openness of space secures particular ways of working. As Thrift (2005: 119) notes, open plan offices orchestrate bodies into 'teams' and 'projects' and he notes how these are 'now regarded as the main way in which bodies can be aligned to productive creativity'.

Indeed, the design and layout of the Buying Office very much performs the company's ethos to be an 'open' and informal organization. For one, it allows for ease of movement—that of people, objects and information—between the different branches of the women's wear department. Merchandisers and buyers sit near each other at their own desks and readily feed information and catch up on news, developments, gossip. The office therefore exhibits the company concern, in recent years, with knowledge sharing and, in addition, the full view it affords serves the purpose of enabling particular kinds of performances on the part of staff and thus the circulation of embodied knowledge about high fashion.

The body is an important 'knowing location' and the open plan office is one 'organizational technology' for bringing bodies 'into alignment' (Thrift 2005: 119), in this case, aligning bodies in terms of style with the effect of disseminating and performing one's high fashion taste. This visibility of bodies, and scrutiny of appearance and fashionability, is not unusual in the open-planned office (Freeman 1993, 2000), but in a fashion retail environment it is particularly noteworthy and even desirable, as it encourages a communal sharing of fashion knowledge and taste. Jane, head buyer for Casual wear, described how the office encourages buyers to 'check out' what others are wearing. She noted how this made her conscious of her own dress and that of others, a consciousness that translates readily into a 'demand' or requirement to dress appropriately (i.e. fashionably). She described in detail the style of her colleagues, noting how members of the team, particularly the head, were always dressed fashionably, often in expensive designer clothes. She also told of how the pressure to wear high fashion was felt all the way down the hierarchy and was a particular problem for junior buyers and merchandisers without the salary to purchase expensive designer clothes. What this buyer described struck me very forcefully in my own observations.

The importance of style, and indeed the similarities in style amongst the team in the office, was very apparent to me. As I surveyed the office on one trip, after a long-ish break from the field, these similarities were particularly striking: I noted about a dozen staff wearing the same pair of 'cult' designer jeans (a pair of which, inciden-tally, I was also wearing at the time. So thoroughly was I immersed in the fieldwork by this time, I had begun to adopt dress not unlike the fashion buyers I observed).

Thus, high fashion style circulates visually in the fertile environment of the open plan office as a form of embodied knowledge; it is knowledge that is worn and car-ried on the bodies of others, who are 'read' in terms of their style as a consequence, as Jane had 'read' the style of the head. It signals that one has the knowledge appro-priate to the company and the business of selling high fashion. Indeed, having and performing this embodied knowledge is critical, as the experience of one of the older buyers, Jane, indicates. She described how she is more inclined to dress in a 'classic' not high fashion way, but went on to note how, in the new, fashion-forward Selfridges 'if you dress too classically, then people assume that you don't *know the fashions*, that you're not trendy and that you don't run with the tide, and you're old-fashioned, and you know, you should be put out to pasture sort of thing!' (emphasis added) As she describes it, working in fashion should translate into looking fashionable; one *wears the knowledge*. However, while she would like to wear 'edgy' fashion clothes, as she 'approaches 40', she feels uncomfortable dressing too fashionably and wor-ries about looking like 'mutton dressed as lamb'. Consequently, she felt a 'horrible pressure to look the part' and was constantly conscious of her dress and vaguely unsure of her style vis-à-vis the company image. The fact that she was responsible for buying the casual and elegant work wear ranges within the store meant her style did, in fact, fit well with her work and was not a problem vis-a-vis the company, but this did little to diminish her anxiety and consciousness of her appearance. What she describes, how important it is to 'look the part' to work in high fashion, cannot be under-estimated, as I have discussed elsewhere (Entwistle and Rocamora 2006) and dressing fashionably constitutes something of the 'aesthetic labour' in this employ-ment market (Entwistle and Wissinger 2006).

High fashion style not only circulates around the office, it is inculcated within it. Though Jane was not noted for her high fashion look, she described how she had modified her style since starting work at the store to fit in with the newly defined Sel-fridges's high fashion image. She first described how she dressed very differently in her previous job working for an Arab company—gold jewellery and much brighter clothes—and noted how this was, at first,

a *conscious effort*, because I kind of thought, "In order to get these people's respect, I'm going to have to start to look a bit more like them." And so I made a conscious effort to buy a few tacky pairs of gold earrings, and buy some sling-backs. But then eventually, what happened is, that *I got quite into it*! (Laughs) Hideous! (emphasis added)

What is significant in this account is how the dress sense she developed in the Arab market was very much a conscious, indeed, cognitive one to begin with, but it became increasingly unconscious through prolonged involvement in this market-place and repeated exposure to this style of dressing. Jane went on to note how, just as she 'just picked up' a style suited to the Arab market, she later 'ditched this style' and evolved a look more suited to Selfridges.

Her experience of dressing to fit in within the high fashion marketplace was not unusual. Other buyers described how their taste had altered—moved 'up market' to-wards more expensive high fashion—as the store re-defined itself as being in the mar-ketplace of high fashion. Indeed, adopting this style seems to have been essential in securing the store's position as a high fashion one. Buyers told of how 'old' Selfridges had been unsuccessful in securing arrangements to stock some designers because its 'middle-of-the-road' image was deemed inappropriate to their brand identities. The successful re-positioning of Selfridges depended upon a re-fashioning of the store's image and this was, in no small part, secured through the fashioning of suitably at-tired and fashion-competent fashion buyers. As I argue in Chapter 8, buyers are im-portant mediators of the store's image to the outside world, performing Selfridges's identity on fashion buying trips in their encounters with suppliers, much like the 'del-egates' that Law (1986; see also Hetherington and Law 2000) describes, performed on behalf of Portugal in colonial encounters. At one buying encounter I observed, one representative of a major designer brand noted how, 'You can tell a lot about a store from the buyer'. We might also say that buyers 'translate' the store's image by becoming increasingly knowledgeable *of* and identified *with* the 'up-market', high fashion way of dressing. This 'fusing' of buyer and store image is complex: buyers' style 'moves up-market' along with the store, but the store does not so much impose this style upon them; it requires buyers who can first understand and translate this style—identify, select, wear, perform it. Identities—buyer/store/product—appear to merge all the time in buyers' dialogue. Maria, head buyer for Contemporary wear at Selfridges, commenting on a colleague's work, described 'how you can see a lot of Jane in what she buys', just as suppliers can see a lot of the store in how the buyer is styled. Understanding the inculcation and mediation of this knowledge can be cap-tured with reference to Bourdieu's notion of 'cultural capital' and 'habitus' as I dis-cuss elsewhere (Entwistle and Rocamora 2006; see also Weller 2007).

To return to the open plan office design, I suggest it encourages a sharing of fash-ion knowledge and style but, more significantly, as a spatial technology, it informs the performance of staff within who come to embody the knowledge and company image (Crang 1994; Entwistle 2004). High fashion dress worn throughout the of-fice helps secure the ethos and style of the company, much like repeated utterances about the company as a 'creative' and innovative one help to perform this identity, as I discuss below. However, the Buying Office is only one 'knowing' location. Fashion knowledge is spatially and materially dispersed across many more locations and ma-terials across the store and beyond. I want to suggest something of the heterogeneous flows of information and knowing locations at Selfridges by examining some of the other objects, spaces and devices gathered together to make sense of fashion.

The Fashion Office at Selfridges

Alongside the Buying Office, one of the key locations of knowledge in the store was the Fashion Office. This Office, established by Radice shortly after he took over as Chief Executive, was given the important responsibility of developing in-house knowledge—of trends in music, fashion, retailing, art and architecture and wider cultural and political developments as well—intended to drive the overall direction of the store and put it at the 'cutting-edge' of retail. The Office was, first and foremost, a 'knowing location' and knowledge-generating mechanism. The importance of developing localized tacit knowledge, to set Selfridges apart, is discussed in more detail in the following chapter. Here I want to examine how the aims and objectives of this Office helped to create belief and confidence in the store and perform its identity as a 'creative' and 'innovative' company.

First and foremost, the Office was involved in research activities; in knowledge gathering and translation. The knowledge generated within and by this Office was gathered far and wide and fed into external promotional activities as well as internally shaping the direction of the store. To take the former, the Office was responsible for co-ordinating major promotional activities, such as the annual promotional event held in the month of May, the first of which, 'Tokyo Now' had been very successful, followed by 'Bollywood' in 2002, during the fieldwork. These events fed through the store in terms of special promotions, new product lines, spectacles and the fantastical styling of the shop floor. They were an attempt to generate a 'buzz' or 'hype' around the store and secure Selfridges's identity as an exciting, 'creative' retail environment. To source ideas, Alice the head and her deputy went with buyers on their bi-annual buying trips and also travelled for purely research purposes to see what is happening and keep abreast of cultural and retail developments globally. The knowledge generated by this Office also fed directly into the internal operations of the store in a large number of ways. It formed part of informal conversations between the Office and buying staff (over coffee, lunch, dinner on buying trips in London and abroad).

The work of the Office translated into numerous forms but most visibly it was turned into formal documents and presentations, such as the bi-annual 'Fashion Directive' (later, 'Fashion' was dropped and it became the 'Directive'). Thus, while Alice prioritized 'intuitive' or tacit knowledge, some degree of codification was inevitable as this knowledge still had to be disseminated across the store in formal ways. Let me examine this Directive in more detail.

This Directive took several forms; it involved the production of a glossy document, circulated internally; it was also disseminated in the form of a bi-annual presentation by Alice to all staff; and it fed through to staff at all levels of the store in follow-up meetings between her and buyers, Retail Ops, VM [Visual Merchandising] and the like. Basically, it set out the company direction for the coming season and, at the event I observed, involved an opening PowerPoint presentation on general cultural and aesthetic trends identified as emerging. This presentation took us on a tour of the world's global cities and cultural spaces—museums, dance performances, international architecture, retailing and innovative Web sites—and also included a talk by a visiting 'expert' speaker (in this instance, Alice Rawsthorne who was then director of the London Design Museum). This occasion was a major one for all employees in the store, a moment when they all came together, albeit at different times (the event was repeated several times in the course of a day) to see and hear 'where' the company would be 'going' next season. This knowledge is then translated and implemented in buying and retailing strategies and follow-up meetings with Alice and retail staff circulate and translate this knowledge further. The translation was not, however, always an easy one. At the Directive I observed a 'new mood among consumers' was noted in the presentation. Following 9/11, Alice suggested that consumers were going to be 'more cautious' and 'spiritual' and 'less interested in celebrity', but this was challenged, in the question time that followed, by one of the head buyers who contended that her customers are still 'celebrity-led'. How then, she asked, was she supposed to think this through in relation to her area? Unfortunately, I did not have access to the meetings following the Directive to know how this difference of opinion was resolved. However, I do know that Alice was considered to have her proverbial 'finger on the pulse' and was well respected among the buyers and, therefore, at the very least, this knowledge was taken very seriously even if it was sometimes at odds with the buyers' experience and knowledge.

Significantly, as a carefully choreographed event, the Directive corresponds to what Thrift calls an 'inspirational' mechanism used to bring an organization together on large scale and 'keep the current of inspiration going' (Thrift 2005: 120). As Thrift also suggests, companies generate 'ideological' narratives which sustain them and these mechanisms can work together. The Fashion Office and Directive that it generated were critical components of Radice's overhauling of the entire Selfridges organization as well as its image. For one thing, the Office and Directive helped to 'inspire' and generate belief (MacKenzie 2004) among staff in the company. Much as MacKenzie describes how financial markets depend upon belief to sustain them, the success of Selfridges as a 'creative' department store depended very much on activities like this one, which generated belief in the company among the staff. The narrative of the company as a 'creative' and 'innovative' one fed a widely expressed sense, articulated in all the interviews, of Selfridges as a 'unique' department store, on a continual quest to be 'cutting-edge' and 'different'. The Fashion Office helped generate the belief among buyers and management in Selfridges's home-grown knowledge as 'instinctive' or 'intuitive'. That this narrative was a powerful one can be seen in the repeated references, across many interviews, to the company's, and their own, 'creative' and 'intuitive' ways in which they make sense of their market. These assertions are not only rhetorical, they are performative (Austin 1962), serving to reproduce and sustain a vision of the store to itself (Thrift 2005).

Thus, as a strategy for knowledge generation and circulation, the Fashion Office was important, but its real influence goes beyond the actual knowledge it created and circulated. As an 'inspirational' and 'ideological' mechanism, the Office set up by Radice was a location for generating 'creative' ideas and therefore critical to his strategy to re-work the store's flagging image. Although I did not conduct any interviews or observations with Vittorio Radice, the staff I interviewed were in no doubt as to his influence in successfully re-inventing Selfridges. His oft-noted 'charisma' and 'inspiring' management style were much in evidence, with strategies, such as the Fashion Office, key to generating new confidence and belief among staff in the store as a 'creative' and 'innovative' place to work.

'Floor Walks'

Selfridges's fashion knowledge is also distributed across other locations as well. Critically, two other important locations for knowledge are the Buying Office and shop floor itself. The boundary between these two is semi-permeable: the Buying Office opens directly onto the shop floor through disguised doors invisible to customers. Buyers move easily between the two spaces routinely in their daily work. This semi-permeable boundary is important for the flow of work, knowledge and information that inform fashion buying at the store. From strategy meetings buyers can immediately go onto the shop floor to check out how the products look, talk to the shop floor staff and observe customers. Knowledge therefore flows between Buying Office and shop floor on a regular basis, although it is routinized in terms of 'floor walks'. These take place each week, usually on Mondays, and involve the head or assistant buyer and merchandiser/s walking around their area with the dedicated floor manager and other sales staff. During these floor walks they discuss 'product'; which brands and items are selling, identifying those that are not and discussing strategies for increasing sales, possible mark downs, and the like. I did two such walks one Monday, through areas on the second and third floors and they reveal the heterogeneous nature of fashion knowledge and its multiple locations.

The first walk took place with head buyer for Casual wear, Jane, who began by introducing herself to Roberto the floor manager, who is new to the area, having just started working that week from the Designer room. They first discussed a new brand to the area, 'Happy Friday'[1] defined as a 'fashion brand' which had a gypsy feel about it (this gypsy, hippy look was fashionable that season). At first Jane said it needed moving: it was 'new and fashion led' and therefore they had to clear the stock quickly as it might not be so fashionable next season. At the moment, it was 'hidden against the back wall' and customers could not see it easily. She suggested switching this brand with another, classic brand, 'Buddha', which 'that customer will find because it is an established brand with a loyal customer who will spend the time seeking it out.' However, Roberto then said that Happy Friday, which had only just arrived in the store on Saturday, had already sold a grand. Jane's response was concern: she had only bought £25K for the month so at that rate, she thought it likely they'd run out of stock. She expressed some hope that she could re-order on this line.

Jane also talked to Roberto about brands which were not doing very well. One in particular was a very new, not established but very expensive designer. It only took in £500 last week, which isn't good as that amounts to about two items. Jane explained this in terms of this designer's little-known identity and noted that the stock cannot be moved or marked down just yet as 'He's coming over soon.' They then discussed what other brands to mark down in the area. As 'the Bollywood promotion was on, they cannot mark things down too obviously'; they can do it, but not advertise it with signage. She then talked about a brand called 'Ragamuffin' which is not doing well (a rail of this was marked down 30 per cent). She noted that she had had a problem buying this stock when, following 9/11 and the cancellation of New York Fashion Week, she had to buy it entirely on CD ROM. She complained that the technology had not allowed her to properly check the colour and quality of the fabric, which proved disappointing on arrival. She went on to note another new label 'Comfort Zone' which was fairly new to the area and, by way of a bit of gossip, described how the designer was a woman who was a bit 'edgy/neurotic'. Looking at the rails she felt it looked rather 'dull' and 'in need of some TLC'—moved around or re-organized. It cannot be marked down, she noted, as it sells mainly 'stables'—apparently, however 'dull', taupe and grey sell well 'so is never to be marked down'. All the time she was discussing these issues, Jane was looking at the clothes and handling them—picking them up to explore their sensual qualities and reminding herself of the product.

The second floor walk was in the afternoon in the denim wear and casual area with the assistant buyer, Sophie, and merchandiser for the area, Monika, and the floor manager Sandra. As with the morning floor walk, a whole range of issues came up that demonstrated the easy flow of information and knowledge between buyers, merchandisers and the retail operations side of the business as to what products are selling well, what customers seem to be liking, what they are trying on and returning, whether something needs to be moved, or whether some products are simply 'not seasonal': one sales manager asking 'Is this a summer product?' and whether the area looks 'dull' or 'messy'. One discussion concerned a 'cult' brand of jeans and how it sold well the previous week. All agreed that the warm weather over the weekend had much to do with this and it was thought that the coming weekend would also be good, weather-wise. Much of the talk concerned the re-positioning of products on the shop floor to make customers see it as new stock: products stuck behind a post or against a wall far from the main 'foot fall' (paths through the shop floor) tend not to sell so well, unless they are well known, with a 'loyal' customer base. Moved to a more prominent position the stock may be mistaken as new, since it might be the first time customers, treading well-worn routes through the store, have seen it. As Callon, Meadel et al. (2005) have suggested, the placement of products is an important component in the 'qualification' of goods and it was certainly true for Selfridges that placement of stock was frequently discussed as part of routine calculative processes of buyers, as an important strategy in generating new sales.

What these two floor walks illustrate is that fashion buying knowledge involves the heterogeneous assembly of elements to make sense of what is happening in the fashion marketplaces of the store. Different assemblages of information are made and routine practices are in place to make sense of the market: for example as noted above, collections are constantly moved to generate new interest on the floor; clothes are marked down when all else seems to be failing, unless the product is identified as a 'stable' (grey or taupe), in which case they should never be marked down; assumptions are made about particular consumers' brand loyalty and shopping practices; how clothes that are not selling one week can sell like hot cakes in warm weather, indeed, how much the weather features as an unreliable, unpredictable element in fashion sales; how the sensitivities of designers feature in whether to move or mark down; how important it is to examine the clothes themselves, to evaluate them and constantly 'test' their properties (colour, texture, cut). All these elements are gathered together to make sense and calculate what is, in effect, an effervescent reality: without a crystal ball, no one really knows what will sell by the end of this week or next. Calculations are made on the basis of a mass of information and from a flow of knowledge from various locations: the buyer, merchandiser, shop floor manager and retail staff are critical knowing locations—there is a lot of trading of knowledge between the buyers, merchandisers and shop floor managers—but so too are the clothes themselves and the shop floor layout, as observations of how these look are regularly made and form the basis of interpretations of sales and calculations of actions in response.

Retail staff provide critical feedback from the customer whom the buyer hardly ever sees: for example the casual wear sales manager, Sandra, spoke very enthusiastically and energetically about what customers were buying. It was commonly noted by retail staff and buyers how important it was to communicate knowledge about brands to the consumer/s. Thus, buyers spoke of how knowledge about a designer and the collection and how to wear it have to be conveyed to retail staff, who can then more effectively understand and communicate the brand and collection to the customer. However, knowledge flows in the other direction, from customer to buyer, again via the mediation of retail staff knowledge. Whether a collection is successful or not depends on whether it is bought and worn, therefore remaining 'close' to customers is important and depends upon regular flows of knowledge from customer to buyer in the form of weekly communication between buyers and retail staff, as well as through the more historical, statistical information generated on a monthly and seasonal basis via merchandising statistics.

Indeed, the consumers' habits and buying are routinely 'captured' and codified through various statistical instruments. An instrument, for Latour (1987: 68) is 'any set-up, no matter what its size, nature and cost, that provides a virtual display of any sort of scientific data'.

Merchandising statistics are a kind of instrument of calculation, seemingly 'scientific' in their apparent objectivity. These statistics produce a 'virtual display' of the fashion marketplace/s, condensing or contracting the effervescent flow of consumer spending week by week, month by month, into orderly, tidy figures that form the basis of other sorts of calculations, such as what to mark down in sales. Ultimately, they feed into a 'virtual display', a way of seeing and assessing the performance of particular labels/designers/brands in the store—what is selling, in what size, shape and colour, that will inform longer-term decisions about what brands to carry in the future. Such statistics are routinely discussed in monthly sales meetings attended by merchandisers, buyers, the head of department and the head of planning and finance. At such meetings, these main agents work their way through thick spreadsheets at break-neck speed, a feat made all the more impressive since the small typeface (point 9) and close text make for difficult reading. Indeed, I was barely able to follow the text and discussion at the same time, as the pace of these meetings was fast, and it was inappropriate to ask questions along the way. What I could observe was the way in which heterogeneous, seeming miscellaneous external factors, such as weather, the pattern of social events (Ascot, wedding season), and general opinions expressed by buyers as to fashion trends, played a key part in the translation of this codified data, so that tacit and codified dimensions of knowledge sit easily side-by-side. Such meetings are a formal attempt to capture, translate and respond to the perpetual motion of the fashion marketplace/s, but one that depends upon informal tacit knowledge shared amongst the team. At times, buyers and merchandisers would enter into a conversation about whether a product was 'on-trend' or not, with opinions about the merits of the collection as it looks on the shop floor shared: a collection might be described as 'dull' or 'on-trend' and its appearance on the shop floor effected 'poor delivery' or 'elements of the collection being cancelled'. In sum, the statistics provide some kind of 'window' or 'display' that is treated as objective and reliable evidence but which is always supplemented by interpretations, based upon tacit knowledge, which, in effect, 'put meat on the bones' of these bare figures. The relationship between formal, codified knowledge and informal, tacit knowledge is, therefore, close, as many (e.g. Howells 2002) have already suggested. This point I return to in Chapter 7.

The Best Laid 'Plans': Financial Planning at Selfridges

Another key element in the formal process of fashion buying that shapes the interpretations of these merchandising statistics is the financial 'plan', and this plays a critical role at merchandising meetings: indeed, it is a central tool for planning and co-ordinating fashion in the store. At face value, the plan is a sales and profit forecast, established each season, which co-ordinates the financial direction of the store—where it is going, what investments it is making in terms of estates and capital expenditure and whether to push aggressive growth or not. While decided 'on high' at senior management level, the plan works its way into the calculations of fashion buying, allocating a figure of how much profit is to be expected in each area of the department. However, here we must step back, momentarily. Such statements of business—like a financial plan—and their relationship to economic practices cannot be taken purely at face value. As Miller (Miller 2004) has demonstrated in his analysis of accountancy, tools of calculation are socially and historically constituted and by no means immutable. However, they do become the basis upon which objects are (momentarily) stabilized and hence rendered calculable. It must be acknowledged that the plan, along with the 'open to buy' (more on this in a moment) set important financial parameters within which buyers must work. Therefore, a key point about such tools is that they are *constitutive* of practice. As Callon (1998b: 23) puts it, 'Calculativeness couldn't exist without calculating tools' and accountancy. Such tools 'do not merely record a reality independent of themselves; they contribute powerfully to shaping by measuring it, the reality that they measure' (1998b: 23). Indeed, the story is more complex than this. The plan is not enacted in a straightforward way: it gets modified and re-configured as it comes into conflict with the calculations of buyers. Indeed, the financial plan traverses a complex path from formal statistical knowledge into practice, as I now want to examine.

The plan begins life over the heads of buyers, established in the planning and Finance Department meetings who, in conjunction with the Directors and Chief Executive, establish the financial projection of the company for the coming season. Since much of this planning happens at meetings to which I did not have access, I was only able to witness how the plan is put into action in very practical and pragmatic ways in the buying department. The planning decisions made at Board level depend upon perceived market conditions 'outside', such as interest rates, inflation and the like. Based on interpretations of these in terms of such things as customer confidence and projections of spending, the store will plan 'cautiously' or 'aggressively' accordingly. If market conditions mean forecasts of higher spending, the store is more likely to be 'optimistic' in its forecast and plan with higher sales and/or profit growth. Thus, the overall plan for the store might be 'to increase sales [or profit] by 10 per cent' (the profit margin is, says one head buyer, 'more important now'). This means, amongst other things, cutting costs in an area, rather than simply buying in more stock. This seemed to be the case during fieldwork: following the buy-out, the store did not replace staff who had left and instead merged buying responsibilities and budgets so that head buyers had to manage more areas than before. The overall financial plan is broken down in terms of buyerships (as discussed in Chapter 5). The planned profit increase is then distributed across the various areas, with buyerships told to increase profit by differently apportioned figures based on a range of calculations and projections of how that area was doing, last season's performance (here the merchandising statistics are important), any plans for expansion/re-fit/re-design, and the like. The plan for the area is further broken down by individual designer/ label, with a figure established for each. With this figure established, each area is allocated an 'open to buy' for the coming season. The 'open to buy' on an established, mid-range (i.e. not high end) designer label for one season might be in the region of £15,000–£30,000, while for a small, independent designer, showing at London Fashion Week, it might be as little as £5,000, which amounts to only a few, maybe just ten, individual pieces from the collection.

The plan is a blunt instrument of forecast and calculation for a number of reasons. For one thing, it is always 'signed off' too late in the season to directly feed into the 'open to buy' allocation, so merchandisers have to estimate and buyers go out with this, not the final figure. As one head buyer, Jane, put it, 'That's ... [a] problem: you almost have to wait until the horse has bolted, it's a very frustrating job in that sense'. This is just one of the many ways in which things do not 'go according to plan'. It is also the case that once the plan for an area is announced there is much discussion between buyer and merchandiser. For one thing, the figure set can prove to be 'too big' but while this can become apparent quite early—'We knew we weren't going to make the plan'—like the proverbial horse, once out of the stable, there is no stopping the plan, even when it is clear that it was the wrong figure to start with. The plan can, therefore, encumber the buyer with an unrealistic target and this has implications for how an area is perceived as a result, as discussed below.

Describing the journey of the plan into practice, Jane noted the many considerations that come into plan when buyers are presented with the figures for their area:

> So the merchandiser will come to us with a global figure, and we'll go to him with a list of tiny little figures, and we've got to get those totals to match. And all the challenges [begin] ... you know, getting more out of particular brands, discontinuing brands that he doesn't agree with, giving brands more space, getting brands up on the density [the amount of stock sold per square metre in the store], getting agreements with brands that they've seen that we've spent too much mark down [sales] on, etc. So, we will challenge him [the merchandiser] on trying to push us too hard on the figures, or not being optimistic enough on the figures, or not taking advantage of the fact that this brand is really trendy, therefore we should try and spend more, or of the fact that we need to spend more up front because we can't get re-orders and things.

In other words, numerous other factors come into play and a dialogue between buyer and merchandiser begins that sees the figure challenged and the calculations of what to buy multiply. In response to a plan that says, 'Increase sales of last year by 5 per cent', the buying team may come back with a whole series of considerations, as Jane continues to describe:

The buyer may say, "Well, I want to re-furbish my area". So you think, "Okay, I'm going to have to make a lot more money, then because we're going to have to pay for the re-furbishment". Or they might say, "I've got a completely new product strategy. I'm going to get rid of all my big money-spinners, and I want to bring lots of new things in, and that's going to cause a bit of risk for about two seasons", so then they'll plan low.

In other words, the simple message of the plan is made more complex once buyers' calculations for their area come into play. The contest will be fought out between buyer and merchandiser in the area. The distinction between buyers and merchandisers is significant for understanding the roles and activities of buying. While merchandisers are responsible for overseeing financial planning in an area and work closely with statistical information, buyers see beyond the statistics and bring a welter of knowledge and information as to what they see happening in their market and in their area. Although the roles and activities merge at times, essentially buyers do the selecting and buying of commodities—going on buying trips and placing orders—while merchandisers tend to stay in the office and co-ordinate the forecasting, arrival, sale and mark-down of commodities, as well as managing the merchandising statistics that track all of this. Jane defined the difference in embodied terms, between 'thinking' and 'feeling': 'A lot of that is our knowledge and it's in our heads, and then ... from the merchandisers' point of view, it's very much geared around formulas, you know, rules, regulations, just basically retailing rules—maths. And so they're the *thinking*, if you like, and we're the *feeling* side' (emphasis added).

'Thinking' and 'feeling' relate to the particular sorts of knowledge—formal and informal or tacit knowledge—with merchandisers responsible for the former and buyers the latter. Merchandisers similarly see their knowledge as being more general and about formulas than intimate market knowledge: one senior merchandiser, described her knowledge as 'more objective'. So, while she feels she needs to understand fashion to understand what the buyers are telling her about new brands, she does not need the same level of intimate knowledge about fashion that buyers need to select on the market. The challenge is to how to marry the two—'thinking' and 'feeling'—so that the store can 'make plan'. This can be put another way: as with model agencies, there is a constant balancing act between the commercial imperatives and the characteristics of the high fashion markets recognized by actors to be high-risk markets. In designer clothing, this is especially risky, because season on season products can vary enormously and collections from designers can do well or they can fail. The Financial Planning Manager Sharon, who is in charge of setting the plan and directly in line managing the merchandisers, described the challenge for the store as follows:

The way it works here, because it's such a *high fashion business* ... I can have a view, I can say, "Well, financially, this is what this brand did, this is what you should be buying next season". But they [the buyers] go and see it next season, it's either a wonderful collection or it's an awful collection. So the Buying Manager and the Senior Merchandiser are responsible for the total amount we sign off for the group, you know, "We said you could spend £10m for that group", if they spend more than that, that's a problem ... or a lot less, that's a problem. But within that, they are expected and allowed to react on the market. (Sharon, senior merchandiser, emphasis added)

As she describes it, the high degree of unpredictability makes objective planning very difficult. Some designers may show a 'weak' collection that a buyer calculates will not sell very well. For this reason, it is imperative that the buyers have autonomy to make calculations when 'out on the market' and confronted with collections. So long as the figures are not way out 'a lot more ... or less' than the 'open to buy' figure, buyers are given the freedom to respond as they see fit. Senior merchandiser Sharon, put it as follows, 'I need the buyers to have that flexibility. Our auditors find it quite scary, actually, you know, when I try to explain this process to them!' This flexibility is expressed in the contingency built into the budget. So she will say to buyers:

> "You've got to spend 80 per cent of your money, and you've got to spend it on any of these brands ... but actually, here's half a million, go and do whatever you want with it ... to make your Department look interesting", because there's no doubt about it, part of Selfridge's success is always looking new and interesting. So *I can't plan for that,* I just have to give them the freedom to be able to do it when they're out there, because they don't see it till they're on the markets. (Sharon, senior merchandiser, emphasis added)

Senior merchandisers and the head of department all felt it important that buyers use their own judgement when 'out' on the market—on buying trips. Thus, while some portions of spending are relatively stable—big labels with their own branded space on the shop floor have to be bought in pretty consistent numbers as the area needs filling with products—beyond this constraint, buyers are told to respond when out on buys. This element of contingency built into the 'open to buy' puts the onus on the calculative abilities of buyers to respond flexibly to the products they encounter. 'Feeling' as opposed to 'thinking' is therefore recognized as an important aspect in the buying process. Indeed, as I shall argue in Chapter 7, 'feeling' may be an embodied way of 'thinking' in a market where some of the qualities of products are intangible and demand an embodied sense and sensibility—or tacit aesthetic knowledge—to be calculated. Suffice it to say here, while mathematical calculations play their part in the planning of fashion buying, the calculative abilities of buyers cannot always be rendered mathematically as they can diverge from the figures set down. The 'best-laid plans' cannot possibly capture the fashion market as it is experienced and captured by buyers.

The plan does, however, perform in more ways than one as the tool by which, ultimately, an area is evaluated as succeeding or failing. However much buyers try to shape it, they have, ultimately, to try to 'make plan'. The performative qualities of the plan are best examined by looking at what happened the previous season in the denim area of the Casual wear buyership. As noted in the previous chapter, the 'denim room' had been re-furbished about two years before the fieldwork so that all the designers or brands selling denim products—jeans and related 'casual' items like T-shirts—where positioned together. Its hip, street-wise 'vibe' was re-inforced by the loud beats of house and hip hop music regularly played on the shop floor. The re-fit had already shown itself to be a big success in terms of a high volume of sales for the previous seasons. However, as noted, the re-fit coincided with denim being 'on trend'. The combined effect of the re-fit and the denim trend resulted in the area being planned 'aggressively' for large profits in subsequent seasons. Jane, head buyer for Casual wear, summarized the reasons for a particular aggressive plan that season as two-fold: 'Because of the cap-ex [capital expenditure], because we had this new re-fit in the denim area, we had to pay for that. But also, because of this big denim trend, the business is expecting denim to carry on doing very, very well.' However, as she went on, this trend 'has got to plateau at some stage, and it's happening now'. With the previous season's figures driving an aggressive plan the effect has therefore been that during the season observed the area was seen to be performing badly: 'If we hadn't been so aggressive ... the figures wouldn't be so bad.' Conversely, she notes, 'In the contemporary designer areas, because they've done so badly previously, and had very low plans, they're doing moderately well.' That is, they have exceeded their plan. When asked to describe the impact of not 'making plan', she noted how:

> It totally demoralises you, it means that you don't get *your* bonuses, it means that the directors' level and the senior management level are looking at your Department and saying, "They are failing in their jobs. Why aren't they coming up with the goods? What's wrong here?" I think it's time for maybe us to cut some slack and give it to somebody else, you know, and next season we'll go very, very small on everything. We'll go flat, or even less. (emphasis added)

That accountancy and management tools 'influence agents' behaviour' (Callon 1998b: 24) is apparent in the role played by the plan in shaping a view of each area in the store. The plan is performative, since it generates a picture of how an area is doing, shaping perceptions of how 'well' or 'badly' an area—and the buyer—is doing which have a real knock on effect. Calculative tools, such as accountancy tools, are, Miller (2004: 180) argues, a 'Technology of government, one of the principal achievements of management accounting is to link together responsibility and calculation to create the responsible and calculating individual.' Such tools enrol actors 'in pursuit of prescribed and often standardized targets ... exacting responsibility from individuals rendered calculable and comparable' (2004: 180). Thus, buyers know they are assessed according to whether they 'make plan' and, while the plan plays heavily in their calculations of what to do in their area—how much to spend, how much risk to carry in terms of other developments (buying new designers, re-furbishing their area, etc.)—they can and do try to modify it through various means so as to reduce its impact. They may challenge the figure given, re-define some of the smaller figures within it, even try to circumvent it altogether by off-setting the risk of a bad plan with alternative tactics—'We'll plan flat'. It seems, in fashion, things 'never go according to plan'.

Conclusion

In contrast to accounts that attempt to define knowledge in terms of particular prop-erties, attributes and locations, I have suggested that fashion knowledge does not have fixed sites or properties, but is dispersed, taking multiple and mutable forms. Through such things as the layout and organization of the office, the embodied style of buyers, statistical tools, regular floor walks and meetings between buyers and mer-chandisers, knowledge about fashion is assembled, circulated, used and performed. Attempts to frame this knowledge formally come in the shape of various tools of calculation, such as the plan, merchandising statistics and 'open to buy'. Formal knowledge, for example merchandising statistics and planning figures, are, however, always rendered into practice in complex ways, translated and may be challenged. Partly this is because such tools are, by definition, imperfect attempts to calculate, since tools of calculation can never perfectly render 'reality' or indeed the 'future', and partly because, in an organization such as Selfridges, which thrives on its 'com-munity of practice' (Wenger 1998), practice is always about creatively sense-making. In this self-consciously 'knowledge-intensive' company, there is much at stake in 'feeling' as well as 'thinking' about the marketplace, something which depends upon the blending of codified knowledge and tacit knowledge. There has, of course, been an acknowledgement in some of the literature on tacit knowledge that codified knowl-edge depends upon tacit knowledge in its interpretation and tacit knowledge de-pends on some form of codification (see for example Howells 2004). However, this literature tends to get bogged down in defining tacit knowledge against its more formal kind, and, as a consequence, tends to maintain a clear distinction between them. Following knowledge-in-use provides one way out of this rather tired debate, as it involves seeing what kinds of knowledge are assembled, seeing heterogeneous combinations of knowledge that make fuzzy the conventional definitions and de-marcations. I remain committed to this approach, even while, in the next chapter, I set about understanding in more detail tacit knowledge in fashion, explicating, in particular, its embodied dimensions.

–7–

Tacit Aesthetic Knowledge: The Fashion Sense and Sensibility of Fashion Buyers

What is fashion knowledge and how can we understand how it circulates? According to Weller (2007: 42),'Fashion knowledge is commonly understood as an aesthetic knowledge, and as an unstable and constantly changing form of knowledge that promotes incessant change without progress'. It is a viscous knowledge that 'depends upon the fortuitous intersection of multiple and variably mobile dimensions, only some of which are embedded in organisations' (41). Moreover, it is spatially complex, in ways that defy the simple codified–tacit binary that is often mapped onto the global/local. Starting from the idea of tacit knowledge as an embodied knowledge and one that is spatially distributed, I challenge conventional thinking on tacit knowledge which is both silent on the issue of embodiment, and assumes a simple mapping of tacit onto the local. In this chapter, I argue that much of the knowledge needed to calculate fashion is tacit in nature but this knowledge is globally mobile. That is to say, tacit aesthetic knowledge in fashion is an embodied knowledge; worn on the body of those who calculate it and 'travelling' with them along global networks.

That fashion's tacit aesthetic knowledge is embodied through style is not surprising: here we have a market concerned *with*, and orientated *towards*, bodies. The ability to intuit what Blumer (1969) refers to as an 'incipient taste', that is, the burgeoning tastes of the day, depends upon informal understandings and the intangible ability to put one's 'finger on the pulse'. Thus, fashion knowledge exceeds formal mechanisms and devices, which are undoubtedly used to track and monitor sales, and is no less valued for that. Indeed, buyers refer to their knowledge in terms of nebulous and less clearly codified systems: 'feeling' working alongside 'thinking'. The feelingful capacities of fashion buyers—what I call *tacit aesthetic knowledge*—allow me to build on some of Allen's (2000, 2002a,b) arguments as to the necessity of expanding our definitions of knowledge beyond the purely cognitive and rational, as well as current thinking about tacit knowledge, which ignores its embodied dimensions. As I shall argue, tacit aesthetic knowledge is both *embodied and expressive* and to understand these qualities I also turn to Bourdieu (1984) and his concepts of habitus and taste.

The body is a knowing location; that is, a site for the enactment and distribution of knowledge. Ultimately, all knowledge is embodied since all markets are constituted out of embodied agents; as MacKenzie (2004), for example has shown, the stock market knowledge is enacted through such things as hand signals and even dress. However, embodiment only surfaces occasionally and incidentally in literature on knowledge and markets, and is, therefore, left largely implicit and unexamined. Since fashion is so evidently a market concerned *with* and orientated *towards* bodies and bodily appearance, analysis of it enables an explicit acknowledgement of the ways in which knowledge is embodied that might be suggestive to other scholars in economic sociology and business and knowledge management literature.

I begin in Defining Tacit Knowledge by summarizing the current debate on economic knowledge, especially the codified/tacit distinction that has been a major preoccupation in so much of the literature. I also define tacit aesthetic knowledge as expressive and embodied knowledge. Since much debate about tacit knowledge argues that it is spatially situated in localities and has difficulty 'travelling', I take up the spatial dimensions of this knowledge in Spatializing Fashion Knowledge, to argue that fashion knowledge is both *locally situated* and *globally circulating*.

Defining Tacit Knowledge

The codified/tacit dichotomy has been a major concern in the literature on knowledge and is closely associated with Michael Polanyi (1967). The distinction between them comes down to 'the degree of formalization' 'and the requirement of presence in knowledge formation' (Howells 2002). Codified knowledge is said to exist in formal language and system (in documents, papers, patents and other materials that circulate within firms). As we have seen in the previous chapter, such knowledge at Selfridges takes the form of merchandising spreadsheets and formal buying plans. On the other hand, tacit knowledge refers to 'direct experience that is not codifiable via artefacts' (Howells 2002: 872). However, this distinction is problematic too. Howells argues that Polanyi's ideas about knowledge have been misunderstood and misrepresented, not least, 'the crude bi-polar dichotomy that is drawn between tacit and codified knowledge' (2002: 872; see also Amin and Cohendet 2004). Instead of seeing them as radically different forms of knowledge, Polanyi sees them existing on a continuum and both are combined in complex ways so that the interpretation of formal knowledge is always dependent upon tacit know-how, while tacit know-how often utilizes codified knowledge. As should be apparent from the discussion in the previous chapter, where I argue that knowledge flows are heterogeneous, Selfridges's knowledge of fashion depends upon the combining of formal and tacit knowledge. So, although I focus on the latter here, I recognize that knowledge is not readily broken down into purely formal/codified and purely informal/tacit.

Having said that, there are particular qualities to tacit knowledge that can be described, albeit rather inadequately, since so much of what constitutes tacit knowledge is, by definition, uncodified and therefore not easily rendered into words. Critically, tacit aesthetic knowledge is an *embodied* knowledge. This is implied but not explored in Allen's (2000) argument, as it is in much of the literature on tacit knowledge. Swart and Kinnie (2003: 63) for example define tacit knowledge as 'a form of knowledge that cannot be explicated and that is *embodied through practice*' (emphasis added), while, similarly, Von Krogh, Nonaka et al. (2000: 6) define tacit knowledge as 'tied to the senses, skills in *bodily movement*, individual perception, physical experiences, rules of thumb and intuition'. For Malecki (2000: 108) tacit knowledge involves an interplay between individual and shared social experiences. He refers to tacit knowledge as 'Privately-held knowledge and shared experience ... Generally, tacit knowledge is *embodied* in people, rather than in written form or in objects' (emphasis added). However, the embodied dimensions of tacit knowledge are not explored further. That embodiment is repressed in much of the literature is all too evident: for example while Howells (2002: 872) defines tacit knowledge as 'direct experience' he immediately goes on to say that 'it represents *disembodied* know-how' (872, emphasis added), which would seem strangely at odds with his definitions of knowledge as derived from 'experience' and the 'knowing self'. Further, while cognition is itself embodied, this fact tends to be repressed or sublimated as 'transcendent rationality', a strange sublimation as recognition is given to the importance of 'being-there' (Gertler 2003) in accounts of tacit knowledge, which implies the embodied presence and practices of workers.

Significantly, embodiment features in accounts that actors in aesthetic markets give of their practice, as well as the practices that define their work: agents say they have to be 'in touch' with, or 'have an eye', for burgeoning tastes not yet fully articulated or evident. When asked to describe how they identify someone with model potential, bookers could only offer 'gut feeling' and their 'eye' as possible explanations (Entwistle 2002). These references to bodily senses and sensibilities are telling not only of the sort of knowledge valued inside these aesthetic markets; they hint at the difficulties actors have in formally capturing their knowledge. This difficulty cannot be easily overcome in the academic account I offer here: tacit aesthetic knowledge evades capture and is hard to formulate into words. For this reason, much of my account centres on describing the scenes observed in an attempt to conjure up something of the aesthetic sensibilities of this world.

Defining Tacit Aesthetic Knowledge

'Expressive' Ways of Knowing. In his critique of reductive definitions of economic knowledge, Allen (2000) provides the basis for a systematic analysis of aesthetic knowledge. As discussed in the previous chapter, the traditional view of knowledge tends towards seeing it in terms of particular sorts of attributes and activities, mainly the valuing of the cognitive, which, in turn, make it appear 'true' and reinforce the idea of knowledge as cognitive. That this becomes 'truth' is all the more the case when one

considers 'that a broad sense of economic knowledge, one which encompasses the *ex-pressive* as well as the analytical, is hard to sustain, given the propensity to formalise, codify innovation and creativity' (Allen 2000: 19, emphasis added). Thus, 'activities which do not fit easily into a schema of abstract symbolism are not immediately considered as part of the driving force of a knowledge-based economy' (19).

Drawing on the work of philosopher Ernst Cassirer (1874–1945) Allen argues for an expanded definition of knowledge that involves the symbolic means by which one comes to know the world. It is worth revisiting some of Cassirer's discussion (Cassirer 1946, 1957, 1979). In his philosophy of knowledge, Cassirer (1979) describes three increasingly abstract, formal language systems we use to understand the world; these are expression, representation and signification. The latter two relate to the realms of language and formal abstract reasoning, both of which demand increasing degrees of abstraction from the world, language being non-representational and abstract knowledge like physics moving even further beyond representation to generate systems and notations. Expressive meaning 'is related directly to *sense perception* and *bodily awareness*' (Allen 2000, emphasis added) and an equally valid way to encounter and know the world even if it 'cannot be readily measured by any cognitive yardstick' (21). As Cassirer (1979: 154) himself puts it, in formal language systems '[Man] [*sic*] loses his immediate experience, his concepts of experience of life fade away ... what remains is a world of intellectual symbols; not a world of immediate experience.' He goes on to note that 'If this immediate, intuitive approach to reality is to be preserved and to be regained, it needs a new activity ... It is not by language *but by art* that this is to be performed' (154, emphasis added). This is not to say that the world of art is a world merely of immediate sensory experiences and emotions. What distinguishes the artist is the ability to translate common, empirical experience and imagination, emotions and dreams into 'a new sphere—the sphere of the plastic, architectural, musical forms, of shapes and designs, of melodies and rhythms' (157). That is, the artistic work is capable of translating our sense-experience and constructing expression that is governed by 'the power of forms' (158) so that 'the horizon of our sense-experience [is] enlarged ... our perspective changed' (160). In other words, the aesthetic experience and aesthetic ways of knowing are about sensory *forms*: 'Art is not reproduction of impression, it is creation of forms. These forms are not abstract, but sensuous' (186). In this way, Cassirer emphasizes the formal qualities of aesthetic expression and insists that these are an important way of encountering and knowing the world, not reducible to codified language but no less valid. Allen develops Cassirer's argument to suggest how accounts of economic knowledge could include knowledge that is 'expressive'. I want to demonstrate this empirically through analysis of fashion buyers' knowledge which is both expressive and embodied in non-cognitive sense and sensibilities.

While fashion is not a pure art form, like poetry or painting, it is a form of aesthetic expression. Thus, while lacking the same status as art, fashion is an aesthetic practice even if that aesthetic is less about lofty ideals of 'beauty' but driven by fluctuating attributes bestowed on certain styles of clothing. Cassirer's point about aesthetic forms is relevant here: fashion has its own formal mechanisms of expression—its own lines and contours—even while these are continually reinterpreted or fluctuating. This aesthetic expression, as the ability to translate sensory experience, can be extended to understand something of the ways of encountering and knowing central to fashion buying and provide the basis for a more expansive definition of economic knowledge. That expressive ways of knowing in fashion are linked closely to 'sense perception and bodily awareness' is evident in the ways in which buyers encounter the clothing they buy. Let me demonstrate this by describing some of the ways in which buyers encounter garments prior to selection.

At routine fashion buys, bodily sense-perception comes into play in the interpretation of clothes on display. 'Fit' models are often employed in studios to enable buyers to see how garments fit and move on the body. Even though fit models do not talk, but walk around the studio like living mannequins (Evans 2005), they may be asked about the clothes—what they feel like and how they fit. I was put in a similar position on a couple of buys with the denim buyer (in New York and London) when she asked me to try on the clothes and give an opinion on their fit and tactile qualities. The denim buyer also tried on various items at times. She described denim as being 'all about fit'—often the focus is on the whether the jeans sit well on the hips and slim and lift the buttocks. It is therefore not surprising that the qualities of denim are thus 'tested' on the body (Callon, Meadel et al. 2005). As I have discussed elsewhere (Entwistle 2006) and in Chapter 8, testing involves examining the sensual and tactile dimensions of clothing—touching the fabric is equally important—and explains why fashion buys are still conducted by being present with the garments. When clothes are bought unseen—as was the case with one buy bought on CD ROM after 9/11 (when New York Fashion Week was cancelled)—the buyer complained that the entire collection was poor and most of it went on sale at the end of the season. Given the importance of sensual testing, it is understandable that the fashion buy involves direct contact with the clothes themselves. According to the buyers, no amount of new technology—Internet or CD ROM—will entirely replace the 'being-there' of the fashion buy, where such things as the quality of fabric and fit are critical.

There are other ways in which sense experiences feature as part of buyers' work. Take the experience of watching a fashion show: fashion buyers attend many such shows over the year, the most important ones being the bi-annual prêt-a-porter collections held in the major fashion cities every January/February and September/October. The fashion show prioritizes the sensory and aesthetic over the purely cognitive or rational. Rather than a direct sales pitch or a cost-effective means of displaying clothes, shows actually make a loss for the designers (Entwistle and Rocamora 2006) and involve what Cassirer and Allen would call 'expressive' meanings and an extended realm of sensory perception. Take, for example how Natalie, Head of Fashion Office, described fashion shows: 'There has to be an element of entertainment, show, theatre, that's what catwalk is. It is to showcase something new or spectacular, or with real content and substance. And sometimes shows don't have that, and there's got to be drama. Drama can be in the clothes.'

The good show is dramatic—an aesthetic event or experience—that renders an aesthetic environment for the clothes. The best fashion shows, as illustrated in the quote above, stimulate the senses and create a spectacle. The drama opens when the first model, usually the most famous model in the show, steps out onto the catwalk and begins her long walk towards the photographers' 'pit' at the very end. Music may be frenzied and loud, as at Vivienne Westwood's show in Paris September 2002, or quiet and ambient, as with John Rocha's show. Often the experience is one of heightened sexuality: as they stride their way down the catwalk, models are subject to the cries of frenzied photographers whose flashbulbs pulsate to generate an electrifying heat and light. The colours, lights, music and models create a theatrical environment or spectacle wherein the clothes are displayed. Here, the show would seem to generate things that are outside of normal cognitive processes involved in markets and difficult to gauge within the narrow confines of economic rationality: 'images, senses, emotions, words, sensualities appear difficult to gauge in economic terms and, when evaluated commonsensically, tend to be by abstract criteria from outside. Non-cognitive activities are recognised less for what they are and more for how they may be reproduced or replicated instrumentally' (Allen 2000: 19).

That shows are not a direct means of selling garments is evidenced in the fact that buyers make their selections in studios before and after the shows and, indeed, hardly need to attend them. What shows offer is something quite different from the display of clothes in the studio, which is often in the form of a very dull presentation by a representative on behalf of the designer (Entwistle 2006). Shows are promotional events, serving to promote the designer and the brand/label, but the event itself is also much more than this: a show attempts to weave meanings and associations around the clothes, albeit ambiguous ones. According to the buyers, shows help them contextualize or make sense of the individual items and the designer's 'vision' for the collection, since shows are often organized in terms of a 'concept' or theme for the season that is then carried through to the shop floor. Indeed, part of the work buyers do is train shop-floor staff in how to understand the collections and, in doing this, they draw on a range of knowledge based on experiences, such as shows, which they try to transmit to staff who sell directly to customers. That something gets lost in the transmission of such tacit, embodied knowledge is inevitable. One buyer in particular expressed her exasperation with the shop-floor staff and how difficult it can be to get them to communicate the clothes to customers, noting that she would do a far more effective job of selling the clothes herself!

The expressive qualities of the show require the experienced eye of the market agent to be fully comprehended and translated. The speed of the models sashaying down the catwalk and the often extreme styles of dress displayed make the fashion show an overwhelming sensory experience and one not readily readable to an outsider. Indeed, as an observer I was often left bewildered by what I saw on the runway and incapable of recognizing with any confidence what trends, colours, shapes of trouser and skirt would be picked up as the style for next season. In other words, I could see no regular pattern or theme. My ineptitude was always thrown into sharp relief by the buyers who could instantly make sense of shows. For example, when asked about the trends she saw emerging on the catwalks in September 2002, immediately following a show at London Fashion Week, the head buyer for Contemporary wear, Maria could, in a moment, isolate some key elements. Far from the sensory overload I experienced she could identify different features: starting with colour, she noted,

> Lots of different ones, metallic and silks, whites, black. Bronzy colours, khakis on bottoms, on tops it is very pretty, glammed up. The utility look is glammed up, not the minimal utility look that was around. Lots of detail, rather than paired down utility. There will be some denim, but mixed in. By the time we get there, 03, some of us will be tired of this look and will be wearing our jeans again. At this end of the market, already you feel like, it starts changing, it's very fast.

Where I saw a seemingly random stream of aesthetic styles, this fashion buyer saw specific colours, patterns and forms. From the selection of the colours for next season, to the summing up of the look ('glammed up utility') the buyer quickly interpreted the show and could make her selections with confidence as a result. Accounting for her knowledge is important in terms of understanding the work of fashion buyers, but it is by no means easy to analyse what is going on here. Indeed, since tacit knowledge is, by definition, difficult to put into words, it rather escapes the buyers themselves and they struggled to give account of it.

Embodied Ways of Knowing.   If the essentially embodied nature of this knowledge is difficult to capture, the work of Bourdieu and his concept of the habitus offer some suggestive possibilities. As Reed-Danahay (2005) notes, this term is first most systematically articulated in *Outline of a Theory of Practice* (Bourdieu 1977), although she suggests it has its origins in earlier anthropological work. In a much-cited paragraph, *habitus* refers to, 'systems of durable, transposable dispositions, structured structures predisposed to function as structuring structures, that is, as principles of the generation and structuring of practices and representations ... objectively adapted to their goals without presupposing a conscious aiming at ends or an express mastery of the operations necessary to attain them' (Bourdieu 1990: 53).

In other words, as a deeply inculcated bodily disposition, the habitus structures ways of being and doing. Habitus expresses Bourdieu's concern to overcome the subjectivist/objectivist dichotomy, since he emphasizes both agents' practice and the structuring principles that generate it. Bourdieu compares the relationship between habitus and field as between 'incorporated history and objectified history' (1990: 66). In other words, as Reed-Danahay (2005: 134) puts it, 'It was in a field, he suggested, that social agents utilize the "feel for the game" or practical sense' and thus come to inculcate and embody objective field values. Although Bourdieu did not refer to tacit knowledge explicitly, 'feel for the game' refers to tacit understandings that are unconscious and embodied in everyday ways of doing things within particular social settings. Habitus can therefore be employed to consider the embodiment of tacit knowledge in historical time and social space. While habitus in Bourdieu's analysis generally emphasizes social class, specifically how class habitus structures particular tastes through family and education, the fashion habitus and taste dispositions I describe are acquired through experiences as an adult, and have no specific class associations. If fashion buyers share any class position, it is as a faction of the petite bourgeoisie who work as 'cultural intermediaries', as discussed in Chapter 1.

Some have argued (Herzfeld 2004) that habitus may not provide the final 'solution' to the either/or of structure/agency, because Bourdieu's model 'suffers from a significant weakness ... He fails to recognise the power of individual agency to overcome the imperatives of ... inculcated habits' (Herzfeld 2004: 38). I would concur with this view that his model is weighted more towards structure than agency, to the point of being too deterministic. This problem has its roots in Bourdieu's rather mechanistic definition of the 'social' and his tendency to focus on theoretical articulation of 'field', within which habitus is situated, rather than empirical application. However, while Bourdieu's own field analysis is flawed, as it becomes divorced from actual fields of practice, as argued in Chapter 2, the concept of habitus can be employed to examine embodied agents and their abilities to do things, specifically, the ways in which bodies come to acquire tastes or 'dispositions'.

The Habitus and Embodied Aesthetic Knowledge.   To be a successful fashion buyer one has to acquire the appropriate fashion habitus, which is a collective disposition. Indeed, habitus is a useful concept for elaborating on Blumer's (1969) idea of 'collective selection' within the fashion world and his concept of 'incipient taste'. The fluctuating aesthetics of high fashion are the product of historical realities and encounters, captured by the idea of fashion organized in 'seasons' and these constitute some of the objectified conditions shaping the fashion habitus. The habitus thus arises out of historical experience but orientates agents towards present and possible future courses of action. As Bourdieu (1990) notes: 'The habitus—embodied history, internalized as a second nature and so forgotten as history—is the active presence of the whole past of which it is the product. As such it gives practices their relative autonomy with respect to external determinations of the immediate present ... The habitus is a spontaneity without consciousness or will' (56).

Indeed, buyers' temporal sense structures their ways of working in pre-reflexive ways. Historical memory is referenced when buyers talk about 'last season' or a 'season or two ago' and this sense-making combines both codified forms of knowledge and rational calculation—merchandising statistics, for example—with agents' 'feel for the game' of fashion into a deeply internalized, pre-reflexive temporal flow of knowledge. This temporal sense orientates agents with regard to present and future courses of action: 'Dispositions guide the actions of social agents through future-orientated perceptions of change for success or failure' (Reed-Danahay 2005: 109). Thus, buyers make temporal sense of designers' collections, fashion shows, garments on display in studios, etc. placing them into some kind of relationship in terms of what styles were in vogue last season, last year, which, in turn, helps them to locate possible future trends. When a trend appears to be 'peaking next season' the buyer may calculate the next trend will react against it or modify it in a new direction but there is nothing rational about making a calculation one way or another; it comes from a 'feel' for what may happen that is only derived through immersion in the fashion flow. Buyers are caught within this flow which affords them 'spontaneity without consciousness or will' and thus the ability to organize, systematically, the flux of products that to an outsider, such as myself, appear disconnected, random and often incomprehensible.

The temporal, sense-making capacities of the habitus would seem to flesh out Blumer's idea of 'collective selection' and the similarities of selections made by fashion insiders each season, as well as the 'incipient taste' they would appear to translate. Blumer suggests that fashion insiders are well positioned to create the trend they appear to spot, although he does not elaborate on this. However, it is evidenced in other markets as well: financial traders, thinking they've spotted a trend, can create it through their very actions by investing it with their belief (MacKenzie 2004). Similarly, fashion insiders become orientated towards an imagined 'future' ('next season') that becomes a reality by their own activities of selecting over fashion week collections. The performative nature of belief, as MacKenzie describes it, is similar to what Bourdieu (1993a) refers to as the 'circle of belief' within art and fashion markets, whereby critics produce the status of artists through their statements of value. By celebrating, selecting and buying particular designers' work, the fashion system supports the very tastes and trends it says will be 'next season'.

Thus, 'collective selection' is the outcome of a shared history amongst the key players in the fashion world that is temporally and also spatially rendered. 'Incipient taste' can be seen as more than arbitrary futurology, derived out of a *situated* and embodied sense and sensibility. This ability to select is beyond the purely cognitive, even while buyers—like the one quoted at London Fashion Week above—can, for the purposes of the interview, rationally order the flow of garments on the runway into discernable trends for next season. In other words, while this knowledge can be post-rationalized in a reflexive encounter like an interview (or possibly in discussions with merchandisers, or team meetings) one could not arrive at the confident statement of the Contemporary wear buyer, as to what styles or trends a designer is presenting, by conscious rationality alone. Instrumental rationality assumes a totally conscious and rational subject is at work, and yet, I suggest that fashion buyers' work involves sensibilities, orientations and ways of seeing that emerge out of deeply internalized knowledge. Selections are arrived at which are based on deeply incul-cated, embodied sensibilities. This is particularly evident in how buyers approach the most solid form of information available to them, namely, the merchandising statistics. According to all the buyers, these will only take you so far. Arriving at a buy Lisa, the buyer for Contemporary wear, noted how,

> You have to do your homework, you have to know what has sold and have that knowl-edge in your mind but then *you can't buy by numbers*, you can't buy exactly what you bought the season before, not at this level of the market. You have to use that info to decide what to buy, keep hold of it but try to make things look different. *So you use that knowledge differently* every season, and you can't have the same *mind set* every season. (emphasis added)

If one can't 'buy by numbers', i.e. if you cannot base your knowledge of what to buy this season on last season's figures but must have a different 'mind set' each season, this is because fashion knowledge exceeds the formal, consciously available knowledge. This is also captured, albeit obliquely, in the following long quote from the head buyer for Contemporary wear. When trying to describe how she buys, and how she has become 'confident' in what she buys, she contrasts the 'fashiony' buy—where things change rapidly—with a buy 'where things look exactly the same':

> Take the example of Prada sport. When you go to that appointment, it is difficult. It is very technical, the differences, nuances very difficult to see. I almost find it easier when the differences are glaringly different, easier to pick. When you go to Prada sport, you have to look at what does sell, there's a certain amount of repetition. But you really have to understand what the nuances are. You also need to look for some kind of newness as well, the customer is quite loyal and they know that Prada is going to do x y z and that's why they spend a certain amount of money. When you look at something much more fashiony it jumps out at you, but then you have to decide what maybe crosses the line, what isn't acceptable and what is going to sell and how you're going to mix it for your particular market. I think over time you get more confident ... and experienced to make things look different one season after the next. And it does become easier. And confi-dence is everything in buying. (Lisa, head buyer for Contemporary wear)

In this quote it is evident that 'confidence' in fashion buying comes from experi-ence and historical memory, both the sorts of things that sold in the past and the sort of customer for that particular label. This comes only from merchandising statis-tics and is also forged out of 'being there' in the market, encountering the products themselves. Tacit and codified knowledge are combined: one cannot buy without the historical knowledge of previous sales but figures alone are not enough, as it takes tacit knowledge to understand products encountered and make sense of the statistics in order to calculate the possible future. Choo and Bontis (2002: 12) argue that the division between tacit and codified knowledge is often too starkly emphasized:

We need to remind ourselves that the two are not only complementary to each other, but are in many ways interdependent ... the exercise of tacit knowledge typically makes references to plans or blueprints, entails the handling of tools and equipment, and involves following written or oral instructions, all of which embody various kinds of explicit knowledge. Conversely, the application of explicit knowledge often requires individuals who can interpret, elaborate, demonstrate, or instantiate the formal knowledge with respect to a particular problem setting.

Indeed, Howells suggests that not only is all knowledge tacit in nature, but makes an important point about the knowledge cycle: often what starts out tacit becomes increasingly codified, thus making the rigid distinction between codified and tacit knowledge rather more difficult to maintain. One other way of putting this is to see knowledge in action or in *process,* and examine the specificities of practice, rather than seeing knowledge as a fixed or finite property or object.

To conclude, tacit aesthetic knowledge is an *expressive* and *embodied* knowledge derived out of a historical and collective disposition, or fashion habitus. This habitus is acquired through extended contact with the high fashion market; through a shared professional position, shared spaces of interaction and regular, routinized encounters in the fashion world. This fashion habitus is shared across markets in high fashion. This explains similarities of body and dress in both the model agencies and Selfridges, and how the dispositions, tastes and aesthetic sensibilities of modelling appear to meet the requirements of those designing high fashion clothing. To those 'outsiders', not sharing this habitus, these styles may be difficult to interpret or seem ugly or esoteric. Indeed, my own inability to make sense of fashion shows and spot future trends, and trends in male models (Entwistle 2002), is some evidence of this, as described in Chapter 3. This embodied sense-making is important but little acknowledged as a dimension of market knowledge.

Thus, the body is an important location of knowledge—one wears the knowledge—and it is to the spatial dimensions of tacit aesthetic knowledge which I now turn to in the second section of this chapter.

Spatializing Fashion Knowledge

Fashion knowledge is not only temporally organized; it is also spatially located. Fashion knowledge is located and distributed across particular cities; circulating around the key fashion cities where the regular bi-annual fashion shows or 'fashion weeks' take place and bring together the important designers, buyers and journalists, as well as models, photographers, stylists and influential celebrities under one roof. However, although shows are widely transmitted by the world's press, fashion week is a relatively closed event, not generally open to the public. This creates field closure or boundaries that have implications for the circulation of fashion knowledge (Entwistle and Rocamora 2006). The bi-annual fashion week collections and other industry events like Premier Vision in Paris are important to the regular, routinized flow of fashion knowledge. The performative nature of fashion week is analysed by Entwistle and Rocamora (2006), where fashion week 'shows' are analysed as an important mechanism for the social reproduction of the field of fashion, enabling the field to materialize to itself and, in doing so, legitimate itself and the players who move within it. However, the local materialization of the fashion field during fashion week also serves to *perform* fashion as a global phenomenon, reproducing the world of high fashion as an encounter between global workers, brands, cities. These events are orchestrated with the express aim of bringing the global community of fashion together. Thus, critical to understanding the expressive and embodied nature of tacit knowledge in this aesthetic market, as outlined above, is understanding the movement of this knowledge and performance of this knowledge, in such spaces of interaction.

It is important to acknowledge the location and transfer of fashion knowledge for a number of reasons. As much literature on knowledge testifies, there are obvious spatial dimensions to knowledge in markets, firms or regions, with terms such as *milieu, clusters, industrial atmosphere* hinting at the spatial nature of knowledge production. Thus, debates about knowledge are inevitably tied to geography: where is knowledge located? How does it transfer? Does it give particular companies/regions/nations competitive advantage in the global economy? Within this literature, a spatial mapping of knowledge along the axis of coded/global, tacit/local has become a major debating point (see for example Howells 2004; Gertler 2003). This long-established distinction suggests that, 'Where some knowledge (codified) is easy to transfer ... other knowledge is dependent on context, and is difficult to communicate others' (Malecki 2000: 110). Thus, tacit knowledge is often described as 'sticky' in that it adheres to particular places and, since it is not codified, is not as readily transferable or able to 'travel' as formal, codified knowledge. Much recent literature has developed such a geography of knowledge. Scott's (2000) analysis for example examines the local relations and networks of production in the film and fashion industries of Los Angeles and Paris (see also Crewe and Forester 1993). However, for Allen (2000: 27) associating tacit knowledge with 'the creation of territorially specific actions and assets—restricted to ... regions, places or other such spatial confines' is 'highly questionable'.

Some recent attempts to elaborate on the non-codified, tacit nature of productive knowledges (see also Crewe and Forester 1993; Salais and Storper 1997; Scott 2000) also emphasize the close associations and local relations and networks that support these knowledge flows and transfers. However, the way tacit knowledge adheres or 'sticks' to particular places or firms is more complex than the simplistic dichotomy codified/global, tacit/local implies. More recently, this mapping has been criticized (Allen 2000; Bathelt, Malmberg et al. 2004) as too 'static', failing to capture the complexities of tacit knowledge flows. Thus recent attempts to map the 'multiple geographies of tacit knowledge' (Faulconbridge 2006: 537).

Further, there is a bias in the literature towards examination of the spatial patterning of heavy industry, science and technology businesses, and thus terms like *industrial atmosphere* have not been modelled on or applied to aesthetic markets and, thus, do not capture the specific spatial dimensions and patterning of aesthetic knowledge. In this section, I argue that fashion knowledge challenges accepted spatial mappings of knowledge. It may be stating the obvious, but it is important to note here the different global circuits or networks within the highly differentiated markets in fashionable clothing. The spaces and places of buying are different at different levels of the market: mid-range stores are denied exclusive access to high fashion shows and are not on the same circuit or network as the buyers for stores like Selfridges. When they travel, buyers in the mid market visit quite different places—factory outlets in Turkey or China, for example—rather than the exclusive salons of designers in Paris or shows in trendy warehouses in Hoxton. The geography of fashion buying at the high, designer end is 'global' and 'local' in the same instance: the map is global, while the actual spaces and activities of buying and retailing are always local. Thus, in mapping tacit aesthetic knowledge in high fashion I want to suggest how simplistic distinctions like global and local do not hold; how tacit aesthetic knowledge is both *locally situated* and *globally distributed*.

Mapping Tacit Knowledge in Fashion: Global Flows

High fashion knowledge depends upon global flows—of people, commodities, images and styles. To be knowledgeable of high fashion one needs to understand and position a universe of designers, design houses, major stores and styles of dress, located all over the world. The garments themselves, and the people who design, style, photograph and buy them for stores, circumvent the globe regularly. Further, images of fashion shows are flashed around by the world's press, while fashion magazines regularly tell readers what will be 'hot' next season. In one sense, fashion, tacit aesthetic knowledge is globally circulating, adhering to particular cities, like Paris, London, Milan, New York or Tokyo, wherein there are hubs or 'clusters' of fashion production. While the actual manufacture of garments may be outsourced—to Turkey or China—the world's global 'fashion cities' (Breward and Gilbert 2006) are the locus for activities concerned with the styling, modelling, marketing and retailing of fashion, as well as the source material, inspiration and backdrop to fashionable display. They are places where the influential people of fashion travel and gather for work. 'Peripheral' cities, such as Stockholm or Sydney, may constantly work to position themselves on the global fashion map, but always in relation to these major cities.

In this way, fashion knowledge is apparently global and free-flowing. Systematic attempts within the industry to capture and codify this knowledge exist in the form of trend forecasts produced by one of the global trend forecasting agencies, such as Worth Global Style Network (WGSN). These agencies trawl the world's cities in search of upcoming trends, attempting to capture and codify something of the unpredictability of fashion. This knowledge, which is not made publicly available but sold to companies on subscription, circulates in the form of books, documents, images and PowerPoint presentations. However, precisely because it is distributed widely, this codified, global knowledge becomes ubiquitous, a fact that undermines its value (Malecki 2000; Maskell and Malmberg 1999). This point is underscored by the main quality defining high fashion, the insatiable quest for newness: to be at the 'cutting edge' of fashion is to have grasped something of the 'new'. Such knowledge is, by definition, not widespread; once high fashion becomes ubiquitous, its meaning as cutting edge or 'cool' is lost. For this reason, tacit knowledge is highly valued within high fashion for it is assumed to be close to actual trends as they emerge and is therefore 'one step ahead'.

Many further spatial concerns need to be foregrounded as they feature in buyers' everyday calculations. Fashion buyers constantly source their ideas for designs in numerous cities across the world and are hooked into a network of similar global aesthetic workers who move regularly between the major cities on a frequent basis. Much time on buying trips is spent just looking and sensing what is going on in other cities, absorbing the 'atmosphere' and sensing the 'mood' of markets abroad. Recognized by Marshall (1920, 1923), 'atmosphere' describes the way in which those clustered in an industrial district come to learn and sense something 'in the air'. While usually applied to heavy industry clusters, it is relevant for understanding the role that cities, as important clusters of aesthetic activity, play in the emergence and dissemination of aesthetic style. From early dandies (Breward 2003; Wilson 2003; Breward and Evans 2005) to post-punk youth subcultures, cities are spaces of fashionable display and many emergent styles 'bubble up' (Polhemus 1994) rapidly from the street. Attempts to codify and capture these, as trend spotters and forecasts try to do, are no real substitute for 'being-there', as such trends rapidly appear and disappear faster than attempts to codify and capture them. For these reasons, research trips are undertaken by Selfridges's buyers for purely research purposes only, with no buying budget: Selfridges's buyers have visited Japan, Brazil, India, Australia and New Zealand in recent years in a bid to keep abreast of developments in these places. Buying trips themselves always involve an element of what is called 'comp' shopping. Walking the streets of SoHo in New York one day with the buyer for denim wear was all about simply seeing and sensing the mood of this influential retail hub. New designers may come to light and ideas garnered for visual merchandising as a result, but the knowledge may not have any direct implementation; it simply ensures the buyers are not 'missing anything' and feeds into Selfridges's sense of itself as located on a global axis, positioned vis-à-vis major department stores across the world, such as Barneys in New York. Selfridges's competitors are, therefore, not just those located within easy reach of the flagship store on Oxford Street, London (Harvey Nichols or Liberty nearby), but are identified in other fashion cities. These movements and the multiple identifications and locations keep Selfridges on the fashion network; without them, the store's identity as a high fashion retailer would wither and die.

This aesthetic knowledge is difficult to label as either 'local' or 'global'. Terms like *buzz* and *noise* (Grabher 2002; Bathelt, Malmberg et al. 2004; Bathelt 2007; Bathelt and Schuldt 2007) portray something of the vibrancy of knowledge captured *in situ,* and the importance of face-to-face contact, but in fashion 'localness' has many spatial dimensions: it is just as important to hang out at a café in SoHo (New York City) as it is in Soho (London), since local buzz is not simply that which is found in the immediate vicinity of Oxford Street. This is because the 'ecology' of local buzz in this market depends upon strong geographical paths of travel that connect global fashion workers to local cultures of creativity in far-flung cities. In other words, geographical distance does not limit what counts as local buzz. Thus, in fashion, 'local' and 'global' are not fixed, spatially bounded terms. One might talk instead about the global circulation of local buzz/knowledge.

Some recent attempts to critique the coded/global, tacit/local mapping of knowledge have focused on how tacit knowledge may not always be as dependent upon spatial proximity, but able to 'travel' under particular circumstances more readily than previously acknowledged. Agrawal, Cockburn et al. (2006: 573) could be describing aspects of the fashion world when they argue that,

> Geography is likely to be less important in mediating social relationships between individuals in the same field since they have various alternative mechanisms through which to establish relationships. For example, individuals in the same community of practice ... or invisible college attend conferences and trade shows together, belong to common associations, and have other institutional settings in which to fraternize and share ideas.

'Communities of practice' (Brown and Duguid 1991; Lave and Wenger 1993) and 'invisible college' (Crane 1965, 1969) suggest how knowledge may circulate beyond particular firms and localities to other firms in similar or related areas geographically far away. Similarly, as Howells (2002: 874) argues, 'the impact of "geographical proximity" is not always (or indeed usually) direct—its influence is often indirect, subtle and varied.' Indeed, geographical space is influenced through things such as organizational or 'relational proximity' and this may be more important than geographical proximity. Nonetheless, as he suggests, geography will have a 'profound impact on these very routines and practices within organisations ... therefore its underlying *indirect* importance remains' (2002: 874).

This focus has obvious application to understanding fashion markets and tacit aesthetic knowledge flows. 'Relational proximity' may account for the ideas, knowledge and people that appear to flow fluidly around the fashion globe, although geography plays a role in this, since much of the work within the fashion industry takes place at global trade fairs. Fashion workers constitute a 'community of practice' and share the characteristics of such a community: they enjoy 'common associations', of meanings, ideas, practices; share places of work and leisure; and are linked via a host of trade events which bring them together in real time and expose them to similar experiences and tastes, as discussed. Indeed, in my travels with buyers, it was apparent that they frequently move as a 'pack', staying in the same hotels, frequenting the same bars, and working in the same enclosed spaces (shows, studios, restaurants and hotel foyers). This global collectivity and connectivity is critical to how they make sense of fashion.

Fashion knowledge is complicated by the fact that it is embodied in the fashion habitus, as noted above, with fashion insiders often wearing the aesthetic style they seek to translate for their consumer/s. This was certainly the case with the high-end designer market, where the styles are highly valued and *have* to be worn for the agent to belong in the market in the first place. Indeed, failure to dress well, that is to be able to understand, translate and wear designer clothes, is an automatic bar to entry into this exclusive world of work: if you do not look the part, you will, quite simply, not 'fit in', as was the case with the US agent described below. In this way, tacit knowledge 'travels' with the buyers themselves, and is globally recognized as the insignia of the fashion workers. What this means, in practice, are remarkable similarities in dress and bodily presentation: on the fashion show circuit, whether in London, New York, Milan or Paris, there are very definite similarities in terms of the style of clothes worn. High fashion style is communicated via the body by clothes, accessories and styles of walking, talking and being; the 'air kiss', for example is a common gesture of affiliation to the fashion set (Entwistle and Rocamora 2006). This communicates fashion 'capital', to use Bourdieu's other valuable phrase. This 'fashion capital' (Rocamora 2002) combines the cultural knowledge of what designers and styles of dress are in fashion, with the ability to select and combine the appropriate clothes and wear them well; that is it is carried through bodily demeanour and comportment as part of the fashion habitus. It is hard, if not impossible, to communicate this habitus on paper, precisely because it is tacit and embodied and therefore does not translate easily into words. As an outsider I know that I did not have it, or did not have it to the same degree as those I observed. Indeed, I had to learn what designers and styles were most valued and my knowledge always lagged behind the buyers. This is not to say I do not understand fashion (indeed, I consider myself a fashionably dressed *academic*) but I lacked the precise, obscure, intricate knowledge of those I observed and the ability to put it together, not least because I could not afford it!

It must be noted that there are different variations of fashion capital at work: 'elegance' is often the characteristic of the older fashion generation and is materialized through the wearing of expensive designers—Chanel, Chloe or Prada—known for their quality material and fine tailoring, while 'edginess' is often the mark of a younger (and poorer) 'fashionista'[1] and involves clever and 'creative' combining of an occasional expensive item, a Prada handbag or Monolo Blanhik shoes, with high street clothes from very fashionable stores like Topshop in London. This ability to *wear the knowledge* returns me to my earlier discussion of the embodied knowledge and is critical to the ease with which insiders move within the fashion network. Without it, it would be hard to access the inner sanctums of high fashion; indeed, failure to embody this style might be fatal. One US agent working for Selfridges in New York was described by one of the buyers as a 'blue rinse, twin set woman' of 'a certain age' who lived in Westchester[2]: indeed, she was also described as 'too Westchester'. What these descriptions attempt to capture was the fact that she lacked the appropriate fashion capital to know what and where to look for designers for the new, fashion-forward Selfridges but even when she did find them, she did not present the store well—people wouldn't meet with her because she did not look as if she was from a fashionable store (more like a rep from a mid-market department store like Macy's or Debenhams). She was eventually fired.

Selfridges's Tacit Knowledge

I have argued that tacit aesthetic knowledge is simultaneously globally circulating *and* locally situated in particular cities and by being worn on buyers' bodies. I now want to examine how this knowledge is deployed in the strategies employed at Selfridges: indeed how it is localized or embedded in the store. In this section I explore the particularities of Selfridges's tacit knowledge in more detail.

Selfridges was often described by the buyers and management as valuing 'instinctive' or 'intuitive' knowledge: tacit knowledge by other names. This was part of a narrative within the store that was articulated in all the interviews; that of Selfridges being 'unique' and on a continual quest for 'difference'. This narrative can be viewed as rhetorical and performative, serving to reproduce and sustain a vision of the store to itself (Thrift 2005). This narrative was critical to the development of new strategies and practices for knowledge generation and management within the store put in place when Vittorio Radice, the charismatic Italian businessman, took over as Chief Executive in 1996. Central to his strategy for re-energizing Selfridges's jaded image was the establishment of the Fashion Office. As discussed in Chapter 6, this office was responsible for developing in-house knowledge to drive the overall fashion direction of the store, ensure that they accumulated the appropriate knowledge and take the lead as to what knowledge to gather, how to promote the store. It was an explicit attempt to produce unique Selfridges knowledge that would ensure they made their own sense of emerging trends and kept abreast of wider trend developments globally. As discussed previously, the Fashion Office helped to generate the belief within the store that it was a 'creative' and 'innovative' company, at the 'cutting edge' of knowledge about retailing and fashion and this was a familiar theme in interviews with buyers and other staff in the store: the buyers spoke readily of the company's—and their own—creative and fluid ways of generating knowledge and the strong emphasis the company placed on tacit knowledge. These assertions echo the rhetoric of many self-proclaimed 'knowledge-intensive' companies who may see themselves as 'creative' and 'innovative' (Nonaka and Takeuchi 1995; Thrift 2005). Such rhetoric proclaims the importance of being not just at the 'baseline', but at the leading edge in order to hold and maintain a competitive advantage (Thrift 2005). Given the emphasis placed upon in-house tacit knowledge, it is no surprise to find that the store shunned ubiquitous trend forecasting information. As the head of the Fashion Office at Selfridges put it, 'We don't subscribe to WGSN. We subscribed to them for a year and I felt that the time we actually spend on it, researching the information, and then out of that information, trying to be different, because everybody will draw on that information, it just took longer than if we followed *our own instincts* right away.'[3]

Thus, the investment in the Fashion Office can be seen both as an investment in tacit knowledge generation and as a performative rhetorical statement reproducing the self-belief and creative confidence that Selfridges has the ability to generate its own unique *localized* fashion knowledge.

From my observations and conversations, buyers were critical to the flourishing of this tacit aesthetic knowledge in Selfridges: it is their calculations that enact this tacit knowledge and, in doing so, secure the flow of appropriate high fashion commodities into the store. Buyers work closely with the Fashion Office, discussing what brands to select and what to 'cull', and thinking through the overall direction of their different areas. Their knowledge, while generated from regular globe trotting and hooked into local 'buzz' in far-flung places, can also be described as 'sticky', in that it develops out of on-going discussions and calculations of the store's direction. It is, therefore, both 'globally' sourced and 'locally' enacted. This 'stickiness' adheres to the unique location of Selfridges's flagship on Oxford Street, and is reinterpreted in the regional stores for the local markets. As I did not have access to the other stores, I cannot comment on the particular ways in which the buyers bought for these stores, but in interviews, it was clear that differences in buying came down to localities. In their calculations of what to buy, fashion buyers factor in locality and buy differently for Oxford Street than the provincial stores of Manchester and Birmingham. For example very 'edgy' London designers, such as newer ones showing on the London Fashion Week schedule, will not be bought for stores in the north, but showcased in the Oxford Street branch. Such expensive and lesser known designers would not appeal to markets outside the metropolis. In this way, buyers' understandings of the market are sensitive to spatial locality.

To conclude this section, tacit aesthetic knowledge has to be seen as both globally circulating and locally situated or enacted. In other words, tacit aesthetic knowledge in fashion depends upon global connectivity but has also to be translated locally by the firm itself. Locally produced calculations and locality of business itself are important to account for in understanding the particularities of the company's strategies for knowledge generation and management and for the way in which the store repositioned itself as a *global* high fashion retailer but bought with local consumers in mind. Selfridges's knowledge, therefore, depends upon a complex spatial ecology. Something of this blend of spatial scales has been acknowledged in recent accounts of knowledge. Malecki (2000: 111) notes that while some firms rely on normal local networks, 'the stronger local environment for firms is one in which both local links are abundant and flows of knowledge to and from other places are common.' Amin and Cohendet (2004) in their discussion of the complexities of 'decentralised business networks' also argue that a blend of global/codified and tacit/local knowledge is preferable within a company to privileging local knowledge. Further, I have argued that while most literature designates local and global knowledge as fixed spatial registers, in fashion, these blur considerably: I have suggested that 'local buzz' need not refer to immediate location, but the 'buzz' of other cities as well, and that for a fashion company like Selfridges to survive, it must be hooked into pathways of tacit knowledge that are globally flowing and locally situated. Geography *is* important, but thinking in terms of spatially separate domains of local and global, and privileging the former as more valuable, is too rigid. Such a simple dichotomy fails to recognize that even the most localized knowledge—that worn by the embodied fashion agent, such as the buyers—'travels' with them, and that to understand the global connectivity of fashion one must be aware of how important this most *local* embodiment is to the *global* circulation of tacit aesthetic knowledge.

Conclusion

Selfridges's buyers pride themselves on knowing their market, but what, precisely, does this mean: what sort of knowledge do they have and how is it organized to make sense of fashion? Pinning down the sort of knowledge that underpins buyers' calculative work is not easy; indeed, even they cannot name it and find it difficult to translate into words. This is partly because the knowledge is largely tacit and therefore uncodifiable. It is knowledge that is expressive and embodied and making sense therefore involves deeply internalized and lived sensibilities that are difficult, if not impossible, to translate into words.

My account of tacit aesthetic knowledge sheds light on hitherto untapped dimensions of economic knowledge more generally and tacit knowledge specifically. I have argued that economic knowledge in aesthetic markets is, in essence, sensual and embodied, features overlooked in accounts of markets and economic knowledge, even in debates on tacit knowledge, possibly because of the bias towards classic markets and those located in science and technology. Directing attention to aesthetic markets, one confronts the limitations of economic knowledge defined as cognitive abilities and rational calculation. Further, I have suggested that in locating economic knowledge in embodied sensibilities one is inevitably spatializing knowledge in turn, since agents are embodied locations of knowledge. However, as discussions of knowledge and knowledge transfer, especially tacit knowledge, neglect aesthetic markets, the spatial features of tacit aesthetic knowledge have not been mapped.

Tacit aesthetic knowledge is thus globally circulating even while the precise aesthetic expression in different locations may vary. Although based on only one case study of Selfridges, I hope my analysis is suggestive to other researchers interested in the other under-researched aesthetic markets and firms.

–8–

The Cultural Economy of Fashion Buying

Fashion buying knowledge, as detailed in the previous two chapters, is put to active use most obviously on the fashion 'buy'. In this chapter, I want to focus in on the micro-encounters of the fashion buy in order to examine at close quarters the calculative processes of fashion buying. This focus is important for understanding the means by which a business, like Selfridges, produces consumption—that is, productively calculates and addresses consumers. The buyer interface is the critical one between 'production' and 'consumption' even while these should not be taken at face value as definitive moments, but processes interlinked through practice, as previously argued. Why look at this interface: why is it important?

UK clothing retailing has become very competitive since the 'retail revolution' of the 1980s (Gardner and Sheppard 1989). In the late 1990s, a number of established high-street businesses, such as the British store Marks and Spencer (M&S) and Laura Ashley, once stalwarts in British retailing, began to experience falling profits. M&S's story, in particular, has been followed closely by the UK press since the 1990s, firstly as a struggling store but more recently for its success in turning around years of falling profits. So while in 2005, a particularly poor year, 'total sales fell to £7.9bn from £8.3bn for the corresponding period last year' ('Profits and sales tumble at M&S' 2005) with women's clothing performing particularly badly, in May 2007 the company announced its highest profits in a decade (almost £1 billion).

One problem M&S has had to counter has been the rise of the 'value' driven 'fast-fashion' stores. As Winship (2000) notes, the M&S brand was founded on 'consumers immense trust in it ... value for money, "quality", but not cheap prices' (Winship 2000: 15), something that does not always appeal to today's 'younger, label-conscious generation' (2000: 17) who prefer the likes of Zara and H&M that deliver high fashion products quickly and at low cost. Thus, unable to compete on fashion or price, M&S lost its way in the late 1990s and early 2000s, failing to capture consumers. It has since addressed this decline under the direction of company boss Michael Rose by introducing high fashion lines in the store and an aggressive advertising campaign featuring the likes of Twiggy.

Whatever its success today, the M&S tale is a cautionary one: if a once dominant retailer like M&S—once so confident of its market position it famously never advertised—struggles with falling profits, then it points to the central issue within all markets, namely, that 'all attachment is constantly threatened' (Callon, Meadel et al.

2005: 38). In other words, 'capturing or "attaching" consumers by "detaching" them from the networks built by rivals is the mainspring of competition' (2005: 38) and this ultimately means no firm's market position, however strong, is guaranteed.

In such a competitive environment as this, I contend that the work of fashion buyers is highly important to the firm's calculations of the market. Buyers are responsible for selecting and bringing goods to the marketplace/store, their work requiring calculations of the market that involve a constant movement between 'production' and 'consumption'. In the process, goods are translated into products for consumers: a 'process of qualification-requalification' (Callon, Meadel et al. 2005: 32). As Fine and Leopold (1993) argue, literature on fashion has tended to plough two separate furrows, with production histories and analyses of work in the fashion industry on the one hand, and studies of consumption on the other. One consequence of this division is a splitting off of explanations of fashion into either supply-driven or demand-driven models. This separation has prevented a full picture of the fashion industry from developing as the critical *relationships* between production and consumption have been systematically overlooked. As detailed in Chapter 5, retailing and the 'middlemen' who work within the sector is one route for reconnecting production and consumption.

The aim of this chapter is two-fold: to examine the *qualification* and *mediation* of fashionable clothing by buyers through analysis of their routine work encounters— with products, suppliers and (virtual) consumers. Taking the first idea, I want to examine the 'active and reflexive role of economic agents in the qualification of products' (Callon, Meadel et al. 2005: 30) in their 'habitual and routine' (Negus 2002: 509) working practices. In other words, I describe how, in their routine encounters, buyers are active in defining, shaping, transforming, qualifying and re-qualifying products. Through this qualification process buyers act upon markets—their selections resulting in the particular assemblage of products on the shop floor that constitute fashionable clothing for that particular retailer at any particular time. Of course, the process of qualification does not stop there, since buyers monitor the effects of their decisions and, in due course, the results (in the form of sales figures) are monitored, digested and translated into the formal and informal knowledge that will form the basis of next season's buying. The circularity of this process is itself evidence of the way in which production and consumption are interlinked or interwoven precisely through the actions of buyers.

However, the problem with this qualification process is that it tends to view the process as linear. To overcome this I draw on Cronin's (2004) idea of 'multiple regimes of mediation', which emphasizes the many directions and mediations that take place between agents in their qualification of products. Indeed, to understand buyers as 'cultural intermediaries' it is necessary to look at the complex processes of mediation, since it is by no means clear what it is buyers, or any cultural mediators, may be said to mediate. Examining the encounters buyers have with objects and agents in their work, it is possible to explore the many mediations involved in buying. That is to say, in these encounters buyers mediate numerous interests, tastes and identities in the process of examining goods to purchase, encounter suppliers and making sense of, and coming to 'know', their customer/s. Focusing on these encounters allows for an 'expanded and nuanced definition of mediation' (Cronin 2004: 352) to emerge and for a critical analysis of fashion buyers as intermediaries hitherto not undertaken.

On face of it, fashion buyers are key cultural mediators between production and consumption in the fashion industry: through their selections they mediate the products set out by designers, selecting them on behalf of their consumer who is actively imagined but not 'virtual' (Carrier and Miller 1998) having left material evidence of their existence through various traces—in merchandising statistics, they leave their mark, and they are the subject of constant conversations with shop-floor staff. As noted in earlier chapters, there has been much interest in ideas of cultural mediation and in cultural intermediaries, deriving out of Bourdieu's (1984) influential work (Featherstone 1990; McFall 2002; Crewe 2003; Nixon 2003; Cronin 2004). However, as Hesmondhalgh (2002) and others (Du Gay and Nixon 2002) have argued, the term has become rather too general, not least because of confusions in Bourdieu's definition and use of the term. Further, the actual *processes* of mediation have tended to be overlooked in favour of analysis of the cultural identities of the mediators themselves, which, while important, is 'only one element in the complex mix' (Cronin 2004: 351) constituting commercial practices. With little empirical work on fashion buying to draw upon, numerous questions have still to be answered: what does it mean to say that buyers are cultural intermediaries and what, precisely, do they mediate—clothing, trends, aesthetics, taste? As I do not have the space to look at all these mediations, I focus particular attention not only on the way buyers select clothes, but also on how they might be said to mediate taste in their encounters with products, suppliers and consumers.

I begin by considering the issue of cultural mediation and to what extent fashion buyers might be said to be cultural intermediaries. I then examine the qualification and mediation of clothing through analysis of the micro processes involved in buying. To do so, I focus attention on the encounters buyers have with suppliers, products and customers and, in doing so, draw attention to the multiple mediations that take place at each encounter. Through this analysis I want to suggest how buyers' qualifications are critical to the operations of the retail practice in positioning itself as a high fashion department store, returning, inevitably, back to the issue of attachment.

Mediating Production and Consumption: Fashion Buyers as Cultural Intermediaries?

Who Are the Fashion Buyers?

Precisely what does it mean to say that buyers mediate between production and consumption? Are they, in fact, cultural intermediaries? To answer these questions, it is necessary to define the term *cultural intermediary*. While Bourdieu (1984) first refers to the 'new cultural intermediaries' as 'the producers of cultural programmes on television or radio or the critics of "quality" newspapers and magazines and all the writer journalists and journalist-writers' (1984: 323), in his later work he drops this and instead refers to symbolic production which is involved in 'the production of the value of the work' (1993a: 37). He claims, as does Featherstone (1990) some time later, that these occupations are expanding and of growing influence within contemporary culture. Since he defined it, the term has been expanded to include an ever-widening band of cultural producers or 'taste-makers' in fields as wide as advertising (Nixon 2003; Cronin 2004), men's magazines (Crewe 2003), women's magazines (Gough Yates 2003), pop music (Negus 1992, 1999, 2002) and fashion design (Skov 2002).

Although, as Hesmondhalgh (2002) suggests, claims as to this expansion tend to conflate cultural intermediaries with the new petite bourgeoisie of which they are a part, there are good reasons for opening up the concept beyond its initial narrow range. This is not least because of confusions in Bourdieu's (1993a) own later analysis of the 'field of cultural production' that would suggest the possibility of including those cultural workers involved in 'the production of the value of the work' (1993a: 37). In this book, Bourdieu suggests that material production of the work of art is just one part of the production of culture; symbolic producers are required to bring art forward to the public and in doing so, add value. This point is also argued by Negus (1992: 46) in his analysis of music producers. He argues that the concept of a cultural mediator refers not only to those involved in 'material' production of objects, but to 'an emerging social grouping concerned with the production and consumption of cultural imagery and information, working in such areas as marketing, advertising, design, public relations, radio and television, journalism, research, consultancy, counselling and the "helping professions" ' (1992: 46). He suggests that 'In these occupations jobs and careers have often not acquired the rigidity of the older bureaucratic professions, and recruitment is frequently via connections, shared affinities, values, and life styles rather than formal qualification' (1992: 46). This is certainly true of many jobs in fashion. As McRobbie (1998: 161) notes, careers in of UK fashion, jobs in journalism and styling for example are characterized by an 'occupational fluidity', dependent more on social networking and unpaid work than on formal training and education.

However, whether these occupations are 'new' or more influential, as both Bourdieu (1984) and Featherstone (1990) claim, is questionable, requiring further historical and empirical analysis to be substantiated (Nixon 2003). Bourdieu himself later drops 'new' to refer simply to cultural intermediaries. Of more direct concern here is the problem that, as Nixon (2003: 27) puts it, the term *cultural intermediaries* is very inclusive, tending to lump together many different occupations by 'family resemblances' rather than examine the specific 'organisational cultures' and 'broader, industry cultures is integral to an adequate understanding of these occupations.' I would concur with this and similarly argue for a more precise understanding of the work of different mediators and mediations. Hence, it is important, from the outset, to establish the ways in which buyers might be said to be mediators and what it is they supposedly mediate, as well as situate them within an occupational and industry context, as I have done in previous chapters.

Buying would appear to be an occupation that fits within the petite bourgeoisie— without the rigid career structure of say, lawyers or doctors—and has become professionalized in recent years: all those interviewed were university educated and some had entered buying directly through graduate schemes. This contrasts with earlier careers in retailing, when buyers would have risen through the organization, starting work on the shop floor. There was one exception to this: in my small sample one of the buyers had worked as a 'Saturday girl', but even she had studied languages at university. This change in education level and, along with it, the status of buying, places buyers in a similar position to other, so-called cultural intermediaries in advertising or marketing, who are similarly university educated and in occupations that have become newly professionalized. In this respect, it would not be inaccurate to see buyers as belonging to the 'new' petite bourgeoisie that Bourdieu (1984) talks of, who work in occupations concerned with symbolic work. This work is gendered: the buyers I followed were all women, with only one male merchandiser interviewed. Although there were other male buyers and merchandisers in other areas of the buying department, they were very much in the minority across the department as a whole. This pattern has its origins in the history of retailing more generally. Since the late nineteenth century, retailing work has been gendered female, with shop work presenting an early opportunity for new white collar work for women (Reekie 1993).

Buyers' Work of Cultural Mediation

If, as I suggest, we consider buyers as cultural intermediaries and their work as one of cultural mediation, we need to explore further what is it they mediate and how. Particular questions highlight the problem: do buyers mediate actual garments, suppliers, consumers' needs/desires, the identity of brands, their own retail business, some general notion of fashion, particular trends or tastes, or some combination of all of these? To begin to answer these questions one must begin unpacking what buyers actually *do* and ask questions of the objects, processes and encounters that constitute their work. It is only by following these that we can begin to unpack the links between production and consumption. As Appadurai (1986: 5) argues, 'We have to follow the things themselves, for their meanings are inscribed in their forms, their uses, their trajectories'. Following the buying process—part of the 'social life' of clothing—involves examining the ways in which clothing is exchanged between supplier and buyer and from buyer to consumer and, in the process, the qualification or valorization of goods/samples in a studio to products for consumption in a shop.

In terms of the work they do fashion buyers can be seen as mediators and 'taste makers', as their work involves much more than selecting and mediating commodities. Fashion buyers at Selfridges describe themselves as multi-taskers, whose work according to Maria, head buyer for Contemporary wear, it 'touches on all aspects of the store'. Jane, head buyer for Casual and Updated more strongly put it, 'From a project management point of view, buying is a dream job, because each season is a project in its own right, involving working with finance, architects, management, training'. Similarly, Julia noted, 'We don't just buy, we get involved in designs of shop fits, we brief the shop fit designers, we have to brief the VM [Visual Merchandising] team, we have to brief the shop floor on what we've bought, going out and seeing new products before they come in ... doing product packs for the shop floor.' Thus, fashion buying involves much more than selecting commodities, but incorporates thinking through a variety of activities and involves a wide range of retailing activities (many of these activities were observed: for example buyers trained and managed staff and worked with VM helping to determine the look of products on the shop floor, all in addition to their buying activities).

In choosing particular designers *and* shaping the look of the shop floor, buyers can be seen to mediate more than actual clothing; they communicate wider fashion and retailing trends as well. Fashion buyers, like art traders (Bourdieu 1993a) or music producers (Negus 1992) act both as cultural agents, symbolically creating value around products and helping to shape and forge tastes in the process and also, by necessity, as economic agents, since their actions are orientated to a marketplace. That is to say, they act as 'shapers of tastes and inculcators of new consumerist dispositions among the wider population' (Nixon 2003: 25). As Nixon (2003: 26) notes, 'The cultural authority they are able to exercise in these areas derives from their position within the increasingly important cultural institutions', namely, their position within the historically significant, internationally renowned Selfridges department store. Their selections are the critical yet invisible link between producers and consumers although, since there has been little analysis of their work, we do not know how they buy what they buy, their encounters with producers, and how they select on behalf of their consumer/s.

However, while broadly speaking buyers can be said to move from production to consumption, this duality needs unpacking since neither production nor consumption are monolithic structures or discrete entities, but are terms that condense complex processes that are critically interlinked. The long-standing separation of literatures on production within sociologies of work and analysis of the global commodity chain from literature on the cultural meanings of consumption has led to an oversimplification of the ways in which these two are linked. In her analysis of South Asian women in the diaspora as producers and consumers of fashionable clothing, Raghuran (2004) challenges the 'productivist' bias and demonstrates the importance of connecting producers to consumption. She addresses the tendency to artificially separate these out with the result that women in the Third World are seen as producers for clothing for Western consumers in the First World. Taking the producers of garments as consumers as well, she envisages the labour of South Asian women in very different ways from global commodity chain accounts or those of feminists interested in gender and development. Agency and pleasure in aspects of their work are brought to the fore as a result.

Similarly, I argue in this chapter that the work of fashion buying demonstrates the semi-permeability of 'production' and 'consumption'. From their position of influence within the fashion retailing network, that is, as some of the key agents of fashion style, buyers are 'producers', although in a rather different way to the women who sew the actual garments. However, much like Raghuran's women, buyers' labour as *producers* merges with their identities as *consumers*. Buyers can and do use their own consumption habits and tastes to guide them and enable calculations of their market, as in the case of the area known as the 'zone' developed by one buyer. Thus, with their own consumption informing their work, these two—production and consumption—can be seen to inform one another rather than existing as separate realms hived off from each other. Further, as indicated in Chapter 6 and discussed below, the consumption patterns of consumers feature directly in the calculations of buying in a feedback loop that includes analysis of merchandising statistics, discussions at monthly sales meetings and talks with shop-floor staff on 'floor walks'.

In the rest of this chapter I want to focus on three points of exchange, three crucial encounters buyers have with products, suppliers and consumers to examine what is involved in fashion buying mediation. These encounters are the moments when buyers stand before the objects and agents critical to their buying work and are involved in 'multiple regimes of mediation' (Cronin 2004). In her analysis of advertising agencies, Cronin (2004: 351) argues that 'the role of advertising practitioners as cultural intermediaries is not restricted to the translation or mediation between producers and consumers', but instead advertising practitioners are engaged in a range of mediations, for example between the agency and client, and within the agency which 'interlink, overlap and conflict with one another in complex ways' (2004: 352). In a corollary to the over-attention given to Creatives, she explores the negotiations that take place between them and Account Managers and Planners, and how the different discourses within the agency itself, and advertising in general, generate conflicts and tensions. Further, the role of ad agencies is not 'limited to channelling tastes in consumption or directing cultural change' (2004: 351). This can be seen in the link between the identities of the agents themselves and the content of the ads they produce. Their work (e.g. on beer ads) often involves them drawing on their own identities and consumption practices as, by and large, young, white, middle-class men, the result being the mediation (reproduction) of existing tastes and consumption practices (of young, white, middle-class men) as opposed to leading the cultural vanguard and forging new tastes. A similar point is made by Nixon (2003) in his analysis of advertising agents. I will return to this issue when discussing how buyers' taste might be utilized in their calculations of markets. First, let me take the buyer/product 'encounter' and analyse what happens here.

Product Encounters

An essential part of buyers' work is the selection of products for the store on 'buys'. Ultimately, the aim of the buy is to encounter the product. Buys usually take place at a studio or showroom where many possible garments are made available for inspection but not all can be chosen. As described in Chapter 6, buyers arrive at buys with an 'open to buy' budget which is an estimated amount of money to spend within their area, broken down by brand, determined by the merchandising plan. With this plan in mind, buyers examine the sample garments on display. The mechanisms of display seem to fall into two sorts. The first is a presentation on the part of a rep who brings out the collection in segments and displays them on hangers, pointing to pertinent features, such as fabric detailing or colour. This was most common in the United States and serves as a mediating encounter between product and buyer, with the rep attempting to assert her definition of the product, possibly to influence the buyer's decisions. During the presentation the rep qualifies the product, rendering its features as attractive, desirable, 'this season', often referring to how well received it has been with other buyers. The second method involves the buyer moving through the rails herself, selecting garments, often hanging them on rail which she then 'edits'. Here the rep stands back but is available to answer questions or arrange for the fit model to display selected samples.

   Callon, Meadel et al.'s (2005: 31) distinction between the 'good' and the 'product' is useful for understanding what happens here. While the good 'implies a degree of stabilization of the characteristics associated with it', the product emerges out of a process, the outcome of 'production, circulation and consumption'. In other words, products are generated through the actions by economic agents who shape, transform and qualify it, whereas goods describes 'a moment in that never-ending process' when its qualities are momentarily abstracted in order to be examined. The studio samples are like goods—temporarily stabilized entities with characteristics that can be examined and 'tested'. However, while Callon, Meadel et al. (2005: 32) recognize 'that agreement on the characteristics is sometimes, in fact, often difficult to achieve', their analysis would appear to describe a linear process, whereby a good is translated into a product along the chain or network of economic agents in their design, production, distribution and consumption. However, examining what happens during the encounter in the studio, between buyer/product/rep, it is apparent that the situation is more complex and non-linear, where different agents face one another with competing definitions of the good's qualities. The presentation method was unpopular with one buyer precisely because it did not allow direct engagement with the product. One buyer said she wants to touch and feel the garment and the freedom to rifle through the collection quickly rather than listen to an entire presentation which, in the case of one brand, was filled with fussy jumpers she dismissed as 'far too Bavarian' and had no intention of buying, despite the best efforts of the sales rep to talk up the product. Here, we might qualify Callon, Meadel et al.'s (2005) qualification process by referring to the two-way mediation taking place between rep and buyer. During such presentations, this particular buyer often fed back her experiences of product, telling reps that qualities they defined as attractive were, in fact, not going to be popular with her customes. She frequently told reps and designers, 'I can't sell racer-back tops' because of the 'bra-problem' (i.e. women have to forgo their bra or display unsightly straps). Thus, it would seem that the good's qualities may be stabilized temporarily in the studio, just not necessarily in the same way by different agents.

This encounter with goods on display is, first and foremost, a sensual one and there is no substitute for this direct encounter. As noted in previous chapters, when, after 9/11, the buyers were unable to go to New York (Fashion Week was cancelled), one whole collection had to be bought on CD ROM and proved to be a total failure. Much of it ended up on the sales rack at the end of the season. On the buy, the qualities of the goods are 'tested'. This testing can take numerous forms—touching, feeling and examining the sample on a hanger, observing it on a fit model, or indeed, by actually trying the garment on if no model is available. In studios without fit models, I was often asked to model the samples and give my opinion on their qualities. Some qualities automatically dismissed samples (racer backs, for example), with no testing, while other products always demanded testing—jeans, for example—which the denim-wear buyer said must be seen. So, while some suppliers in the United States, where she buys most of her jeans, do monthly 'drops' where they send cards showing new products, this constituted 'blind shopping'. Jeans, she noted, could not be bought this way, but need to be seen and felt and worn, the main qualities of selection being their fit on the body and detailing in the fabric—for example 'distressing', 'whiskers' (tiny lines around the crotch and knee) and wash—all of which cannot be reproduced faithfully in two-dimensional form. The encounter with the product is, therefore, a direct, face-to-face one in which the buyer stands in front of the object and inspects it. Sometimes the qualities are hard to discern. On a casual-wear buy, filled with garments variously described in colour terms as 'parchment', 'sand', 'pebble', 'alabaster' and 'stone', the head buyer became increasingly confused, unable to differentiate. Indeed, she requested a quick run-through the next day to clarify precisely these colours, asking for the differences to be explained/displayed yet again so she could be sure of her decisions. The fact that this was an Autumn/Winter buy in the United States—the so-called cruise collection—and the colours were largely pale, summery ones also laid heavily on her mind, with her describing to the rep the effects of such pale colours on the pallid complexions of white skin in the middle of November when the light would be failing. (Here, the buyer would seem to be assuming the consumer for this designer is Caucasian, although she did note how such colours would look great on black skin.) These characteristics of colour were, to her, a real problem for how the whole range would look in the store ('dull') and, ultimately, a threat to its saleability. She bought the odd item in 'banana' just 'to add a bit of colour' and 'interest' to the area.

Testing is not just about intrinsic qualities; as Callon, Meadel et al. (2005) note, factors of time and space are part of the testing process, as are seasonality, fashionability and availability. Buyers bear such considerations in mind and will ask about the delivery slot of all the products which may be critical to selectability. If something is to arrive either too early or too late in the season it may not be suitable, since an early slot means either problems of space in the storeroom or its arrival on the shop floor ahead of season where it will quickly lose its value as 'new' and 'fashionable'.

This process of testing garments sets in motion the journey of 'good' to 'product'. Once tested, products are set against other products in the wider universe of commodities. As Callon, Meadel et al. (2005: 29) suggest, all markets are about classification: economic agents, such as buyers, 'devote a large share of their resources to positioning the goods they design, produce, distribute or consume, in relation to others'. Thus, buyers establish where this product will sit in relation to the others they have seen or may see, quite literally spatializing it by visualizing where it will be positioned on the shop floor, as well as situating it within the overall universe of similar products that might be bought in the immediate vicinity of Oxford Street. If it looks like something Topshop might do for a third of the price, it may be rejected.

What is being mediated in this interaction? It is assumed in the literature that cultural intermediaries are arbiters and mediators of taste, responsible for introducing the public to new tastes. However, this assumption is too simplistic to describe what happens in the processes of fashion buying. The mediation may appear straightforward—the garment moves from studio to shop floor—but more is being mediated than the clothes themselves. While in the product/buyer encounter the flow would appear one-directional—inanimate object/good chosen by buyer—it is the product's sensual qualities that partly determine the outcome of selection. The idea of an actor-network that binds different actors together is perhaps more appropriate to understand what is going on here. Thus, the buying encounters I describe are interactive, since buyers do not simply bring to the studio their own, pre-determined ideas about products and taste and select on the basis of this; products also assert themselves in the encounter. In this way, buyers' ideas and tastes are actively shaped, that is heavily influenced by their encounters on buys. It may seem strange to say that products assert themselves upon buyers and influence their decisions, but as one buyer put it, 'You do end up being influenced by what you're buying, you end up liking it more'. An interaction, an active mediation, takes place between buyer and product. Indeed, buyers can be so heavily influenced by their encounters with the products they buy that it shapes their taste and consumption habits. Two of the buyers Jane and Melanie were most emphatic about the ways in which their taste develops out of encounters with product markets they work within. As noted previously Melanie, buyer for denim, described how she has progressively 'moved up-market' in her consumption and taste as a result of buying high-end designer clothes; indeed, moving into high-end designer denim as a direct result of buying it for the store. Jane described how her experience of buying products in the Middle East shaped her taste in ways she felt uncomfortable about: 'In some cases it's the *product that* [changes] *the individual*. I mean, I used to buy for the Middle Eastern market, and after I'd been there about four and a half years, and I started to wear lots of gold, I thought, "No, it's time for me to move on!" I'd never worn gold in my life!' (emphasis added).

Taste would, therefore, seem to be a dynamic force, a hybrid, forged out of on-going, sensual relationships and encounters with product markets. As Callon, Meadel et al. (2005: 31) put it, 'The product (considered as a sequence of transformations) describes, in both senses of the term, the different networks coordinating the actors involved in its design, production, distribution and consumption. *The product singles out the agents and binds them together* and, reciprocally, it is the agents that, by adjustment, iteration and transformation, define its characteristics' (emphasis added).

The 'binding' of product and agency noted above captures the ways in which buyers, such as the ones I observed, talked of their connections and relationships to products, the subtle ways in which product markets worked on and through them. In this way, taste is not something buyers impose *on* markets but emerges out of active engagement between buyer and products, and so too with other features, such as the store's taste, discussed in my account of supplier encounters below.

The qualification of products does not stop at their selection in the studio. Buyers (along with merchandisers) mediate the entry of goods from warehouse to shop floor and are active in qualifying it on its journey. All products come with an assortment of meanings and values; none more so than big brands and designer labels, whose identities have to be carefully managed and negotiated vis-à-vis the interests of both the brand and the store. These meanings and associations are added to in the process of the goods' arrival on shop floor and journey to consumer. Buyers are involved in placement of products on the shop floor—discussing where new and established labels should be situated. Much as Callon, Meadel et al. (2005: 36, citing Cochoy 2002) suggest, product identities are derived 'against a background of similitude' and one way to manage the identities of products on offer is 'the establishment of a socio-cognitive arrangement that situates the different products in relation to one another: a particular point on the shelf; packaging' (2005: 36). The Contemporary wear fashion buyer for the über-fashionable area, known in the department as the 'test-tube', described how she introduced new and 'cutting-edge' labels by careful placement next to highly visible and known brands. Indeed, she saw her role as instructive, almost pedagogic, in educating customers in this area about the newest labels. Here, she noted how she could rely on the 'trust' that customers have in Selfridges: they will assume a new label is 'hot' by virtue of its very selection.

The pedagogic role of store placement is illustrated by the arrival of a 'cult' denim brand whose identity was confirmed—re-qualified—by its placement in the 'Test-tube' area of Contemporary wear, as opposed to the usual location of jeans in the Casual wear area. As discussed in Chapter 5, this new kind of denim jeans troubled the boundaries between buyerships, particularly the Contemporary and Casual and Updated buyerships, and product categories—that of 'fashion' versus 'commodity' products—as jeans would normally be seen as the latter but were re-interpreted as 'fashion'. Normally, all jeans automatically go in the 'denim room' of Casual wear, but the arrival of a 'cult' pair of jeans from the United States challenged this. 'Cult' status is not a guaranteed quality but meaningfully constructed—qualified and re-qualified. Initially, these jeans were qualified as 'high fashion' by their location in the high fashion arena of the 'Test-tube', next to cutting-edge designers like Vivienne West-wood. However, as Maria the head buyer for Contemporary wear noted, all products have a 'life span' and she expects that it will eventually 'migrate' to the Casual wear area. As she notes: 'A lot of products have migrated from Contemporary into Casual wear ... once they're not as cutting edge any more, once they become a bit more established, [they] can easily migrate to Casual wear.' This is exactly what happened: about eighteen months after their arrival in the store, the jeans were moved into the 'denim room'. The qualification process of products is, therefore, never-ending, right through to the eventual demise of long-held labels that have to be 'culled' when deemed wrong for the store. Thus, in contrast to the goods in the studio, with their temporarily stabilized qualities, products have a 'life span' and qualities that are con-stantly qualified and re-qualified. This may be especially true in the fast-paced world of women's fashions, where fashionability, by very definition, is about the incessant search and construction of the 'new'.

Supplier Encounters

While buyers have to look 'upstream' (White 2002) towards production, examining their encounters with suppliers complicates the idea that buyers straightforwardly mediate between production and consumption. In the realm of high fashion, some suppliers are big-name brands headed by a single, known (famous) designer, often designing under his or her own name, as in the case of Muccia Prada for Prada and Mui Mui or Marc Jacobs. Others suppliers are famous brands with anonymous designer/s, as in the case of MaxMara or Theory. For the most part, designers do not appear at buys and leave the selling of their products to representatives. Indeed, out of a total of seventeen buys I attended, the designer was only present at two of them. The majority of buys are therefore conducted by representatives of the designer or independent studios acting on behalf of a number of designers (and something of the work these reps do on the buy has already been discussed). Thus, as Negus (2002) argues, between production and consumption lie numerous gaps that are not neces-sarily plugged by cultural intermediaries, or that are plugged by agents whose work tends to fall outside the usual definition of cultural intermediary and who remain invisible as a result. Since rarely do they meet the garment makers or designers themselves and may, therefore, know little of the origins of the clothing they select, the buyers' role is not one of direct articulation or mediation of production, at least, not in the normal run of things. Jane, involved in the store's annual promotion event (which was 'Bollywood' in 2002) had spent some time in India directly sourcing designers, even helping them translate their designs for Western consumers. However, this kind of direct collaboration is rare at this level of the market.

Nevertheless, even if the encounter with producers is mediated, how buyers source products and manage relationships with suppliers is critical to the store's success. In recent years, research has tended to argue that large retailers are in powerful positions to exert influence over suppliers, in terms of design, price and quality of products (Gardner and Sheppard 1989; Crewe and Davenport 1992; Wrigley and Lowe 2002). While major multiples like Marks and Spencer and those within the Walmart group are able to do this very successfully, and it is common in the supermarket business (Wrigley and Lowe 2002), this pattern may not necessarily be repeated across all sectors of fashion retail. Selfridges is not a multiple equivalent in size to M&S, and this must be factored into the findings, but my research would seem to point to a picture of supplier/retailer relations and flows of influence and power that are quite complex. Indeed, the suppliers the store has dealings with are major global brands who exert considerable power and influence over retailers, controlling all aspects of their brand image as well as co-ordinating the supply of products to ensure exclusivity.

Indeed, prior to the transformation of Selfridges's market identity by Vittorio Radice into a cutting-edge retail outlet, many leading fashion brands would not trade with the store. Big brands are especially protective of their image and need this re-qualified by retailers with an image, or taste level, that is similar. According to the Selfridges buyers, designer wear suppliers can be very picky about who they trade with. Again, if we ask, what is mediated in the interaction between suppliers (or their reps) and buyers, it would seem that it is more than the clothes themselves. The Selfridges brand, newly invigorated, had first to be sold *to* designers *before* the designers would sell to the store. For Radice's strategy to work, buyers had to not only know the 'right' brands to bring in, but be able to secure relationships with powerful suppliers. Thus, what had to be mediated in those initial encounters (not observed since they took place several years before the fieldwork, but referred to by the buyers) was the new image of Selfridges as 'fashion-forward' or 'cutting-edge'. Along with the head of the Fashion Office, buyers are the public face of the retail practice at industry events, such as the bi-annual fashion weeks (Entwistle and Rocamora 2006) and had to literally embody—in their clothing, style, demeanour—the new, high-fashion image. That is, buyers had to convince some brands of the value of Selfridges, with this image mediated *by* the buyers *to* the suppliers in their face-to-face encounters with suppliers.

This brings us back to my discussion in previous chapters (see also Entwistle and Rocamora 2006) on the requirement of buyers to 'look the part'—that is have high 'fashion capital', in the form of knowledge of fashion trends, brands, names in the business, etc.—and embody this in their self-presentation. As discussed in Chapter 5, buyers all felt the importance of dressing fashionably and were conscious also of the dress of others they worked with. That is to not only know, but be able to wear, high fashion clothes. Thus, Selfridges's buyers had to embody and mediate the store's re-configured identity, their taste seeming to merge with that of the newly fashioned Selfridges. This binding or merging of buyer and store identity might be said to start at recruitment. Since I was not present at interviews for buyers, I am speculating here, but it is highly likely that buyers are recruited partly on the basis of their embodied capital or 'aesthetic labour' (Warhurst, Nickson et al. 2000; Nickson, Warhurst et al. 2001; Pettinger 2004; Entwistle and Wissinger 2006). This may, perhaps, be evidenced in the similarities between bodies in the store—all, without exception, were relatively slim, young, attractive and 'stylish'. Once inside the business, these embodied capacities are shaped in interactions with the store (as well as with the products they encounter, as discussed above), in the form of their own on-going 'aesthetic labour' shaped through their encounters with product markets. In subtle ways, the movement of Selfridges 'up-market' and into high fashion is reflected in the sensibilities of buyers who, in turn, are responsible for communicating this new image to suppliers. Thus, it is not just the supplier's products—clothing/garments—that are mediated to the store; the store's identity has also to be mediated to the supplier in order to secure these products coming into the store in the first place.

Further evidence of the ways in which Selfridges has to mediate itself to suppliers was provided by the buyers who referred to brands they had courted for some seasons before finally securing them, suggesting that the model of retailers as controlling supply is not true in all cases. Suppliers can and do limit the flow of their products, developing exclusive arrangements with some stores, for example to protect the value of their products. Big, exclusive brands are very protective of their product and image and have the power to make demands, as to how their products are sold, displayed and marked down. However, these relationships are varied and dependent on the power of the brand, with smaller labels and new designers having little influence compared to big brands and established designers who are well positioned to exert considerable influence in their negotiations. Once top brands are established in the store, buyers describe how they enter into complex social and political relationships that have to be very carefully and diplomatically handled. Considerations of market distribution, geographical location and relationship to other distributors, as well as the reputation of the store, are important to whether or not a designer decides to supply the store. Thus, in their interactions with suppliers, buyers not only mediate the clothes produced by brands, but the identities and images that these big brands bring with them. Part of what happens in the mediation of branded clothing is the qualification of those brands' very identities and a virtuous circle of value has to be established. The brands bring in high value products, the identities of which are re-confirmed or qualified by their very selection and by such things as their placement on the shop floor. In turn, Selfridges's identity as a high fashion store is confirmed and qualified (see Aspers 2001; Entwistle 2002 for discussion of aesthetic markets).

Customer Encounters

The third and final encounter I focus on is that of buyers and consumers. The first thing to note is that buyers rarely, if ever, directly meet their customers, at least, not in the way they meet/encounter products and suppliers (touching, feeling, talking to them). While there are ways in which some stores might try to talk to their customers (via focus groups, for example) at Selfridges they prided themselves on not using such formal knowledge systems, relying instead on 'gut instinct' and 'assumptions' as one buyer put it. However, even these buyers use various forms of information, alongside 'guts'. Indeed, there are numerous ways in which buyers encounter consumers, albeit in highly mediated ways. First, they rely heavily on merchandising statistics, which tell them what consumers were buying last week, month, season, and in what volume. In terms of the mediation between buyer and customer, this data provides an 'interface', i.e. it is an artificial object, 'the organisation of data by one system for communication with another' (Lury 2004: 49), through which buyers interact with customers and learn of their evaluations of products. These statistics are important to weekly and seasonal calculations of stock (when to hold sales, what mark-downs might be needed, for example) and ultimately help form part of the plan and 'open to buy' for the next season. However, even these statistics have to be interpreted or qualified at weekly and monthly meetings. These can be according to the qualities of the product itself, such as when a jeans brand, not doing too well, is described as not having enough of a 'fashion element', or when external factors, like poor weather, staffing problems, shop-floor location, are used to account for low sales volume. Raw data on the product is, therefore, constantly digested and qualified and used as an imperfect guide to assessing customer evaluations of products. Since this picture is historic, it does not allow one to predict ahead with total certainty: as one buyer put it, 'You can't buy by numbers, you can't buy exactly what you bought the season before, not at this level of the market.' The range of decisions that buyers must make within the 'open to buy' are numerous: out of the entire collection, the buyers have to choose what styles fit their customer profile, decide what numbers, colours and sizes to purchase. They may return from a buy having under-spent because it was a poor collection and some contingency is built in to the process, with buyers able to hold back monies for the odd new label they might come across on their trips.

Another important, mediated encounter with the customer/s is the weekly 'floor walk', discussed in Chapter 6 when buyers meet the shop-floor manager and walk through the floor, discussing products, sales and customer feedback. Shop-floor staff obviously encounter customers daily and are in a position to mediate customer impressions and experiences of products. This mediated encounter with the customer may be supplemented with buyers' own observations on the shop floor. Indeed, as part of a discussion during a taxi ride between buys in Paris, my buyer went on to say that 'the shop floor is my interface, the eyes and ears' that give her access to her customer/s.

Thus, buying knowledge accumulates through some combination of formal merchandising knowledge and intuition, or 'guts', as well as from an on-going engagement with products, markets and customers. Maria, buyer for Contemporary wear, noted how it might take a while—a few seasons—to feel confident about what one is buying. She described how she found it hard, at first, to differentiate between products on some buys and feel confident with her buying decisions. Experience and regular contact with products are what establish a link to the customer, a picture of whom builds up in due course. Many of the buyers could describe, in close detail, their consumer/s in terms of taste, lifestyle and shopping habits. These ideal-type customers or 'virtual' consumers were often personified and given names. For example, Maria, described a typical customer as a 'West end girl', while Jane, the head buyer for Casual wear, used the names of characters from a popular UK comedy series—'Shobbian' or 'Dorian'—to describe some of her typical customers. Through experience, buyers build up a picture of their ideal consumer, and it becomes possible for them to make decisions based on an understanding of customer expectations: for example a pair of trousers by a 'conceptual designer' may seem 'difficult', but 'actually, that's what that customer of that designer expects'. Thus, buyers depend upon 'skill and judgement in saying, as Jane noted, "Well, I think, knowing my customers as I do, I think they will go here, or they will go there"'.

Merchandising data and floor walks provide the opportunity for a mediated encounter with the customer, and, here again, we might ask, what is mediated through these mediations? Is it merely customer 'demand' or taste? Obviously these encounters map, retrospectively, 'demand' but buyers do not, cannot, merely follow this since 'demand' is too fluid to be captured entirely by what sold yesterday or last week. Tomorrow's 'supply' depends upon the active interpretation of this fluidity—upon buyers' active interpretation and mediation of tastes. This active mediation of taste/s is critical to the store's success. However, while all the buyers spoke of how it is possible, indeed essential, to be able to buy outside of one's own taste, the process of taste formation within the store is more complex than simply capturing tastes 'out there' in the marketplace or heads of consumers. For one thing, these very tastes are themselves subject to change. When asked if it helps to have the same taste as her customers, one head buyer said, 'I think having the same taste as them helps you in the beginning, but then it can actually hinder you, because customers change, markets change'. Likewise, as I have argued, the tastes of buyers are fluidly forged out of encounters with products, as well as from their identifications and contact with the store itself, which in the case of Selfridges had moved up-market. Calculations of taste are less rigid than the idea that buyers merely follow demand suggests. However, as I now discuss, buyers may use their own experience and taste as part of their calculations of markets.

In Nixon's (2003) and Cronin's (2004) work on the subjectivities of advertising agents and Gough Yates's (2003) analysis of women's magazine editors, they note how the identities of these cultural intermediaries—their class, status, gender and taste dispositions, along with the institutional culture of the workplace—have implications for the work they do as arbiters of taste and culture. This subjective knowledge finds its way into their commercial practice, enabling them to calculate markets and consumers they themselves are close to. To this I would also add the importance of embodied knowledge, acquired by being 'inside' a particular field of cultural production (Entwistle and Rocamora 2006). The clearest example of how buyers draw on their own identity and taste came from the head buyer for Casual wear's descriptions of how she developed an area called the 'zone'. Jane described how she drew on her experiential knowledge and taste to develop this area a few years earlier. The 'zone' was based 'almost on people in the business; the buyer, and the architect, the advertising girl, the press agent, the girl who works in the City but is a little bit kookie and doesn't want to wear the pin-stripe suit ... who is business-like, quite fashion conscious but not a fashion victim [and] knows quality'. (An apt description of her own style in fact!) While the area addressed a perceived gap in the market—many of these targeted customers, as she notes, had been saying for some time, 'I can't find anything to wear'—this example demonstrates the complex forging of taste, rather than an illustration of customer 'demand' being exercised over the store. For one thing, 'demand' came not from objective statistics, such as market research, but forged out of the experiential knowledge of the buyer drawing on her own taste and culture: indeed, her experience as a *consumer* was as much part of the mix of calculations for the area as was her identity as a professional buyer. Rather than illustrating some straight forward, abstract notion of demand, it might be seen, in part, as the store setting out to 'capture' particular sorts of consumers it feels are appropriate to its brand image.

Indeed, demand-led explanations do not explain why the store decided to cull a large number of brands on the third floor. This coincided with the redesigning of the entire floor, which had begun to look 'tired' in comparison to the high-energy, visual impact generated on the first and second floors. Towards the end of fieldwork this generated much discussion and, although the changes were not implemented till later, the Head of Department told me that about thirty brands were to be 'culled' from the floor, because they were perceived not to be 'working' in terms of the store's newly formed, high fashion market position. In the process, she realized this might 'lose', or 'detach' customers, just as it may have lost some loyal customers in its redesigning of the Casual wear area on the second floor a couple of years previously. However, while changes to the area might alienate an older, less fashion-conscious customer, it was necessary to continue the store strategy to become 'fashion-forward'. Again, these decisions did not emerge directly from formal, abstract notions of customer demand, or market research, not only because the culture of the store did not place particular emphasis upon such knowledge, but because this demand is not 'out there', but is actively configured, interpreted, managed, and, ultimately tested. That the other areas had been so successful and the identity of Selfridges had been established provided enough basis upon which to proceed with this development.

Conclusion

In contrast to the other two encounters, the buyer/customer encounter is a highly mediated one since buyers do not confront consumers directly. However, this meeting is critical and returns us to the central issue in all markets, raised in the Introduction, of 'attachment'. The ability of buyers to know what products to purchase, actively calculating taste in the process, is critical to Selfridges's ability to capture—'attach'— customers and, thus, carve out a place for itself in the marketplace. Assuming that buyers either shape or follow demand over-simplifies the mediating processes of fashion buying, which are fluidly forged out of the encounters buyers have with products, suppliers and consumers. So, while buyers have to develop an 'imagined' consumer, often buying things they personally do not like, they do not merely 'meet demand', as a common sense view of them might suggest. On the other hand, the degree of influence they exert over markets and tastes should not be over-emphasized. While early literature accords cultural intermediaries some considerable influence in directing or shaping taste (Bourdieu 1984; Featherstone 1990), I argue that the meeting point of buyers and consumers is more complex than this.

For this reason, the qualification process, described by Callon, Meadel et al. (2005) has limitations because it would seem to suggest a linear flow of objects and influences along the chain from production to consumption. However, using Cronin's (2004) 'multiple regimes of mediation' affords the possibility of analysing the multi-directional flows of objects and mediations. If, as I have argued, alongside the clothes themselves, taste is also mediated in buying encounters it should not be seen as a priori belonging to either consumers or buyers, with one or other driving the buying process, but as a hybrid forged out of the negotiations, or mediations, between buyers and consumers in conjunction with the interactions taking place between buyers and products, buyers and suppliers and, indeed, buyers and the store itself. In other words, buyers do not always lead or forge tastes or merely 'follow the customer' slavishly, but some negotiation, or mediation, between them occurs. Ongoing encounters with products, suppliers, consumers and, indeed, the commercial culture of the store itself would appear to provide the basis for market calculations.

Conclusion

This book represents an attempt to understand the workings of particular markets that have hitherto been neglected by economic sociology and business literature. For want of a better term, I call them *aesthetic markets* and I have detailed how they operate through the careful balancing of 'cultural' and 'economic' calculations. The theoretical framework I use to understand these markets I refer to as the 'aesthetic economy', borrowing of course from 'cultural economy', to emphasize the idea that aesthetics are rendered calculable within a market. This framework, drawing on Callon's ANT-inspired economic sociology and Bourdieu's field theory, is perhaps a controversial one but enables me to examine the ways in which things ordinarily seen as 'cultural' and 'economic' can be assembled in meaningful ways to make sense of the products that circulate within aesthetic markets; in my case studies, fashion models and high fashion clothing. As I suggest, aesthetic markets have their own specific 'local rationality' (Abolafia 1998) and I examine the precise nature of their rationality and practice.

In Chapter 2, I argue that attending to aesthetic markets demands we see economic and cultural calculations as merged, and this theoretical point, developed also in 'cultural economy' approaches, I demonstrate more concretely in Chapter 3. Here I examine how model bookers aiming to promote models merge 'economic' considerations as to what jobs models should do at what price with more complex 'cultural' issues, such as the status of the job or client, and whether it will transfer value to promote a model's career in the long term. These considerations were examined vis-à-vis fashion buying in Chapters 5 through to 8 where I analyse how the retailing of high fashion clothing at Selfridges depends upon calculations that combine seemingly economic decisions—what to purchase in what volume, whether to invest in a new area on the shop floor, whether to cull a number of designers—with more nebulous so-called cultural concerns about the store's overall identity, the complex nature of imagined consumer habits and identities and the identities of buyers themselves.

In examining these calculations, I draw on both Bourdieu and Callon for their sensitivity to markets as practised, as I argue in Chapter 2. My arguments closely echo Callon's insistence on an anthropological view of markets and Bourdieu's similar arguments as to the need to look at economics in practice, rather than abstract economics. One important dimension to the work of both which is very much critical to my own analysis is the attention to the spatial relations of markets. Space is critical to understanding markets as bounded locations—fashion shows, trade shows and the like—and important to understanding the dissemination and circulation of market knowledge within. However, what they and others in economic sociology do not always attend to are the ways in which knowledge in markets is embodied. This point is one that my analysis of aesthetic markets throws into sharp relief. That is to say, one key spatial zone of markets, especially ones in aesthetic goods, is the body, as the location and locus of aesthetic market practice. This tacit aesthetic knowledge or embodied market knowledge extends what we know already about tacit knowledge, as I argue in Chapter 6. As I have argued in Chapters 6 and 7, aesthetic knowledge is tied to the body, enacted upon it, communicated through it and thus performative, it is market knowledge that is embodied and expressive.

While the spatial dimensions of fashionable clothing and modelling are different in many respects, they also frequently converge, most obviously and literally during the bi-annual fashion weeks, when fashion journalists, buyers, designers, models and the like are gathered in the same place to observe the new season's collections. These spatial encounters are, as I have argued in Chapters 6 and 7, critical to the circulation and dissemination of fashion knowledge and are spaces for spectacular bodily enactments of fashion knowledge. That these sensibilities are embodied is also evidenced in the role the body plays in the performance, circulation and dissemination of fashion knowledge. In fashion, you demonstrate you are 'in the know' (of high fashion) through embodied presentation and performance. This is not to say that other markets do not appreciate intuition or instinct, or that bodily performance is not a feature in the shared practices and knowledge of other markets. In other aesthetic markets, the knowledge may also be worn on the body or, perhaps, demonstrated through other tangible means which are extensions of one's embodied taste—in one's taste for home interiors, art or design.

In drawing out the dimensions of space, I suggest that the idea of network, as a spatialized metaphor drawn from Callon, is helpful for understanding how aesthetic objects become entangled and acquire meaning and value. This is true for models, as I discuss in Chapter 3, and clothing as analysed in Chapter 8. What is clear is that the aesthetic object has no intrinsic aesthetic quality: its aesthetic value is attributed to it through the way in which it is meaningfully connected to and entangled within relationships across the network. Models need to be photographed by the top fashion photographers and seen in all the right magazines and shows to be successful; likewise, fashionable clothing has to be located in the top fashion stores, situated alongside the top fashion designers, to acquire its value as 'this season'.

These points then—concerning market practice as spatially bounded and networked, and centred around embodiment—form the critical and interlinked elements of my analysis that, whilst applied to only two case studies, provide the basis of analysis which could be extended to similar aesthetic markets, such as art markets, design or flowers, as discussed in Chapter 3, as well as critical comparisons between these markets and others. As discussed in that chapter, there are significant similarities between flowers (Hughes 2004) and fashion and furniture (Reimer 2004) but to what extent are the sorts of calculations I examine found in other related areas such as cultural policy and regional development through culture (Neitzer 2008; Pratt 2004a,b)? How much of my analysis is relevant to related aesthetic goods and services, such as boutique hotels that do not trade entirely on aesthetics, but for which aesthetics are a key component?

These broader questions go beyond fashion and I suggest that while this book may have particular appeal to scholars within cultural studies and fashion studies, providing some answers to questions concerning the nature of fashion and, in particular, the silent and largely invisible world of fashion buyers, fashion models and brokers, and their work of cultural mediation between 'production' and 'consumption', I hope equally to have inspired those economic theorists and business academics to reconsider their ideas about markets. By no means a complete theory of aesthetic markets, this book, I hope, opens up economic sociology to 'softer' markets in aesthetic goods and helps students and scholars interested in markets of any kind to examine how these elements are brought together in other markets.

Of course, I can only hypothesize that my findings of fashion are expressed in other markets. However, until now, we have not been treated to an analysis of such markets because they have not been examined. The bias towards 'hard' markets—in industrial, chemical, technological or financial products—is strong and has restricted our understandings of markets as a result. As I have argued, the narrow range of markets and businesses examined in the economic literature has generated a narrow range of skills and attributes defined as economic knowledge. I hope I have suggested how 'softer' markets in 'cultural' products throw up further questions for future analysis. If nothing else, my (perhaps contentious) idea of the aesthetic economy and my analysis of two particular aesthetic markets both addresses this bias with empirical evidence from a different sort of market, and, through this empirical material, provocatively challenges some of the definitions and taken-for-granted assumptions and repressions that this narrow focus has engendered.

Notes

Chapter 1

1. The Economic and Social Research Council funded the entire cost of this fieldwork. Award reference: R000223649.

Chapter 3

1. These are only meant as a very rough guide and the estimates were valid at the time of fieldwork.

Chapter 5

1. All names have been changed.
2. This comment came from the Selfridges's designer wear buyer in May 2008, at a meeting about the designer wear sector and, while strictly falling outside my fieldwork, was worth mentioning, as evidence of an interesting development in the designer-wear buying cycle.
3. At the time of my observations, the women's wear buying department was organized in terms of five 'buyerships': Contemporary, Designer wear, Casual and Updated collections, Intimate Apparel, and Accessories. I concentrated attention on the first three, largely because I did not have the time to follow all of the buyers, but also because I chose to focus on women's outer wear since these constitute the bulk of what is considered fashionable dress (although handbags, lingerie and the like are also subject to the fluctuations of fashion).

Chapter 6

1. All companies' names have been changed.

Chapter 7

1. *Fashionista,* a term coined by the popular press in the United Kingdom, refers to the fashion insider. It is the style of the fashionista that is most often picked up and parodied in fashion journalist accounts of fashion shows.

2. Westchester is a quiet, leafy suburban region of New York located outside New York City. It was regarded by the buyer as quintessentially middle class and middle-aged—not the qualities Selfridges was seeking at this time.

3. An informal contact has since informed me that they have renewed their subscription to WGSN, and, while I have no way of verifying this, it is worth noting at least in passing. Without access to the company I cannot speculate on what this may tell us about the store's knowledge management practices.

Bibliography

Abolafia, M. Y. (1998), 'Markets as Cultures: An Ethnographic Approach', in M. Callon (ed.), *The Laws of the Markets,* Oxford: Blackwell.

Agrawal, A., I. Cockburn and J. McHale (2006), 'Gone but Not Forgotten: Knowledge Flows, Labour Mobility and Enduring Social Relationships', *Journal of Economic Geography,* 6/5: 571–91.

Allen, J. (2000), 'Power/Economy Knowledge and Spatial Formations', in J. R. Bryson, J. P. Daniels, N. Henry and J. Pollard (eds), *Knowledge/Space/Economy,* London: Routledge.

Allen, J. (2002a), 'Symbolic Economies: The "Culturalization" of Economic Knowledge' in P. du Gay and M. Pryke (eds), *Cultural Economy,* London: Sage, 39–58.

Allen, J. (2002b), 'Living on Thin Abstractions: More Power/Economic Knowledge', *Environment and Planning A,* 34: 451–66.

Amin, A. and P. Cohendet (2004), *Architectures of Knowledge: Firms, Capabilities, and Communities,* Oxford: Oxford University Press.

Amin, A. and N. Thrift, eds (2004), *The Blackwell Cultural Economy Reader,* Oxford: Blackwell.

Appadurai, A., ed. (1986), *The Social Life of Things: Commodities in Cultural Perspective,* Cambridge: Cambridge University Press.

Arnold, M. (1932), *Culture and Anarchy.* Cambridge: Cambridge University Press.

Aspers, P. (2001), *Markets in Fashion: A Phenomenological Approach,* Stockholm: City University Press.

Austin, J. L. (1962), *How to Do Things with Words: The William James Lectures Delivered at Harvard University in 1955,* Oxford: Clarendon Press.

Barber, J. (2006), *Intangible Assets and Competitive Advantage in the Knowledge-based Economy,* London: Department of Trade and Industry.

Bardot, B. (2003), *Casting Couch Confidential: The Good, the Bad and the Ugly Business of Beautiful People,* Sydney: Macmillan.

Barthes, R. (1985), *The Fashion System,* London: Cape.

Bathelt, H., A. Malmberg and P. Maskell (2004), 'Clusters and Knowledge: Local Buzz, Global Pipelines and the Processes of Knowledge Creation', *Progress in Human Geography,* 28/1: 31–56.

Bathelt, H. and N. Schuldt (2007), 'Between Luminaries and Meat Grinders: International Trade Fairs as Temporary Clusters', *Regional Studies,* 42: 853–868.

Bathelt, H. (2008), 'Buzz-and-Pipeline Dynamics: Toward a Knowledge-Based Multiplier Model of Clusters', *Geography Compass,* 1/6: 1282–1298.

Baudrillard, J. (1981), *For a Critique of the Political Economy of the Sign,* St Louis, MO: Telos.

Becker, H. (1982), *Art Worlds.* Berkeley: University of California Press.

Berger, J. (1972), *Ways of Seeing,* Harmondsworth: Penguin.

Blumer, H. (1969), 'Fashion: From Class Differentiation to Collective Selection', *Sociological Quarterly,* 10: 275–91.

Boisot, M. (1998), *Knowledge Assets: Securing Competitive Advantage in the Information Economy,* Oxford: Oxford University Press.

Bordo, S. (1993), *Unbearable Weight: Feminism, Western Culture and the Female Body,* Berkeley: University of California Press.

Bourdieu, P. (1973), 'The Berber House or the World Reversed', in M. Douglas (ed.), *Rules and Meanings,* Harmondsworth: Penguin, 98–110.

Bourdieu, P. (1977), *Outline of a Theory of Practice,* Cambridge: Cambridge University Press.

Bourdieu, P. (1984), *Distinction: A Social Critique of the Judgement of Taste,* London: Routledge and Kegan Paul.

Bourdieu, P. (1990), *The Logic of Practice,* Cambridge: Polity Press.

Bourdieu, P. (1993a), *The Field of Cultural Production: Essays on Art and Literature,* Cambridge: Polity Press.

Bourdieu, P. (1993b), *Sociology in Question,* London: Sage.

Bourdieu, P. (2005), *The Social Structures of the Economy,* Cambridge: Polity Press.

Braudel, F. (1981), *The Structures of Everyday Life: The Limits of the Possible,* London: Fontana.

Breward, C. (1995), *The Culture of Fashion,* Manchester: Manchester University Press.

Breward, C. (2003), *21st Century Dandy,* London: The British Council.

Breward, C., and C. Evans, eds (2005), *Fashion and Modernity,* Oxford: Berg.

Breward, C., and D. Gilbert, eds (2006), *Fashion's World Cities,* Oxford: Berg.

Brown, J.S. and P. Duguid (1991), 'Organizational Learning and Communities-of-Practice: Toward a Unified View of Working, Learning, and Innovation', *Organization Science,* 2/1: 40–57.

Butler, J. (1993), *Bodies That Matter,* London: Routledge.

Butler, J. (1994), 'Gender as Performance: An Interview with Judith Butler', *Radical Philosophy,* 67.

Callon, M. (1986), 'The Sociology of the Acts in This Work: The Case of the Electrical Vehicle', in M. Callon, J. Law and A. Rip (eds), *Mapping the Dynamics of Science and Technology,* London: Macmillan.

Callon, M. (1991), 'Techno-economic Networks and Irreversibility', in J. Law (ed.), *A Sociology of Monsters: Essays on Power, Technology and Domination,* London: Routledge.

Callon, M. (1998a), 'An Essay on Framing and Overflowing: Economic Externalities Revisited by Sociology', in M. Callon (ed.), *The Laws of the Markets,* Oxford: Blackwell.

Callon, M. (1998b), 'Introduction', in M. Callon (ed.), *The Laws of the Markets,* Oxford: Blackwell.

Callon, M., ed. (1998c), *The Laws of the Markets,* Oxford: Blackwell.

Callon, M. (1999), 'Actor-Network Theory: The Market Test', in J. Law and J. Hassard (eds), *Actor Network Theory and After,* Oxford: Blackwell.

Callon, M., J. Law, and A. Rip (1986), *Mapping the Dynamics of Science and Technology,* London: MacMillan.

Callon, M., C. Meadel and V. Rabeharisoa (2005),'The Economy of Qualities', in A. Barry and D. Slater (eds), *The Technological Economy,* London: Routledge.

Carrier, J.G. and D. Miller, eds (1998), *Virtualism: A New Political Economy,* Oxford: Berg.

Cassirer, E. (1946), *Language and Myth,* New York: Dover Publications.

Cassirer, E. (1957), *The Philosophy of Symbolic Forms, Vol. Three: The Phenomenology of Knowledge,* New Haven, CT: Yale University Press.

Cassirer, E. (1979), *Symbol, Myth and Culture: Essays and Lectures of Ernst Cassirer,* New Haven, CT: Yale University Press.

Chalayan, H. (2005), *Hussein Chalayan,* Rotterdam: NAI Publishers.

Choo, C.W. and N. Bontis (2002), *Strategic Management of Intellectual Capital and Organizational Knowledge,* Oxford: Oxford University Press.

Cochoy, F. (1998), 'Another Discipline for the Market Economy: Marketing as a Performative Knowledge and Know-how for Capitalism', in M. Callon (ed.), *The Laws of the Markets,* Oxford: Blackwell.

Coe, N.M. and N. Wrigley (2007), 'Host Economy Impacts of Transnational Retail: The Research Agenda', *Journal of Economic Geography,* 7/4: 341–71.

Cole, S. (2000), *Don We Now Our Gay Apparel,* Oxford: Berg.

Cook, I. and P. Crang (1996), 'The World on a Plate: Culinary Culture, Displacement and Geographical Knowledges', *Journal of Material Culture,* 1/1: 131–53.

Corner, L. (2001), 'Introducing the New Model Army: What Does It Take to Make It as a Male Model These Days?', *The Independent,* London, October 8.

Coward, R. (1984), *Female Desire,* London: Paladin.

Crane, D. (1965), 'Scientists in Major and Minor Universities: A Study of Productivity and Recognition', *Sociological Review,* 30: 699–714.

Crane, D. (1969), 'Social Structure in a Group of Scientists: A Test of the "Invisible College" Hypothesis', *American Sociological Review,* 34: 335–52.

Crang, P. (1994), 'It's Showtime: On the Workplace Geographies of Display in a Restaurant in Southeast England', *Environment and Planning D: Society and Space,* 12/6: 675–704.

Crewe, B. (2003), *Representing Men: Cultural Production and Producers in the Men's Magazine Market,* Oxford: Berg.

Crewe, L. (2004), 'Unravelling Fashion's Commodity Chains', in A. Hughes and S. Reimer (eds), *Geographies of Commodity Chains,* London: Routledge.

Crewe, L. (2008), 'Ugly Beautiful? Counting the Cost of the Global Fashion Business', *Geography,* 93/Part 1: 25–33.

Crewe, L. and E. Davenport (1992), 'The Puppet Show: Changing Buyer-Supplier Relationships within Clothing Retailing', *Transactions of the Institute of British Geographers,* 17/2: 183–97.

Crewe, L. and Z. Forester (1993), 'Markets, Design, and Local Agglomeration: The Role of the Small Independent Retailer in the Workings of the Fashion System', *Environment and Planning D: Society and Space,* 11: 213–29.

Crewe, L., N. Gregson and K. Brooks (2003), 'Alternative Retail Spaces', in R. Lee, A. Leyshon and C. Williams (eds), *Alternative Economic Spaces,* London: Sage.

Cronin, A. (2004), 'Regimes of Mediation: Advertising Practitioners as Cultural Intermediaries?' *Consumption, Markets and Culture,* 7/4: 349–69.

Department for Culture, Media and Sport (1998), 'Designer Fashion', *Creative Industries Mapping Document,* http://www.culture.gov.uk/reference_library/ publications/4740.aspx (accessed 20 June 2008).

Department for Culture, Media and Sport (2001), 'Designer Fashion', *Creative Industries Mapping Document,* http://www.culture.gov.uk/reference_library/pub lications/4632.aspx (accessed 20 June 2008).

Du Gay, P., S. Hall, L. Janes, H. McKay and K. Negus (1997), *Doing Cultural Studies: The Story of the Sony Walkman,* London: Sage.

Du Gay, P. and S. Nixon (2002), 'Who Needs Cultural Intermediaries?' *Cultural Studies,* 4/1: 495–500.

Du Gay, P. and M. Pryke, eds (2002), *Cultural Economy,* London: Sage.

Dwyer, C. and P. Jackson (2003), 'Commodifying Difference: Selling EASTern Fashion', *Environment and Planning D: Society and Space,* 21: 438–56.

Entwistle, J. (1997), 'Power Dressing and the Fashioning of the Career Woman', in M. Nava, I. MacRury, A. Blake and B. Richards (eds), *Buy This Book: Studies in Advertising and Consumption,* London: Routledge.

Entwistle, J. (2000a), *The Fashioned Body: Fashion, Dress and Modern Social Theory,* Cambridge: Polity Press.

Entwistle, J. (2000b), 'Fashioning the Career Woman: Power Dressing as a Strategy of Consumption', in M. Andrews and M. Talbot (eds), *All the World and Her Husband: Women, Consumption and Power,* London: Continuum International Publishing Group.

Entwistle, J. (2002), 'The Aesthetic Economy: The Production of Value in the Field of Fashion Modelling', *Journal of Consumer Culture,* 2/3: 317–40.

Entwistle, J. (2004), 'From Catwalk to Catalogue: Male Models, Masculinity and Identity', in H. Thomas and J. Ahmed (eds), *Cultural Bodies: Ethnography and Theory,* Oxford: Blackwell.

Entwistle, J. (2005), 'Between Production and Consumption: Fashion Buyers and Cultural Intermediaries', R000223649, Economic and Social Research Council, Swindon, Final Report.

Entwistle, J. (2006), 'The Cultural Economy of Fashion Buying', *Special Issue: Encounters in the Fashion Industry, Current Sociology,* 54/5: 704–24.

Entwistle, J. and A. Rocamora (2006), 'The Field of Fashion Realized: The Case Study of London Fashion Week', *Sociology,* 40/4: 735–50.

Entwistle, J. and E. Wissinger (2006), 'Keeping up Appearances: Aesthetic Labour in the Fashion Modelling Industries of London and New York', *Sociological Review,* 54/4: 774–94.

Evans, C. (2003), *Fashion at the Edge: Spectacle, Modernity and Deathliness,* New Haven, CT: Yale University Press.

Evans, C. (2005), 'Multiple, Movement, Model, Mode: The Mannequin Parade 1900–1929', in C. Breward and C. Evans (eds), *Fashion and Modernity,* Oxford: Berg.

Faulconbridge, J. (2006), 'Stretching Tacit Knowledge beyond a Local Fix? Global Spaces of Learning in Advertising Professional Service Firms', *Journal of Economic Geography,* 6/4: 517–40.

Featherstone, M. (1990), *Consumer Culture and Postmodernism,* London: Sage.

Fine, B. (2002), *The World of Consumption: The Material and Cultural Revisited,* London: Routledge.

Fine, B. and E. Leopold (1993), *The World of Consumption,* London: Routledge.

Flügel, J.C. (1930), *The Psychology of Clothes,* London: The Hogarth Press.

France, L. (2009), 'We might need to see you without your bra, he told me. I was 14. I didn't even have breasts yet', *The Guardian,* 7 June 2009, http://www.guardian.co.uk/lifeandstyle/2009/jun/07/sara-ziff-teen-modelling-fashion (accessed June 7, 2009).

Freeman, C. (1993), 'Designing Women: Corporate Discipline and Barbados's Offshore Pink Collar Sector', *Cultural Anthropology,* 8/2: 164–85.

Freeman, C. (2000), *High Heels and High Tech in the Global Economy: Women, Work and Pink-collar Identities in the Caribbean,* Durham, NC: Duke University Press.

Garcia, M.-F. (1986), 'La construction social dun marché parfait: Le marche au cadran de Fontaines-en-Sologne', *Actes de la Recherce en Sciences Sociales,* 65: 2–13.

Gardner, C. and J. Sheppard (1989), *Consuming Passion: The Rise of Retail Culture,* London: Unwin Hyman.

Gereffi, G. (1999), 'International Trade and Industrial Upgrading in the Apparel Commodity Chain', *Journal of International Economics,* 48: 37–70.

Gereffi, G. and M. Korzeniewicz, eds (1994), *Commodity Chains and Global Capitalism,* Westport, CT: Praeger.

Gertler, M.S. (2003), 'Tacit Knowledge and the Economic Geography of Context, or the Undefineable Tacitness of Being (There)', *Journal of Economic Geography,* 3/1: 75–99.

Gough Yates, A. (2003), *Understanding Women's Magazines: Publishing, Markets and Readerships,* London: Routledge.

Goworek, H. (2007), *Fashion Buying,* Oxford: Blackwell.

Grabher, G. (2002), 'Fragile Sector, Robust Practice: Project Ecologies in New Media', *Environment and Planning A,* 34/11: 1911–26.

Granovetter, M. (1983), 'The Strength of Weak Ties: A Network Theory Revisited', *Sociological Review,* 1: 201–33.

Gregson, N. and L. Crewe (2003), *Second Hand Cultures,* Oxford: Berg.

Gross, M. (2004), *Model: The Ugly Business of Beautiful Women,* London: Bantam.

Hartwick, E. (1998), 'Geographies of Consumption: A Commodity-Chain Approach', *Environment and Planning D: Society and Space,* 16/4: 423–38.

Haug, W. F. (1986), *Critique of Commodity Aesthetics: Appearance, Sexuality and Advertising,* Cambridge: Polity Press.

Haywood, G. (1998), *Addressing the Century: 100 Years of Art and Fashion,* Exhibition at the Haywood Gallery, London, in collaboration with the Kunstmuseum, Wolfsbury, Germany.

Heelas, P. (2002), 'Work Ethics, Soft Capitalism and the "Turn to Life"', in P. Du Gay and M. Pryke (eds), *Cultural Economy,* London: Sage.

Herzfeld, M. (2004), *The Body Impolitic: Artisans and Artifice in the Global Hierarchy of Value,* Chicago: University of Chicago Press.

Hesmondhalgh, D. (2002), *The Cultural Industries,* London: Sage.

Hollander, A. (1993), *Seeing through Clothes,* Berkeley: University of California Press.

Honeycombe, G. (1984), *Selfridges Seventy-five Years: The Story of the Store 1909–1984,* London: Park Lane Press.

Hopkins, T. K. and I. Wallerstein (1986), 'Commodity Chains in the World Economy', *Review,* 10: 157–70.

Howells, J. R. L. (2002), 'Tacit Knowledge, Innovation and Economic Geography', *Urban Studies,* 39/5–6: 871–84.

Howells, J. R. L. (2004), 'Knowledge, Innovation and Location', in A. Amin and P. Cohendet (eds), *Architectures of Knowledge: Firms, Capabilities, and Communities,* Oxford: Oxford University Press.

Hughes, A. (2004), 'Retailers, Knowledges and the Changing Commodity Networks: The Case of the Cut Flower Trade', in A. Amin and N. Thrift (eds), *The Blackwell Cultural Economy Reader,* Oxford: Blackwell.

Hughes, A. and S. Reimer, eds (2004a), *Geographies of Commodity Chains,* London: Routledge.

Hughes, A. and S. Reimer (2004b), 'Knowledge, Ethics and Power in the Home Furnishings Commodity Chain', in A. Hughes and S. Reimer (eds), *Geographies of Commodity Chains,* London: Routledge.

Jackson, P. (1999), 'Commodity Cultures: The Traffic in Things', *Transactions of the Institute of British Geographers,* 24: 95–108.

Jackson, P. (2002), 'Commercial Cultures: Transcending the Cultural and the Economic', *Progress in Human Geography,* 26: 3–18.

Jackson, P., M. Lowe, D. Miller and F. Mort, eds (2000), *Commercial Cultures: Economies, Practices, Spaces,* Oxford: Berg.

Jackson, P., N. Thomas and C. Dwyer (2007), 'Consuming Transnational Fashion in London and Mumbai', *Geoforum,* 38/5: 908–24.

Jackson, T. (2001), *Mastering Fashion Buying and Merchandising Management,* Basingstoke: Macmillan.

Jameson, F. (1991), *Postmodernism or the Cultural Logic of Late Capitalism,* Durham, NC: Duke University Press.

Jobling, P. (1999), *Fashion Spreads: Word and Image in Fashion Photography since 1980,* Oxford: Berg.

Kawamura, Y. (2004), *Fashion-ology: An Introduction to Fashion Studies,* Oxford: Berg.

Knorr Certina, K. and U. Bruegger (2004), 'Traders' Engagement with Markets: A Postsocial Relationship', in A. Amin and N. Thrift (eds), *The Blackwell Cultural Economy Reader,* Oxford: Blackwell.

Koda, H. and A. Bolton (2005), *Chanel,* New York: Metropolitan Museum of Art.

Lash, S. and J. Urry (1994), *Economies of Signs and Space,* London: Sage.

Latour, B. (1987), *Science in Action: How to Follow Scientists and Engineers through Society,* Milton Keynes: Open University Press.

Latour, B. (1991), *We Have Never Been Modern,* Hertfordshire: Harvester Wheatsheaf.

Latour, B. (2005), *Reassembling the Social,* Oxford: Oxford University Press.

Latour, B. and S. Woolgar (1979), *Laboratory Life: The Social Construction of Scientific Facts,* Princeton, NJ: Princeton University Press.

Lave, J. and E. Wenger (1993), *Situated Learning: Legitimate Peripheral Participation,* Cambridge: Cambridge University Press.

Law, J. (1986a), 'Laboratories and Tests', in M. Callon, J. Law and A. Rip (eds), *Mapping the Dynamics of Science and Technology,* London: Macmillan.

Law, J. (1986b), 'On the Methods of Long Distance Control: Vessels, Navigation and the Portuguese Route to India', in *Power, Action and Belief: A New Sociology of Knowledge? Sociological Review Monograph,* London: Routledge and Kegan Paul.

Law, J., ed. (1991), *A Sociology of Monsters: Essays on Power, Technology and Domination,* London: Routledge.

Law, J. (2001), 'Notes on the Theory of Actor Network. Ordering, Strategy and Heterogeneity', in Warwick Organizational Behaviour Staff (eds), *Organizational Studies: Critical Perspectives on Business and Management,* London: Routledge.

Law, J. (2002), 'Economics as Interference', in P. Du Gay and M. Pryke (eds), *Cultural Economy,* London: Sage.

Law, J. (2003), 'Notes on the Theory of the Actor Network: Ordering, Strategy and Heterogeneity', *Lancaster Online Papers,* http://www.lancs.ac.uk/fass/sociology/papers/law-notes-on-ant.pdf (accessed February 2008).

Law J. and M. Callon (1988), 'Engineering and Sociology in a Military Aircraft Project: A Network Analysis of Technological Change', *Social Problems,* 35: 284–96.

Law, J. and K. Hetherington (2000), 'Materialities, Spatialities, Localization', in J. R. Bryson, J. P. Daniels, N. Henry and J. Pollard (eds), *Knowledge/Space/Economy,* London: Routledge.

Leslie, D. and S. Reimer (1999), 'Spatializing Commodity Chains', *Progress in Human Geography,* 23/3: 401–20.

Lloyd, M. (1999), 'Performativity, Parody, Politics', *Theory, Culture and Society,* 16/2: 195–213.

Lury, C. (2004), *Brands: The Logos of the Global Economy,* London: Routledge.

MacKenzie, D. (2001), 'Physics and Finance: S-Terms and Modern Finance as a Topic for Science Studies', *Science, Technology and Human Values,* 26/2: 115–144.

MacKenzie, D. (2004), 'Physics and Finance: S-Terms and Modern Finance as a Topic for Science Studies', in A. Amin and N. Thrift (eds), *The Blackwell Reader in Cultural Economy,* Oxford: Blackwell.

Malecki, E. J. (2000), 'Competitiveness: Local Knowledge and Economic Geography', in J. R. Bryson and N. H. a. J. P. PW Daniels (eds), *Power/Knowledge/Space,* London: Routledge.

Marshall, A. (1920), *The Principles of Economics,* London: Macmillan.

Marshall, A. (1923), *Industry and Trade: A Study of Industrial Technique and Business Organization; and of Their Influences on the Conditions of Various Classes and Nations,* London: Macmillan.

Maskell, P. and A. Malmberg (1999), 'The Competitiveness of Firms and Regions: Ubiquification and the Importance of Localised Learning', *European and Regional Studies,* 6/1: 9–25.

McFall, L. (2002), 'Advertising, Persuasion and the Culture/Economy Dualism', in P. Du Gay and M. Pryke (eds), *Cultural Economy,* London: Sage.

McFall, L. (2004), *Advertising: A Cultural Economy,* London: Sage.

McRobbie, A. (1998), *British Fashion Design: Rag Trade or Image Industry,* London: Routledge.

McRobbie, A. (2002a), 'Clubs to Companies: Notes on the Decline of Political Culture in Speeded up Creative Worlds', *Cultural Studies,* 16/4: 553–69.

McRobbie, A. (2002b), 'Holloway to Hollywood: Pleasure in Work in the New Cultural Economy?' in P. Du Gay and M. Pryke (eds), *Cultural Economy,* London: Sage.

Miller, D. (1987), *Material Culture and Mass Consumption,* Oxford: Basil Blackwell.

Miller, D., ed. (1997), *Material Cultures: Why Some Things Matter,* London: UCL Press.

Miller, P. (2004), 'Governing by Numbers: Why Calculative Practices Matter', in A. Amin and N. Thrift (eds), *The Blackwell Reader in Cultural Economy,* Oxford: Blackwell.

Mintel International Group (2002a), *Clothing Retailing in Europe—UK: Retail Intelligence,* London: Mintel International Group Ltd.

Mintel International Group (2002b), *Department and Variety Store Retailing: UK, European Retail Intelligence,* London: Mintel International Group.

Mol, A. and J. Law (2004), 'Embodied Action, Enacted Bodies: The Example of Hypoglycaemia', *Body and Society,* 10: 43–62.

Moore, C. (2000), 'Streets of Style: Fashion Designer Retailing within London and New York', in P. Jackson, M. Lowe, D. Miller and F. Mort (eds), *Commercial Cultures: Economies, Practices, Spaces,* Oxford: Berg.

Mulvey, L. (1988), *Visual and Other Pleasures,* Bloomington: University of Indiana Press.

Neff, G., E. Wissinger and S. Zukin (2005), 'Entrepreneurial Labor among Cultural Producers: "Cool" Jobs in "Hot" Industries', *Social Semiotics,* 15/3: 307–34.

Negus, K. (1992), *Producing Pop: Culture and Conflict in the Popular Music Industry,* London: Edward Arnold.

Negus, K. (1999), *Music Genres and Corporate Cultures,* London: Routledge.

Negus, K. (2002), 'The Work of Cultural Intermediaries and the Enduring Distance between Production and Consumption', *Cultural Studies,* 4/1: 501–15.

Neitzert, E. (2008), 'Making Power, Doing Politics: The Film Industry and Economic Development in Aotearoa/New Zealand', *Sociology,* London: London School of Economics.

Nickson, D., C. Warhurst, A. Witz and A. M. Cullen (2001), 'The Labour of Aesthetics and the Aesthetics of Organisation', in I. G. a. H. W. A. Sturdy (ed.), *Customer Service: Empowerment and Entrapment,* London: Palgrave.

Nixon, S. (2003), *Advertising Cultures,* London: Sage.

Nonaka, I. and H. Takeuchi (1995), *The Knowledge-creating Company: How Japanese Companies Create the Dynamics of Innovation,* Oxford: Oxford University Press.

Nonaka, I., R. Toyama and A. Nagata (2000), 'A Firm as a Knowledge-creating Entity: A New Perspective on the Theory of the Firm', *Industrial and Corporate Change,* 9: 1–20.

Pettinger, L. (2004), 'Brand Culture and Branded Workers: Service Work and Aesthetic Labour in Fashion Retail', *Consumption, Markets and Culture,* 7/2: 165–84.

Polanyi, K. (1957), *The Great Transformation: The Political and Economic Origins of Our Time,* Boston: Beacon Press.

Polanyi, M. (1967), *The Tacit Dimension,* London: Routledge and Kegan Paul.

Polhemus, T. (1994), *Streetstyle: From Sidewalk to Catwalk,* London: Thames and Hudson.

Pollard, J. and A. Leyshon (2000), 'World in Promotion? Worlds of Production, Evolutionary Change and Contemporary Retail Banking', in J. R. Bryson and N. H. a. J. P. PW Daniels (eds), *Power/Knowledge/Space,* London: Routledge.

Pratt, A. (2004a), 'The Cultural Economy: A Call for Spatialized "Production of Culture" Perspectives', *International Journal of Cultural Studies,* 7/1: 117–28.

Pratt, A. (2004b), 'Mapping the Cultural Industries: Regionalisation; The Example of South East England', in A. J. Scott and D. Power (eds), *The Cultural Industries and the Production of Culture,* London: Routledge.

Pratt, A. (2008), 'Cultural Commodity Chains, Cultural Clusters, or Cultural Production Chains?' *Growth and Change,* 39/1: 95–103.

'Profits and Sales Tumble at M&S' (2005), *BBC News,* 24 May 2005, http://news. bbc.co.uk/1/hi/business/4574353.stm (accessed 25 May 2005).

Raghuran, P. (2004), 'Initiating the Commodity Chain: South Asian Women and Fashion in the Diaspora', in A. Hughes and S. Reimer (eds), *Geographies of Commodity Chains,* London: Routledge.

Ray, L. and A. Sayer, eds (1999a), *Culture and Economy after the Cultural Turn,* London: Sage.

Ray, L. and A. Sayer (1999b), 'Introduction', in *Culture and Economy after the Cultural Turn,* London: Sage.

Reed-Danahay, D. (2005), *Locating Bourdieu,* Bloomington: Indiana University Press.

Reekie, G. (1993), *Temptations: Sex, Selling and the Department Store,* St Leonards: Allen & Unwin.

Rocamora, A. (2002), 'Fields of Fashion: Critical Insights into Bourdieu's Sociology of Culture', *Journal of Consumer Culture,* 2/3: 341–62.

Roodhouse, S. (2003), 'Essential Facts: The Nature of Designer Fashion and Its Markets', Bolton, Bolton Institute of Higher Education: 1–35.

Rooney, D., G. Hearn and A. Ninan, eds (2005), *Handbook on the Knowledge Economy,* Cheltenham: Edward Elgar.

Ross, A., ed. (1997), *No Sweat: Fashion, Free Trade, and the Rights of Garment Workers,* London: Verso.

Salais, R. and M. Storper (1997), *Worlds of Production: The Action Frameworks of the Economy,* Cambridge, MA: Harvard University Press.

Sassen, S. (1991), *The Global City: New York, London, Tokyo,* Princeton, NJ: Princeton University Press.

Scott, A. J. (1999), 'The Cultural Economy: Geography and the Creative Field', *Media, Culture and Society,* 21: 807–17.

Scott, A. J. (2000), *The Cultural Economy of Cities,* London: Sage.

Simmel, G. (1971), *On Individuality and Social Forms: Selected Writings of Georg Simmel,* Edited by D. N. Levine, Chicago: University of Chicago Press.

Simmel, G. (1990), *The Philosophy of Money,* London: Routledge.

Skov, L. (2002), 'Hong Kong Fashion Designers as Cultural Intermediaries: Out of Global Garment Production', *Cultural Studies,* 16/4: 553–569.

Slater, D. (2002a), 'Capturing Markets from the Economists', in P. Du Gay and M. Pryke (eds), *Cultural Economy,* London: Sage.

Slater, D. (2002b), 'Markets, Materiality and the "New Economy"', in J. S. Metcalfe and A. Warde (eds), *Market Relations and the Competitive Process,* Manchester: Manchester University Press.

Slater, D. and F. Tonkiss (2001), *Market Society: Markets and Modern Social Theory,* Cambridge: Polity Press.

Strathern, M. (1996), 'Cutting the Network', *Journal of the Royal Anthropological Institute,* 2: 517–35.

Swart, J. and N. Kinnie (2003), 'Sharing Knowledge in Knowledge-intensive Firms', *Human Resource Management Journal,* 13/2: 60–75.

Thrift, N. (1997), 'The Rise of Soft Capitalism', *Cultural Values,* 1: 29–57.

Thrift, N. (2005), *Knowing Capitalism,* London: Sage.

Tokatli, N. (2007), 'Asymmetrical Power Relations and Upgrading among Suppliers of Global Clothing Brands: Hugo Boss in Turkey', *Journal of Economic Geography,* 7/1: 67–92.

Tokatli, N. (2008), 'Global Sourcing: Insights from the Global Clothing Industry— The Case of Zara, a Fast Fashion Retailer', *Journal of Economic Geography,* 8/1: 21–38.

Tonkiss, F. (2002), 'Between Markets, Firms and Networks: Constituting the Cultural Economy', in J. S. Metcalfe and A. Warde (eds), *Market Relations and the Competitive Process,* Manchester: Manchester University Press.

Tsing, A. (2004), 'Inside the Economy of Appearances', in A. Amin and N. Thrift (eds), *The Blackwell Cultural Economy Reader,* Oxford: Blackwell.

Veblen, T. (1953 [1899]), *The Theory of the Leisure Class,* New York: Mentor.

Von Krogh, G., I. Nonaka and K. Ichijo (2000), *Enabling Knowledge Creation: New Tools for Unlocking the Mysteries of Tacit Understanding,* Oxford: Oxford University Press.

Warhurst, C., D. Nickson, A. Witz and A. M. Cullen (2000), 'Aesthetic Labour in Interactive Service Work: Some Case Study Evidence from the "New" Glasgow', *Service Industries Journal,* 20/3: 1–18.

Webb, I. R. (2008), 'Male Models: Where's the Beef?' *Sunday Telegraph,* 11 April 2008, http://www.telegraph.co.uk/fashion/main.jhtml?xml=/fashion/2008/04/12/sm_malemodel.xml (accessed 14 April 2008).

Weller, S. (2007), 'Fashion as Viscous Knowledge: Fashion's Role in Shaping Transnational Garment Production', *Journal of Economic Geography,* 7: 39–66.

Wenger, E. R. (1998), *Communities of Practice,* Cambridge: Cambridge University Press.

Wenger, E., R. McDermott and W. Snyder (2002), *Cultivating Communities of Practice: A Guide to Managing Knowledge,* Boston: Harvard Business School.

White, H. C. (1993), *Careers and Creativity: Social Forces in the Arts,* Boulder, CO: Westview Press.

White, H. C. (2002), *Markets from Networks: Socioeconomic Models of Production,* Princeton, NJ: Princeton University Press.

White, N. (2000), *Reconstructing Italian Fashion: America and the Development of the Italian Fashion Industry,* Oxford: Berg.

Wilcox, C. (2001), *Radical Fashion,* London: V&A.

Williams, R. (1963), *Culture and Society 1780–1950,* London: Penguin.

Wilson, E. (2003), *Adorned in Dreams: Fashion and Modernity,* London: I. B. Taurus.

Winship, J. (2000), 'Culture of Restraint: The British Chain Store 1920–1939', in P. Jackson, M. Lowe, D. Miller and F. Mort (eds), *Commercial Cultures: Economies, Practices, Spaces,* Oxford: Berg.

Wissinger, E. (2007a), 'Modeling a Way of Life: Immaterial and Affective Labor in the Fashion Modeling Industry', *Ephemera: Theory and Politics in Organization,* 7/1: 250–69.

Wissinger, E. (2007b), 'Nice Work If You Can Get It: Labor in the New York Fashion Modeling Industry', Unpublished doctoral dissertation, University of New York, New York.

Wissinger, E. (2007c), 'Always on Display: Affective Production in the Fashion Modeling Industry', in P. Clough and J. Halley (eds), *The Affective Turn: Theorizing the Social,* Durham, NC: Duke University Press, pp. 231–60.

Wissinger, E. (2009), 'Modelling Consumption: Fashion Modelling Work in Contemporary Society', *Journal of Consumer Culture,* 9/2: 275–98.

Witz, A., C. Warhurst and D. Nickson (2003), 'The Labour of Aesthetics and the Aesthetics of Organisation', *Organization,* 10/1: 33–54.

Woodward, S. (2007), *Why Women Wear What They Wear,* Oxford: Berg.

Wrigley, N. and M. Lowe (2002), *Reading Retail: A Geographical Perspective on Retailing and Consumption,* London: Arnold.

Index